RAINDROPS KEEP FALLING
ON MY HEAD

RAINDROPS KEEP FALLING ON MY HEAD

MY AUTOBIOGRAPHY

IAN REDFORD

BLACK & WHITE PUBLISHING

First published 2013
by Black & White Publishing Ltd
29 Ocean Drive, Edinburgh EH6 6JL

1 3 5 7 9 10 8 6 4 2   13 14 15 16

ISBN: 978 1 84502 735 3

The publisher has made every reasonable effort to contact copyright
holders of images in the picture section. Any errors are inadvertent and
anyone who for any reason has not been contacted is invited to write to
the publisher so that a full acknowledgment can be made in subsequent
editions of this work.

A CIP catalogue record for this book is available from the British Library.

Typeset by Iolaire Typesetting, Newtonmore
Printed and bound by ScandBook AB, Sweden

I dedicate this book firstly to my mum and dad. Over the years I have come to appreciate more and more just how difficult it must have been for them both, two wonderful people devastated and torn apart by losing a child in such a way: simply put, any loving parents' very worst nightmare.

To my three aunties – Isla Redford, Rose Petrie and Margaret Robertson – who I remember offered such strength and support to Mum, Dad and all of us.

To my family: Janine, Natalie and Ian. With my love.

CONTENTS

FOREWORD   IX

INTRODUCTION   XI

 1 MY CHILDHOOD   1

 2 ERROL ROVERS   23

 3 DUNDEE FC   59

 4 PLAYING FOR RANGERS: THE JOHN GREIG ERA   95

 5 THE OLD FIRM AND OTHER SCOTTISH FOOTBALL   113

 6 THE RETURN OF JOCK WALLACE   187

 7 DUNDEE UNITED   221

 8 BARCELONA   242

 9 MOMENTUM BUILDING   257

10 THE TRACTOR BOYS   290

11 GOING BACK TO MY ROOTS   308

12 BRECHIN UP WAS SO HARD TO DO   316

13 FROM UKRAINE WITH LOVE!   325

14 MY LIFE AS A FIFA LICENSED AGENT   340

15 REFLECTIONS   358

16 INJURY TIME   364

APPENDIX: YOUTUBE LINKS   369

FOREWORD
BY GRAEME R. COCKBURN

In my thirty years working in audiology, I have met some remarkable individuals who have had to overcome the many challenges which a severe hearing loss presents. In his or her own way, each one of these people has learned to cope with the difficulties they have had to face from a very young age. Ian Redford is one such person.

Ian's hearing loss is identified as a 'monaural' loss (little or no hearing in one ear and reduced hearing in the other). This means that the ability to localise or identify where a sound is coming from is greatly reduced. The brain's processing power is therefore much slower. For example, in the classroom with all its background noise, making sense of what you are hearing is extremely difficult.

At the age of six, Ian's hearing loss was diagnosed and the specialist advised him not to participate in contact sports of any kind to avoid the risk of further damage to his residual hearing. It goes without saying, Ian chose not to take that advice! Instead, he followed his dream and became a professional footballer playing at the highest level.

Never underestimate the combination of the human spirit, strength of character – a can-do approach to life – and the brain's capacity to utilise what natural hearing remains. Ian very quickly learned, from a young age, various strategies he could employ in order to disguise his disability. Perhaps the most challenging of situations would be in the players' dressing room, travelling in the team bus or socialising in the hotel. Ian knew that by being first into the dressing room or onto the team bus, he could gain an advantage by strategically placing himself where he would hear best.

For many people with hearing difficulties there is a constant anxiety when working in groups and with unfamiliar voices, especially when there is also background noise. To live and work in a team environment meant Ian having to constantly be more aware of where people were. This was something he could never take for granted.

I am delighted to say that the more recent significant advances in digital hearing instrument technology mean that hearing loss can now be effectively addressed, ensuring that some of the old barriers associated with this disability have been removed.

Graeme R. Cockburn
HCPC registered, FSHAA

INTRODUCTION

What basically started as a hobby six or seven years ago has become the publication of the story of my life. The journey has been long and the numerous rewrites sometimes very arduous and painful. As is typical with me, I only tend to learn, or at least improve, by making mistakes!

The first manuscript I delivered to a publisher, almost two years ago, was well over 200,000 words and was not great. However, from that starting point, and with the patient help of my English teacher and her red marker pen – my wife Janine! – I have managed over the years to knock it into some sort of shape, at least good enough for a publisher to say yes!

I am grateful to Campbell and Black & White Publishing for taking the time to read it and go with it.

Ian Redford

1

MY CHILDHOOD

I was born Ian Petrie Redford on 5 April 1960. My mum was Elizabeth Mary 'Elma' Redford Petrie and my dad was Ian John Redford. My sister Jill was born three years before me, and later we'd also welcome my brother Douglas into the family. Mum was from farming stock in Perthshire and spent most of her early life on the farm Ladyfield at Sheilhill, Stanley, in Perthshire, where her brother, my uncle Gilbert, still farms today. Dad was born the son of a blacksmith in 1928 and was brought up at Kinclaven 'smiddy', or the blacksmith's cottage, near Stanley in Perthshire.

Some of the earliest recollections of my childhood were when my cousin Gavin and I would go to stay with Dad's parents, my gran and granddad, at Kinclaven smiddy. We had such great fun during these times and Old Pap (Granddad), as we called him, could be both very funny and very grumpy. Wee Granny just spoiled us both completely!

We used to love exploring the workshop of the smiddy. I remember the musty smells, the bellows cranking up the heat of the fire and the old anvil. Pap would be hammering away at the molten metal with sparks flying everywhere. Health and safety? No chance!

Gran was a cook and had worked in the kitchens of the neighbouring Ballathie estate. I can still smell the bacon and

1

eggs sizzling away in the big frying pan on the stove in the tiny kitchen of the cottage they had. It was cholesterol heaven. Gran kept big lumps of suet, or cooking fat, at the side of the stove and didn't spare any when it was time for a fry-up. The open coal fire in the adjacent lounge was always warm and glowing, it was very cosy. Pap had already done half a shift by breakfast time and would come in from the workshop that adjoined the cottage to scrub up. It was always a cooked breakfast and always a cooked lunch. They didn't have much but it seemed in other ways like they had everything. There was always a good feeling about the place.

It was a haven for Gavin and me in those very early days. Lizzy, as Pap would call his wife, totally spoiled us both when it came to food. She knew that Gavin's favourite dessert was syrup sponge pudding but mine was spotted dick. So when she was making dessert she'd make both but in the same bowl. Half would be syrup sponge and half would be spotted dick. With loads of custard poured over the top, we were in sweet paradise. It was typical farmhouse kitchen food. We ate lots of broth, stews, mince and tatties, and nearly always a sponge pudding and custard for dessert.

Things were not always sweet pudding and custard though. One particular day, Gavin and I fell out with old grumpy Pap. We'd probably been doing something we shouldn't have and had been ticked off about it. But anyway, we'd decided enough was enough and we were going to walk home from the smiddy at Kinclaven all the way over the hill and home to Errol, approximately fifteen miles away in the Carse of Gowrie. So with bags packed and well in the huff, we upped and duly announced to both Gran and Pap we were leaving to go home. We couldn't have been any older than five or six but I can still remember them both standing at the side of the road waving us goodbye

2

as we set off on this incredible journey. A journey which would begin by passing Kinclaven Primary School, which was literally next door to the smiddy. However, this incredible journey was to get no more than a few yards past the school gates, because Old Pap had an ace up his sleeve.

'Cheerio, boys,' I can still hear him say, 'hope you have a good journey home, but please be very careful when you get to the corner past the school because that is where Big Wally the Weasel lives, and he has been known to go after young boys and girls and give them a very nasty bite.'

Well, that was it . . . As neither Gavin nor I had the stomach to confront Wally the Weasel, it was about-turn and back we came to the relative safety of the smiddy. I am sure Gran and Pap had a real chuckle at that one.

The funniest (though this depends on whose side you take here) and most lasting memory I have though is the story of the mysterious disappearance of Johnny the Cockerel – JC for short. Pap used to keep a run of chickens out in the back yard and Johnny was his prized cockerel. Johnny, however, was one evil son of a bitch cockerel and did not take kindly to strangers in his territory or yard. One morning whilst out with Pap feeding the chickens, I unwisely strayed off on my own to explore other things in the run. But within no time at all, JC jumped on my back and started clawing at me with those vicious talons. Luckily he didn't get me in the eye. Old Pap was quick on the scene though, and the aim with his bucket was spot on. He caught Johnny a beauty, knocking him off my shoulders onto the ground. But the bird got up no problem and shuttled off up the run, non-plussed. Yes, those old metal buckets were lethal weapons in the hands of such a deadly marksman as my Old Pap! Of course, I was never in any danger, but no doubt that had Pap hit me instead of JC, it may well have knocked some much needed sense into me!

My cousin Gavin was my best buddy at the time. We grew up together, and although we did have the odd punch-up here and there, the animosity never lasted! Sometimes he'd beat me and sometimes I'd beat him. Naturally, I made Gavin aware of what had just happened in the chicken run, seeing as he'd been otherwise occupying himself in the kitchen with Gran, licking out the remains of the sponge pudding mix that was to be his steamed pudding! The discussion between us after lunch was of retribution and how we were going to take revenge and make that bird pay! Pap had gone out somewhere in the afternoon, and with Gran busying herself in the house, we were left to our own devices in the yard.

So, we took the law into our own hands! Cautiously we approached the chicken run and lair of JC, picking up some of the biggest stones we could get our hands on. We began lobbing them over the fence into the run in the hope we'd hit him. I think we really only wanted to teach him a lesson, albeit one he'd never forget! We had to re-establish the status quo. We couldn't have this bloody cock-sure cockerel ruling the roost!

Never for one minute did we think the events of that afternoon would turn into a murder inquiry! After many fruitless attempts, Gavin, who was a consistently better aim than me, picked up the biggest stone he could carry, never mind throw. Somehow he managed to lob it over the fence in the general direction of the psycho bird. Unfortunately for JC, it caught him, slam-dunk, right on the back of the head! I had never seen a severely concussed chicken before and I will never forget the way JC staggered off up the run. His wings were low and flapping aimlessly and his legs had gone, like a boxer struggling to make the count. Gavin and I just looked at one another in total shock, both of us knowing what the other was thinking: *Christ, what have we just done!* We decided it was best just to play dumb and not to mention a word about it. The thought of what would happen next if we told our Pap was too much to contemplate at our early stage of development!

The next morning at breakfast Pap was talking to Gran, telling her how strange it was that JC was nowhere to be seen in the run. There was total silence across the table but our reddening faces might have given up the game had old Pap decided to eyeball the two lads sitting opposite. Next morning, worse was to follow.

'Lizzy, I've just found Johnny dead under one of the hutches. I cannot for the life of me understand what's happened to him.'

Old Pap was really upset, Johnny was his prized bird, but now he had gone to that eternal chicken run in the sky – and with one almighty 'sare heid'.

If I told you just how much we feared the wrath of Old Pap, you will understand why it was not until Gavin and I were in our late teens and Old Pap was nearly ninety before we confessed to the killing of JC! I can still remember the look on his face when we told him – it said it all! We didn't mean to do it, Pap . . . honestly. We only wanted to teach him a lesson! Gavin and I were to get into some serious scrapes together as we grew up, but more of that later!

Dad was a time-served blacksmith but he decided from an early age that he didn't want to spend the rest of his life working for someone else. So by the age of approximately eighteen he left home with no more than twenty pounds in his pocket and the words of Old Pap ringing in his ears: 'You'll be back.'

He moved to Errol in the Carse of Gowrie, Perthshire, and started his business life with just a litter of pigs, spending all he had on his first crop of livestock. He was totally skint. This was not long after World War Two. I can remember Dad telling me that, as a boy growing up at Kinclaven, for their 'war effort' he and some of his pals used to ambush the Italian prisoners of war who were riding home on their bikes after a night on the town in neighbouring Blairgowrie, and pelt them with rotten tatties!

He managed to rent some old sheds down at the Grange beside Errol Airfield, which had been used during the war. He struggled for years and he told me he often had to hide from creditors and lived off nothing more than bars of chocolate. Eventually, however, with dogged determination and relentless hard work, his business began to grow. He would drive his pigs down to England, sell them in the market then drive straight home again – trying very hard not to fall asleep at the wheel in the process!

In 1956 he married Mum and by the time my sister Jill was born, one year later in 1957, Dad had bought the family home, Holmlea, at Errol Station, just about a mile from the village of Errol. This was where I was brought up. Dad was becoming more and more successful but he was a workaholic. In the early years I can remember him taking me everywhere with him in his van. I think this was the main reason why my parents had such difficulty in getting me to go to school. School was no fun but being with Dad on the farm was fantastic. He'd take me into the pen with his pigs and they were so huge that I was looking up at them. He also moved into poultry, and so at six or seven years old, I used to follow him into the rearing pens where he kept all the thousands of chicks that were reared for the battery-caged pens. It was never considered in those days that this was cruelty to animals, but I can honestly see why some people would not be happy to see chickens live in this way. It is said, though, that a happy chicken will lay eggs and an unhappy chicken won't. He certainly never reared free-range hens and, in the main, never seemed to complain about how many eggs his chickens produced. It's not really for me to say, but I couldn't see myself wanting to make a living out of caged birds. However, to say it's cruel is maybe not quite as easy to determine as it would seem.

It was also about this time I can clearly remember kicking a football, which my dad had introduced me to virtually before I could walk. Apparently I used to spend ages kicking this ball against the kitchen door (left foot only). It was my party piece when anyone came to the house, but it got so incessant that my left leg began to grow out of shape. As a result, for many months I had to wear a brace on my leg in bed at night as a corrective measure.

School for me was Errol Primary, about a mile up the road from us, in the village. It took me a while to accept that going to school was something you just had to do. There were days when I would take it upon myself that I'd had enough for the day and would walk home at playtime. The school would phone Mum and Dad to tell them I had gone AWOL and I'd be picked up on the road by one of them and taken straight back to the classroom!

I was not really interested in lessons, but as I got a little older there was one aspect of school I really began to enjoy, and that was playing for the Errol Primary football team, which was formed by the school's sports-mad headmaster, Eric Duncan. I remember wanting to play football in the playground all the time. In the morning before the bell, at lunch time and sometimes even after school. From kicking a ball around the house as a toddler, it quickly became an obsession. I can even remember trying to play 'keepy up' whilst sitting on the toilet! I remember at that time, though, I was so into footie that I'd cycle a mile to school in the morning, cycle home at lunchtime, gulp down a large cooked lunch, jump on my bike and cycle back up the road, in order to get as much footie in the playground as possible before the afternoon classes. I think Errol Brae was a metaphor for me because it was all uphill going to school and downhill coming home. I would get up as much speed as possible and almost freewheel all the way!

Gavin and I were standouts in football from an early age, both being selected for Perth and Kinross County, at around ten years old, when we were still involved in primary football. During our time on the school team, though, Errol Primary began to win things it had never done before. Our great rivals were Stanley Primary School. Stanley was a small village like Errol but on the other side of Perth. They had the mainstays of a certain Raymond Stewart (Scotland, West Ham, Dundee United) and Mark Williamson, who, like me, was a naturally left-footed player, who also went on to sign for Dundee United. We had some great battles with Stanley Primary and they seemed to come out on top more than we did. Our biggest success, however, was when we won the Robertson trophy, beating Caledonian Road Primary School from Perth in the final. It was pretty obvious that the likes of Raymond Stewart, Mark Williamson, Gavin and I were pretty decent and showed some promise.

It was with this in mind that some of the local dads decided to get together and form a Juvenile team, and it was named Errol Rovers. The 'Rovers' joined the highly competitive Dundee Sunday Boys League, and it was there I really began to develop my game.

Round about this time during my primary school years a problem was discovered that would have a profound effect on my life. The audiologist came once a year to test everyone's hearing. One by one we were called out to the front of the class and told to sit down facing the class with headphones on. Different-pitched sounds were played and you had to put your hand up to signify when you heard them. When it came to my turn, I remember facing the class and seeing some of my classmates waving at me, like they were gesticulating for me to put my hand up. I had no idea what they were on about – but by then the pitches had reached such a level that everyone in the class could hear them without headphones!

The results, unsurprisingly, showed that I was stone deaf in my left ear. As a result, I was sent to see a specialist in Dundee, where I was put through some more extensive hearing tests to try and establish what had caused the deafness. Finally the specialist told me that a nerve had been damaged and there was nothing more they could do to save my hearing. He asked me if I played any sports. I told him that I played football for the school primary team. But he then went on to say that contact sports were no longer an option for me because if I received any blow to the head it could damage the other ear and I would be completely deaf. He assumed that the hearing loss was caused by some sort of virus, perhaps measles. There was no way in my mind I was going to stop playing football. For me it was just never going to be an issue. Nothing was going to stop me doing what I loved. I was determined to play no matter what.

The memories I have of my family life in the early days were that of a mum and dad who were happy and caring. I have watched some old cine movies of my dad at this time and what struck me about him was how happy and contented he looked. Dad loved kids and it showed, as no matter how busy he was, he always seemed to have time to spend playing with us. It was Dad who taught me how to hunt and fish, teaching me how to fly cast for trout and salmon and drilling into me all the safety aspects of using a gun. Fishing became his passion later on in his life, but, as I said, he was a complete workaholic in the early days of building his business and rarely took any time off. When I was about eleven years old Dad took me salmon fishing to the Cargill beat, near Kinclaven, where he was brought up. In those days when you went to any salmon beat on the River Tay there was rarely a moment when you would not see a fish leaping out of the water. What a day we had, and I caught my very first salmon, spinning with a silver toby for bait. What a thrill it was and it gave me such a fight I thought my arms would fall off when I eventually landed it. The tradition was – or maybe still is – to be blooded by your first catch or kill. So I went around for the rest of the day with a big splotch of the fish's blood on my forehead.

Nowadays I would probably only ever kill one salmon and if I caught any more I would release them back into the water. Actually, fresh Tay salmon baked on a barbecue is one of my favourite foods! But over the years I have become much more appreciative of the life cycles and spans of these magnificent creatures. How cruel is it when you think of what the salmon goes through just to get up the river to spawn. They are a truly remarkable species. They have to contend with the seals at the estuaries, and they take them by the thousand. It's a numbers game. Every female fish killed means the loss of approximately 20,000 eggs, or potential fish. Many of the natural spawning beds have also been destroyed over the years by deforestation and various modern farming methods using pesticides, fertilisers, etc. Unbelievably, in Dad's time many of the fish they caught weren't consumed and were just caught, killed, counted then thrown away. What a criminal waste when I think about it now!

We were a very happy family and I can't remember being anything other than a normal, happy child who just loved being outdoors playing football or just running around the farm. Dad was becoming a successful pig and poultry farmer and Mum was happy to be at home looking after her kids. Mum was tall and a very strong woman. She was not to be tangled with and seldom did my sister Jill or I step over the line. She had the forearms of a man and when she lost her temper with you, which was rare, you took cover! Dad was only about 5ft 8in in height but was very powerful. His hands were that of someone who had grafted all his life. His fingers were so huge that, years later when I got engaged, my engagement ring only managed to sit on the very tip of his pinky! His hands were quite literally twice the size of mine.

I was told a story about him that is apparently true but I find very hard to believe. He was in his local pub one night in the village of Errol, where he used to meet with all his cronies. He'd had a lot to drink and accepted a bet that he couldn't karate chop and break the wooden handle of a besom. The besom was set up sticking over the bar counter and he broke it in half at the first attempt!

I remember lots of family trips up to the smiddy at Kinclaven on a Sunday. Gran would always have a three-course meal prepared, and Dad and Pap would sometimes take us worm fishing for trout on the Tay down at Ballathie estate, which was within easy walking distance of the smiddy. Having fished there when he was a boy, Dad knew all the hot spots and often we'd catch some brown trout. It was great fun. There was an old lodge house or cottage on the grounds quite near the entrance to the estate. It was set very much on its own, almost hidden amongst the trees. We used to call it 'the witches' cottage' and would scare ourselves to bits when going anywhere near it. It really was a very spooky place, and when walking back past the cottage, Dad would scare Jill and me, telling us there was a ghost that lived in it. Often when I neared the cottage I would take off and run as fast as I could to get away from it! One time Mum came fishing too, and I remember her nearly choking on a boiled sweet when very near the witches' cottage. I think it was Dad who somehow managed to dislodge it. Funny, the

11

things you remember, and I suppose that experience didn't help my feelings of uneasiness towards that area of Ballathie estate!

Things all seemed very normal to me, and I remember being happy and feeling very secure in my early childhood. It was around about this time when Doulgas, my brother, Mum and Dad's third child, was born – 10 December 1965, to be precise. I'm not sure if it was planned or not, as there was a five-year gap between Douglas and me. I don't remember too much of him when he was a baby, but I remember him being left with Gran and Pap when we went off on a family cruise of the Canary Islands. This was a real family affair because Dad's brother, my uncle Phil, and his wife, my aunt Isla, came along, together with my cousins Elaine, Phillip and, of course, my partner in crime Gavin. Mum's brother, my uncle Joe, or 'Smiler' as he was known, and his wife, my aunt Rose, made up the rest of the party. It was a real squad. From what I remember, everyone had such a great time and there were lots of laughs, particularly from my aunt Rose, who had the most infectious laugh I have ever known. Nicer, kinder people you could not wish to meet. Aunt Rose would have everyone in stitches. One day all the adults went to a vineyard for a wine-tasting session in Madeira and the kids were all dragged along. We came back in two huge open-top taxis. I still have this vision of teetotal Aunt Rose laughing her head off at something ridiculous. No doubt within seconds everyone was joining in!

The only other family holiday I can remember is when we went to Butlins in Ayrshire, or Butlitz as it became know. Again it was all such good fun. Gavin, Phillip and I were seemingly allowed the run of the place and definitely made the most of it. From memory, Douglas was not with us at Butlins either. I can also remember Mum and Dad going off to Switzerland one year and taking Jill but leaving me behind at the smiddy along with Gavin!

This was a time when Dad must've felt he had everything. A happy marriage, three kids and a successfully growing business. He worked for it and he'd earned it.

When Douglas was around two or three years old and I would be around seven, we were all supposed to go on holiday to Ireland. Dad's all time favourite movie was *The Quiet Man*, starring his favourite actor, John Wayne. The film depicts the beauty and charm of the countryside of Ireland and we were all looking forward to going. Tragically, something happened that changed everything and that holiday was cancelled. Douglas had not been well and Mum had taken him to the doctor's. Initially as a matter of course the doctors took a blood sample and the results were the beginning of our worst nightmare. Douglas had leukaemia. Jill and I, being so young, were not aware his illness was life-threatening. We knew he was not well and had to go hospital regularly for treatment, but because so much of his illness was kept from us, we had no idea of the gravity of the situation.

I would regularly say things like, 'When will Dougie be better, Mum?'

And she would reply, 'Oh, he needs to go to hospital for one more treatment then he'll be well again.'

As the years went by, his illness just never seemed to be going away but I still never considered for a minute he might be dying. When he began going to school he was teased because he had lost his hair and was fat. This was because of the chemotherapy and having to take steroids, which affected his weight. I hated the thought of him being teased by other kids when he wasn't well. I never teased him about his hair or his weight.

Douglas looked very much like Dad and had fair hair and

blue eyes. Like me, he was left-footed and loved playing football whenever he was well enough. We'd play football in the garden but I would never let him win. He would go running off inside, crying to Mum, and she would come out and give me such a rollicking. I couldn't understand why Mum and Dad seemed to go way over the top when giving me a row over Douglas.

One night at the dinner table I recall saying something quite nasty to Douglas. In reality, it was nothing more than typical sibling stuff. The reaction from Mum and Dad towards me was again excessive, and I was really struggling to understand why it seemed they were giving Douglas all the attention and being so short with Jill and me. I suppose the hurt and anger my parents were feeling at the time must've made it very difficult for them to be anything other than over protective of him. Occasionally there were incidents at home which scared me. One in particular I vividly remember. Douglas was lying on the couch in the family 'good room', his special room inside our house. He started coughing badly and brought up a huge amount of horrible green phlegm. Dad was with him and told him to spit it out on the carpet. Jill and I just sat and looked at each other. I was both horrified and frightened by this.

Douglas had such spirit and was such a fighter, but he also had a temper! Once when he was feeling better I had been winding him up a bit and he hit me on the head with a wooden toy, which knocked me semi-unconscious! Gran had been staying with us to help out and I remember her actually giving Douglas a telling-off, but when I fully came round, I also got it from my gran for teasing him. Had I known he was so ill I would never have done this and to this day I sorely regret not knowing more about his condition at the time. I suppose Mum and Dad only thought they were doing the right thing keeping the facts from us. They were obviously praying he'd get well again, and I know they would not have wanted Jill and I to be going through what they were.

The amount of time Douglas spent at hospital with Mum meant, of course, that Jill and I were missing out and had to fend for ourselves emotionally more and more. Looking back, deep down, I must've resented this. Jill and I would sometimes talk about how Douglas was their favourite. The atmosphere around the house was not what it had been before Douglas was born and so probably subconsciously I was blaming him for the way all our lives seemed to be changing. There were many things that I only really began to find out years later. For example, Dad couldn't face going to see him in hospital; therefore Mum was the one who directly took all the strain by going to see him every day when he was receiving his treatment and talking to his doctors. Mum later told me that on the very odd occasion Dad did go, he would turn up right at the end of visiting hours, just in time to say cheerio.

Douglas would ask, 'Where is Dad? Why is he not coming to see me?' I cannot imagine what Mum must've felt like when she could not give him an honest answer.

As a family we'd been to Monifieth a couple of times, where we rented a caravan. Then one year Dad decided to buy a holiday home in the area and so, when I was around nine or ten, he bought a small cottage, named Craigknowe, at East Haven, right on the beach just a mile along the coast from Carnoustie, not far from Monifieth. I think the idea was to try and give us somewhere proper to stay for a family holiday but also from where he could easily travel back and forth to the farm. So during the summer holidays we'd all, most often apart from Dad, head down to the cottage at East Haven. I used to love swimming in the sea and never gave a thought to any potential dangers, though we really did have to be careful – as I soon found out!

15

I often think that nowadays we are too protective of our kids and never give them any chance to find things out for themselves. Accidents can and do still happen but I think you are more prone to danger if you have never sensed or experienced it before. Nothing seemed to bother me though and I'd go swimming no matter what the weather or temperature was like.

One day, again left to my own devices, I was climbing on a tree in the neighbour's garden. I was leaning on a branch when it snapped and I fell onto the spiked metal fence below. Luckily for me, the spike only went into my leg! Mum rushed me up to A&E at Arbroath Hospital to get the wound stitched up. It was a real nasty one and I still have the scar to prove it. To this day I cannot believe how lucky I was. Had my body landed on the spike, I would've been killed.

When I got back from the hospital, Dad had arrived at the cottage. He started to goad me by saying there was nothing wrong with me and that what I'd had to endure was nothing compared to what my brother was going through. There was a nastiness to him I had never seen before. It was out of character and very destabilising for me. I think what was really going through his mind was that he'd come close to losing another child. Looking back, I realise I was just on the receiving end of a lot of his obvious pent-up anger and frustration, but for me, as I did not really know what my brother was going through, it was difficult to accept what he was saying, my interpretation probably being that he only really cared about Douglas.

To take the pressure off Mum, an au pair girl was hired to look after us and take Jill and I places during the day. Her name was Sheena Dunbar, a student from Dundee. Her boyfriend at the time was none other than Dundee FC's star striker John Duncan. Sheena brought him out to the cottage one day and he gave me a footballing lesson in the garden. He certainly knew how to score goals. John was someone who I got to know better much later in my career, when he signed me for Ipswich Town, but I've not forgotten my earliest memory of him at the cottage.

Aunt Rose was also with us a lot at Craigknowe and she helped enormously with everyone. Jill and I loved her to bits, but she was no pushover – far from it. Like a drill sergeant barking out her instructions, she would not allow one single grain of sand across the threshold. This was very hard for me to adhere to since the cottage was no more than thirty yards from the beach! Yes, Aunt Rose was a pillar of support for the whole family. By this time Jill was around thirteen or fourteen and I was about ten or eleven. Douglas was with us at the cottage when he was well enough and not in hospital. I know he enjoyed some good times there.

I am sure Dad, in his own way, was trying to do some special things for Douglas, as deep down he was thinking he maybe wouldn't live very long. One thing he did, which I think was mainly for Douglas, was build a swimming pool in our back garden. Believe me, no one had a swimming pool in those days. We had a field that adjoined the back of our house at Holmlea, so Dad used a bit of the land and extended our garden. He built an indoor heated swimming pool with a Scandinavian-type sauna bath beside it. Douglas loved the water, as did Jill and I. A lot of the kids from Station Road did too.

We started a life-saving club and had an instructor from the village. His name was Forbes Winchester and he came down once or twice a week. Eventually we all sat our life-saving proficiency tests. Jill and I both got our Grade 4 survival and Grade 4 distance awards. Dad was very generous, allowing practically all the neighbours free access to the pool any time they wanted. About the only two who didn't use the pool much were Mum and Dad. Mum in particular was a very poor swimmer. My uncle

Phil, Dad's brother, nearly drowned because, insanely, he dived in at the deep end knowing he couldn't swim but had calculated he would be able to surface, catch on to the side and pull himself up. He badly miscalculated and had to be rescued! I went on to swim for Errol Primary in the county swimming galas and got a credible second at the freestyle event. I didn't have much by way of technique but was certainly enthusiastic!

It was around this time I think that Mum began drinking. Douglas was still having regular treatment and Auntie Rose would go with Mum to the hospital in Edinburgh. Whilst Douglas was receiving his chemotherapy, Mum and Aunt Rose would stay in a hotel nearby. Aunt Rose told me many years later that Mum would have the minibar cleared out in no time. Aunt Rose was very much against alcohol because her husband, Mum's brother Uncle Smiler, was an alcoholic. To her credit, I think she understood Mum's reasons and didn't judge her at the time.

By the time I was aged twelve Douglas was approaching seven. He'd been ill for approximately five years and his condition was deteriorating. The first inclination I had that my brother was very seriously sick during that whole period was actually not long before he passed away. I was out and about in the van with Dad when he suddenly stopped and pulled into a lay-by. He sat quietly for a few minutes before saying to me, 'I hope you are praying for your brother.'

This was a bombshell for me. I remember feeling frightened and confused, wondering why he'd said this. I finally thought to myself, Douglas cannot be that ill. He's surely not going to die, is he? Maybe I was in denial of what I now realised was actually really happening.

I was in my first year at Perth High School when he died.

He'd become too sick to go to school and latterly I can only remember him either being away in hospital or at home, too ill

18

do anything. I have some vivid memories and some not so vivid. There was one night when I was aware of him being taken from our room in the middle of the night and then finding out the next day he was in hospital. This must have been getting close to when he died.

The day he died I will never forget. I was playing football for Perth High School on a cold Saturday morning on 16 December 1972, only days after his seventh birthday. We were playing away in Fife, at Bell Baxter Academy I think. Normally Gavin and I joined the school bus on the Saturday morning but would get a lift home from our dads after the game, as they never missed a match. During the game I became aware that Dad and Uncle Phil were no longer on the touchline. I thought this was very odd and wondered where they had gone and what was wrong. I think the police had been contacted and told to inform them to go to Perth Royal Infirmary immediately. At the end of the game nothing was mentioned but Gavin and I were told to take the team bus back to Perth, with no explanations as to why. From there we were picked up and taken back to Isla Villa, near Errol, which was Gavin's home and only a couple of miles away from our Holmlea. Later on that day, approximately early evening, we were sitting in the kitchen. I don't remember what we were doing, but Dad suddenly appeared. I could tell immediately something was wrong. He said, 'I have some very bad news about your brother: he only has hours to live.'

So, after five years of wondering what his illness was all about, finally came the realisation. Douglas, my wee brother, was going to die. I bolted from the kitchen through to Gavin's room, threw myself on the bed and sobbed my heart out. Dad followed but he didn't put his arms around me to console me but tried to keep the stiff upper lip and said something like, 'It's okay to cry; I've had my cry.'

19

He then went on to tell me about how well he thought I had played in the match earlier but we had to be brave now because there was nothing we could do about what was happening. He must've been as completely and utterly devastated as I was. Looking back, it was all such a shock. Whilst Mum and Dad had probably come to realise and accept for some time Douglas was not going to get well, for Jill and me it was the opposite. The shock of that day is something I have never forgotten and never will. Thinking it was in our best interests, Mum and Dad had tried to protect us by keeping the facts from us. In doing so, when that day finally came, it was much harder to accept or bear. The emptiness I felt during that time is something that still haunts me to this day.

Eventually Dad and I returned to Holmlea to wait for the final call from the hospital. I am sure that he and Mum had both said their goodbyes earlier in the day when he'd slipped into a coma. When I got home with Dad I just went through to the lounge and sat staring at the TV in disbelief, totally numb and in complete shock. I was thinking, 'Why couldn't I see him? Why can't I say sorry? This can't be happening. I don't believe this is happening.' Inevitably, later in the evening the phone rang. It was the hospital to inform us that he'd finally passed away. Mum was hysterical. Aunt Rose and I could only look at each other and say nothing. Dad was trying to console Mum; Jill, as I recall, was in her room, on her own. It was a total unforgettable nightmare. My life felt like it had just imploded with the shock of it all. I don't remember anything else of that night apart from Mum crying and Aunt Rose sitting with me. My recollections of the next day were of being in the garden just kicking a football against the wall nonstop for what seemed like hours and hours in the cold rain. I never spoke to anyone for what I remember as an eternity. I have very little recollection of how my sister Jill coped. I don't remember her saying or doing much, but I know she must've felt pretty much the way I did.

On the day of the funeral, Jill and I were sent off to school. On that very blackest of days, I can recall climbing the stairs to go to class and being teased. I used to get teased a lot about the fact that I tend to speak out the side of my mouth – it is connected to the nerve damage which caused my deafness. It doesn't bother me now but at the time it was hurtful to me and I hated it. There were a couple of lads in particular who used to love winding me up about it. I happened to meet one of them on the stairs that day, and when he started to wind me up I grabbed him by the neck and was going to give him a real doing when I was dragged off. Just as well, for the way I was feeling I don't think I would've ever stopped hitting him that day had I really got started. When we returned home from school, the house was full of people all dressed in black.

Christmas came within days of the funeral and somehow, for Jill's and my sake, Mum found the strength to make the effort, but Dad made it clear he wanted no part of it. From when Douglas died I cannot recall a single Christmas at home that was not a very tense, anxious and depressing affair. For years after his death it was taboo to even mention his name. I can't remember Dad talking about him to me or even mentioning his name again until I was in my late teens.

When someone in the family dies, normally they are old, and it's almost expected. Growing old gradually is just nature's way of preparing us all for the inevitable. But when a parent loses a child or a child loses a brother or sister who has not even lived to be a teenager, it's catastrophic. There can be nothing worse for a parent to endure. Douglas died pretty much a stranger to me. I so regret not being able to say sorry for resenting the attention he got and sorry for teasing him and hurting his feelings and sorry that I didn't understand how badly he suffered with his illness. I would say how much I admire him today because of how brave and courageous he was and, at the very least of all, how sorry I was that he got ill in the first place. Being a parent myself I cannot even begin to know what emotional torture Mum and Dad went through, from the start to the end. However, what was possibly forgotten was that a lot was kept from my sister and me. I had terrible feelings of guilt due to how I had sometimes treated Douglas because of what I perceived as favouritism. In truth, we treated him no different to how most brothers and sisters would've treated him under normal circumstances. As a young child I simply didn't know. In hindsight, my behaviour was probably pretty normal. Certainly over the years I have rationalised this and forgiven myself.

If, God forbid, any of my kids ever got seriously ill, I would want the other to know and understand all about the illness. You see, at the end of it all, the heartache is no less but at least with it will come a greater sense of understanding.

Many years later a psychologist explained to me that what had affected me most was a strong sense of guilt. I had somehow deep down believed it was my fault, my punishment. It seems flippant to say – this is only normal human behaviour – but it was all very real to me.

There is a photograph of Douglas and me together with our football strips on; he loved to play football when he felt well enough. Unfortunately these days were very few and far between. Every year Jill and I put a wreath down at the family grave up at Kinclaven cemetery in memory of Douglas, our brother; Dad; Mum; Gran; and Pap; and all the other family members who've since passed away.

2

ERROL ROVERS

As mentioned earlier, my prowess as a footballer had been evident since I was very young. It was my obsession. I'd be kicking a football around all the time – in the garden, in the house and basically anywhere I could get away with it! Dad introduced me to football more or less when I was old enough to walk. As I got a little older he would often take me outside into the garden and throw a ball in the air for me to head or trap. He would throw the ball diagonally in the air for me to jump and head against the garage door, which was often used for target practice. He had been a keen player himself but had only played at Junior level until he went off to build his business, during which time he rarely did anything other than work 24/7.

It was said of my dad that he was a skilful player whilst his brother, my uncle Phil, was a take-no-prisoners, thou-shalt-not-pass, old-fashioned typical Scottish centre-half – well, according to what Dad told me! As I mentioned earlier, it was mainly due to the success of Errol Primary School football team that some of the parents decided to get together and form a Juvenile team, named Errol Rovers. I would have been around ten at the time, and in the first photos taken of the team we are in the old Southampton strip of red and white vertical stripes, with black shorts and red and white socks. Douglas was also in the original team photo. At that time he must have been undergoing chemotherapy, as his hair was very thin on top. Probably part of the reason why Dad also decided to get actively involved with the running of Errol Rovers was to give him something else to try and take his mind off things. Typically, though, when Dad decided to do something, he put everything into it.

Eventually the Rovers went from the red and white vertical stripes of the old Southampton strip to the red and white of Ajax – I think largely because of that great Dutch team in which Johan Cruyff was the brilliant young star. I'll never forget the thrill of lining up against him one night at Ibrox, years later. Incredible to think that I was playing against the man who I had idolised when I was a boy. Yet there he was, right opposite me on the pitch at Ibrox! At the time he was playing for Feynoord along with a very young but emerging Rudd Gullit. For the record, Cruyff may have been well past his sell-by date in the mid-1980s, but he just oozed class and still had that grace of movement more akin to a ballet dancer than a footballer. Ruud Gullit was just about the biggest, strongest-looking player I had ever seen. He looked more like a rugby player than a footballer. Although he didn't have the poetic motion of Cruyff, his sheer power on the ball was incredible. It was another level altogether. But more on that part of my life later.

Originally Errol Rovers were more or less a combination of the primary schools of the two small Perthshire villages of Errol and Stanley. Stan Clark, my pal who lived almost next door to me on Station Road, was the original goalie for Errol Rovers FC. Stan and I used to play for hours out on the pitch, along with his brothers Robbie and John. And when it was dark we'd play under the streetlights of Station Road – no laptops or Play Stations in those days! There were also old outbuildings and sheds that we used to go into when the weather was really bad.

In particular there was an old barn that Dad converted into the away dressing room. It was much like a loft with wooden stairs leading up to it. The floor was wooden and I'm sure full of woodworm because a lot of the wood panels were spongy and would splinter easily. There were no windows but Dad had put power in so we had indoor floodlights! Normally there would be the four of us – the three Clark boys and me. Any more and it became a tight squeeze. We'd set up a brick at either end of the loft and play 1-v-1 or 2-v-2. It was much easier to defend your own brick than it was to attack your opponents, so goals were difficult to come by. Sometimes, after what seemed like hours of play, there would only be a handful of goals scored. It was also very dusty and with very little by way of ventilation. By the end of a long session our throats were burning dry and we were gasping for a drink. We had some real tussles up in that attic. The three Clark boys were John, the eldest and two years older than Stan, who was my age and the middle child; and Robbie, the youngest and two years younger than Stan and me.

Sometimes Robbie would go off in the huff when things weren't going his way. Normally, to even out the age average, it was Stan and me versus John and Robbie. Because it was such a tight, confined space and goals were hard to come by, I have no doubt this type of constant practice was largely responsible for me developing good close control.

John also went on to become a decent player. He had a brief spell at Aberdeen under Billy McNeill but more than established himself with Forfar Athletic. I remember when he played against me when I was with Rangers in a Scottish Cup semi-final tie at Hampden. Incredibly, we drew with them 0–0. Only for us to beat them soundly in the replay. I remember that game in particular because I came very close to gambling everything I had on us beating Forfar that day. I didn't have much money at the time – maybe only around four or five thousand pounds in total. From memory, the odds would've got me my money back plus about a grand. However at the last moment I bottled out of it and didn't put the money on. Thank goodness, as Forfar came pretty close to causing one of the biggest major upsets in Scottish football!

Errol Rovers began playing in the Dundee Juvenile Sunday Boys League Under-13s. For the first couple of seasons we seemed to get thrashed nearly ever week, mainly because we were all still virtually Under-11s and too young for the age group. But once we'd had a couple of seasons under our belts, two things emerged. One, we were now playing against boys our own age and were so used to getting thumped we no longer had any fear of anyone. Two, we also had Raymond Stewart from Stanley. He was an outstanding player for his age at that time. Originally when he came down to Station Park for practice he didn't even have a pair of boots so Dad took care of that and bought him his first-ever real football boots. Ray was as hard as nails and up for anything, against some of the roughest and toughest that Dundee had to offer. It wasn't long before Jim McLean, manager of Dundee United, snapped him up on an S-form, along with his Stanley buddy Mark Williamson, who also showed a lot of class for his age. Mark probably should've gone on to make it at a higher level but for some reason didn't. Kenny Johnston from Perth was another player who attracted some attention from senior clubs and I think also had a spell on S-form with Dundee United.

We were initially very much seen as the country bumpkins, as the rest of the league was comprised of teams from inner-city Dundee. I think there was probably also some jealousy in that we were seen as being more affluent because of the swimming pool Dad had built in our back garden and the fact that he allowed all the away teams to use it after the games. They must've thought we were loaded, what with our own swimming pool and not only that, but our own pitch! As opposed to away matches, where it was mainly on the community public football pitches of Dundee that we played.

Station Park, our home turf, sat right next to the railway track beside Errol Station and directly across the road from where we lived, which, as far as I was concerned, was great! It was basically set in just a small four- or five-acre field which Dad owned and had used mainly for grazing cows. He acquired a set of gang mowers and in no time we had our own pitch marked out, along with proper wooden goal posts and, of course, nets, which were a rare thing in the Dundee public parks at that time. Nothing could be further from the truth of course, but the bottom line was, we were seen as the aristocrats of the Dundee Sunday Boys Juvenile League and we became the team everybody wanted to beat.

I used to love waking up on Sunday mornings when we were playing at home. One of Dad's employees, farm worker Willie Mowbray, would be out on the park on his tractor, armed with gang mowers, cutting the grass. Then he'd touch up the lines with whitening. I was only interested in helping out by putting up the goal nets! I probably used up more energy in the mornings kicking balls into the empty nets than I used during the actual match in the afternoon!

Errol Rovers were no ordinary Juvenile team. For starters, we had our own team doctor, Nick Taylor. Nick was a medical student from Essex who was living in one of the cottages at Errol Station that Dad owned. He rented it out to some medical students studying at Dundee University. 'Doctor' Nick, as we called him, even though he was still a long way off qualifying, was also our club physio. He was the one who would administer the magic sponge when required. Coming from Essex, Nick was an avid West Ham supporter. His heroes growing up were the likes of Jimmy Greaves, Bobby Moore and Trevor Brooking. So with an official team doctor; Willie, our official grounds man; home dressing room (an old brick-built round house Dad used as his farm office); an away dressing room (the aforementioned converted loft); and our own swimming pool complete with Scandinavian sauna, it was easy to see why we became the envy of the league!

Originally Dad had acquired Holmlea, the family home, as his business began to grow. It was not a typical farmhouse because it is a semi-detached sandstone villa situated on a street less than a stone's throw from Errol Station. It is on three levels comprising a ground floor with kitchen, utility room, lounge, dining room, 'wee sitting room' and WC, first floor where there were four large double bedrooms but only one bathroom and the second floor, which comprised of two large rooms. At one time I was very keen on table tennis and persuaded Mum and Dad to buy a full-sized table tennis table and install it in one of the rooms in the attic. I would spend hours up there in the winter. For me the worst thing about Holmlea was it had no central heating. Fortunately, my bedroom, which I shared initially with Douglas, was next to the airing cupboard, so at least I got a little extra heat from the hot water tank. Mum and Dad did at least try to improve things and installed two old-fashioned brick storage heaters – one in the hall and one on the upstairs landing. I swear they hadn't a clue how to use them though, because they always seemed to come on at night when you were in your bed. During the day, however, when we needed the heat they were stone cold! If I was ever off school sick in the winter, I would stay in bed until Mum put the coal fire on in the 'wee sitting room'. Despite it all, Mum had certain rigid routines. The coal fire was never lit before 10am and the tatties for tea were never put on before 5pm!

I remember scraping the ice from the inside of my bedroom window regularly. I took really bad coming back to Holmlea after I had been away from home for a few years. Janine in particular felt the cold of Holmlea really bad. We had the place re-christened 'Ice Station Zebra'. By this time of course I had become a big city softy! As things progressed and Dad's business grew, he got the chance to acquire some of the other properties that lay between Holmlea and Errol Station.

To give you an idea of how close we all were to the railway line, the house actually vibrated every time a train passed! Of course over the years we'd all got used to it, but when we had guests staying, they couldn't believe the noise and vibration! The other acquired cottages provided a bit of rental income. The main cottage was large and had approximately six bedrooms and it was rented out mainly to medical students from Dundee University.

This was great for me and my street pals, mainly Stan and Gavin, because we used to love playing pranks on them and winding them up. They were definitely seen as targets and fair game. Occasionally at the weekends they would have typically wild student parties when the whole place would be rocking! I'd be over the wall and sneaking around pretending I was James Bond, trying to get a peek at what was going on inside. I knew how to get on the roof and how to access upstairs by shimmying up a drainpipe. Sometimes we'd break in during a party and cause all sorts of mayhem!

When it came to the practical jokes, club physio Nick Taylor was usually the main victim. One morning after a big party when he was still in bed suffering from a major hangover, Gavin and I sneaked into his room to waken him up and offered to make him his breakfast and to take him a cup of tea or black coffee to help sober him up. This really was all just a ruse to get him off

29

guard. Under our sleeves were some raw eggs, which we craftily broke and had mashed up in his shoes when he wasn't looking. Eventually of course when he got up and put his slippers on he had a nice surprise waiting for him! Nick went bonkers at this and hunted us down for hours and when he finally caught us we were both chucked into the pool headfirst and fully clothed. Not without putting up a good fight though!

In 1973, when I was thirteen, Errol Rovers took a major step forward and landed their biggest coup in recruiting ex-Lisbon Lion and Celtic Tommy Gemmell as head coach. Big Tam, as he was known, had recently signed for Dundee after a spell in England with Nottingham Forrest. I'm not really sure how this had come about, but in any case, this was a huge thrill for every-one at the time. Big Tam was a genuine Scottish football legend. Without doubt, he played a big part in my early development as a professional because he eventually became my manager only a year after I became a full-time pro with Dundee. Big Tam was an extrovert in more ways than one; he was a colourful character who played hard and lived hard. I was very much in awe of him as he was so famous. He was a great coach for kids too and his sessions were never anything other than great fun.

As in all good things, Errol Rovers was very much a team effort as we also had lots of support from a lot of the parents. There was never any shortage of mums or dads to give us lifts to Dundee when we were playing away from home. Subsequently and unsurprisingly, it wasn't long before we were becoming the force to be reckoned with and Station Park was becoming our fortress.

We also began tempting the top players from Dundee and added the likes of Gary Murray, who went on to play with, among other clubs, Hibs, and goalkeeper Derek Hunter, both from Duncraig Boys Club. Duncraig were among our biggest rivals and the two were among the best players in the league at the time.

With the squad getting stronger and stronger, we got to the semi-finals of the Scottish Cup in 1974, a truly remarkable feat that such a small village green team from rural Perthshire could be competing with the very best from the West of Scotland, including Celtic boys, Gartcosh, Eastercraigs and Fir Park boys. In that semi-final match I can remember it was the first time I had ever felt nervous before a game. This was something I knew I was going to have to get used to!

It was Errol Primary School headmaster Eric Duncan who formed the primary school football team. Eric was a real sports enthusiast and a qualified Grade 2 referee. From time to time he was called upon to referee the home games at Station Park. Eric Duncan was a great guy and my idea of the ideal and perfect headmaster. As long as you were good at sports, you got away with murder!

Originally when I began watching football I was a St Johnstone supporter. I would annoy Dad to take me with him to see them when I knew he was going. It was a real thrill for me when Eric Duncan organised for Willie Coburn and Alex Gordon, both legends of a great St Johnstone team at the time, to come out and do some coaching sessions with all the Errol Primary kids at Station Park. Looking back it was all basic stuff, with mainly passing drills where you would get a ball between two and work on passing and control. Inevitably it always finished with a game; it was never too serious and always great fun. I loved every aspect of it with a passion.

My first real life football hero was John Connolly. I watched him play often for Saints when he was an up-and-coming young player with lots of potential. John was an old-fashioned inside forward with great control and balance. He would glide past defenders with ease and had a very silky, deft touch on the ball. He was the first player who actually made me star-struck. I loved the way John would glide past opponents with ease. He would drop the shoulder, throwing his opponent off balance then glide past him as if he wasn't there. To me at the time it was like magic!

We used to go to watch St Johnstone at old Muirton Park in a group. There would be Mum, Dad, Uncle Phil, Auntie Isla and Jimmy Galloway. Jimmy and his Danish wife, Didda, were great friends of Mum and Dad. Both were all-round sports fanatics. Jimmy was a real character who loved a debate. He and Dad were opposites politically and it got really heated sometimes. Jimmy also seemed to bear the brunt of many of the practical jokes that were played on the drunken nights in our kitchen. Didda loved playing golf, and I can remember her taking Gavin and me to Dunning to play the nine-hole golf course. One of the highlights of the day would be a stopover at the Glencarse Hotel for high tea, on the way back after the match. One particular Saturday when we stopped off I was nearly gobsmacked. I walked into the lounge behind everyone but was first to notice the guy sitting at the window with his wife, or more likely his girlfriend. It was my hero, John Connolly! Embarrassingly, I shuffled over and asked him politely if he would sign his autograph for me. He was a real star in my book and, as I remember, he couldn't have been nicer. It goes to show that when a player takes the time to do that type of thing with a young fan it creates a nice memory that is never forgotten.

Not only did Eric Duncan form the primary school football team but the cricket team too. Subsequently we also became the best primary school cricket team in Perthshire. Basically only the colours changed – not the personnel! The football team more or less just swapped the blue football strips for the cricket whites.

The weird thing about me was that I was a left-handed batsman. Despite the fact that over the years since I retired from football I became a right-handed scratch golfer! Yet even today if you handed me a cricket bat I'd still want to bat left-handed! Actually, in one of my first ever introductions to golf, Eric organised a sponsored golf marathon at Gleneagles, where Gavin, Dave Logie and myself played 81 holes round the then Princes course in one day, to earn money to pay for the school mini-bus. We were also joined by my favourite teacher at the time, Miss Todd (who I confess to having a crush on) and who herself was a very keen golfer. People like Eric Duncan were the main reason why young kids like myself became interested and good at different sports. He was a real enthusiast and thought nothing of giving up his time after hours to take us to matches against other local villages.

Hilariously, though, Eric habitually morphed into the devil when he donned that black uniform! Sometimes it was as though he would deliberately try to infuriate some of the more zealous spectating parents with some of his decisions. Not many of them seemed to appreciate the fact he was giving up his own free time for very little reward to do this for us. Once, he sent one of our own players, Neil Donaldson, off for saying, 'Put the boot into them!' This nearly caused a riot on the touchline. Typically, in his official referee's match report, which was submitted to the league management committee, there was reference to the whole incident! Certainly my Errol Primary headmaster could never be accused of being a 'homer'!

It's funny when I look back and remember how excited some of the parents would get. I could just never imagine this type of thing happening in Juvenile football in Spain, Italy, France or Holland, where there is only emphasis on developing skill and technique and the parents are kept at arm's length. Some of the parents did take things to ridiculous lengths and got so caught up in it all. We had a goalkeeper, Grant Carcary from Perth. His parents Edna and Gregg were fanatics and loved coming to watch every game. I remember one year we were playing in a Cup final in Dundee and one of our players went down injured. The referee for some reason waved play on. The next thing we knew, Edna took to the pitch with play raging on around her to tend to the injured player. It was obviously not a serious injury, but to Edna that was not the point. The passions ran high from both sets of parents. It was not taken too kindly by some when Errol Rovers came to Dundee and won Cup finals.

Typically after our home games on a Sunday our kitchen would be full of players' parents. Dad would get the whisky out and, as usual, it was flowing freely. When you were invited in to Holmlea, you were never offered tea or coffee, no matter what time of the day. Over the years I witnessed some agricultural sales reps literally stagger out of our kitchen before lunchtime and actually even on occasion at breakfast time! Meanwhile, Dad typically would not look as though he'd drunk anything! So, yes, our kitchen was the hub of all après match social activity. There was also so much cigar and cigarette smoke you would've thought the whole place was on fire. One afternoon, though, things went a bit too far and the drinking exploits of one parent nearly caused the ruination of British Rail!

As I've already mentioned, Station Park was named so because it was right beside Errol Station. The pitch was so close to the rail track that any shots fired over the bar inevitably landed on the railway line behind the goal. At that time we also had the old-fashioned railway gates with signal box and signal duty man. The signal duty man was a parent who supported the Rovers and liked a dram. One Sunday afternoon in particular, though, his after-match celebrations in our kitchen were not appreciated by the occupants travelling on the main Glasgow to Aberdeen train. It was stranded at Errol Station due to the fact Archie was AWOL! The train was just stuck there blasting its horn in anger, with a whole bunch of very disgruntled passengers. Eventually word of BR's predicament filtered through to our kitchen.

'Aye, they can bloody wait a bit a longer,' was the cry.

He, though, reluctantly drank up and staggered off to put BR back on track!

The après match entertainment really used to frustrate me because I was always starving after the game and just wanted everyone to go so that we could eat. Mum, much to her credit and no matter what, always cooked a traditional three-course Sunday dinner. Apart from the football, Mum's Sunday dinner was the highlight of my week. She was a fantastic cook. Usually she would do a pot of homemade broth or lentil soup, followed by a roast or casserole of some description. Her liver casserole was awesome. Then it would be something like an apple sponge pudding with custard. It was real old-fashioned farmhouse cooking. By that time she must've been working solely on autopilot. Along with the cigarettes and the booze I think cooking was one of the few things that she actually got any satisfaction from. She did have one really heartbreaking night in the kitchen, though. She'd spent nearly all day preparing the most wonderful-looking steak and kidney pudding I have ever seen. We were all sat round the kitchen table, which was always set with a proper tablecloth, place mats and appropriate cutlery. As she very carefully began to bring her creation out of the oven it looked absolutely delicious. It was perfection. Disastrously, however, somehow it slipped from her grasp and fell onto the floor. Immediately the dogs moved in for the kill and it was so good to them they seemed unconcerned about their mouths getting burned!

There was utter silence. No one in that kitchen dared speak. I could see Mum was literally in tears. Dad, as usual, didn't show much sympathy and I could feel the tension rising around the table. It was horrible. I felt sorry for Mum that day and maybe the reason I remember that day so well is because it was also a metaphor for our lives at the time.

The more successful the Rovers were becoming the more critical Dad had started to become of me. There were the usual after-match inquests at the dinner table, by which time he'd nearly always had a few drams. It was always worse when he'd been drinking. My sister Jill and Mum used to get really fed up of it. Jill couldn't understand what all the fuss was about and Mum just didn't like it when Dad picked on me or anyone. Actually, tellingly, Jill only ever saw me play football once in my entire career! She came to the Scottish Cup replay when I played for Rangers and we beat Dundee United 4–1. Maybe she should've come to more Cup finals!

Quite often things would get so bad round the table that I'd just get up and leave the kitchen, my dinner only half eaten. Dad would goad me about how poorly I had played or how I should've done this or that better. He seemed to need to keep it all going until he got a response from me. Eventually I would take no more and get up from the table and go through to the lounge. Sometimes I'd just sit there in the dark, feeling very depressed about everything. Incredibly, my own spirit always seemed to rally and by the end of the next week I was always looking forward to the next game. I think it was an indication that there was a certain resilience to my character. However, Dad was like Jekyll and Hyde and a couple days later he'd be telling me how great I'd played again. This stuff all began not long after Douglas had died. That was when I most noticed that everything seemed to have changed within the family. I think Dad took a lot of his hurt and anger out on his family because we were easy targets, your immediate family being less likely to fight back and retaliate. His mood swings began to make life difficult and it was like treading on eggshells with him, and especially when he'd been to the pub – which was nearly every night.

I think basically Dad thought the harder and more critical he was of me, the more determined it would make me. Perhaps in spite of him? Whilst I do concede it did certainly make me more determined, it could so easily have backfired had I not been quite so passionate about playing football. It certainly didn't do much for my self-esteem or confidence, which had been shattered after Douglas died. Dad's disapproval and approval were the two most difficult things for me to handle psychologically. I felt that my form as a football player was how he judged me as a person. In reality that probably wasn't true but it's just how he made me feel.

It wasn't just me who was getting it. Mum and Jill were both also subject to his mood swings. He was never violent in the physical sense. In 1977, on the night before Jill got married, there was a classic. Jill was marrying Graeme Fitzgerald, who had practically become like a family member. Graeme lived locally just beside Errol Station and they'd been going out together for what seemed like two or three years. With the wedding arrangements all apparently going to plan, Dad came home from the pub on the Friday night. It was the eve of Jill's big day but we could all tell he was in a mood just by looking at him. In those moments you could cut the atmosphere with a knife. First of all, he started on at Mum until he had her in tears. Then he started on at Jill and was going on and on about her fiancé Graeme.

Ironically, Dad had just taken Graeme into the family business as farm manager! There was no rhyme or reason to it when Dad was like this. It was as if all the poisonous, pent-up feelings just came out when he'd been drinking. Mum was in tears now, Jill was in tears and I'd had enough of it. Finally I snapped and challenged him to shut up and leave everyone alone. He'd got me so wound up and angry about it I was ready to hit him, my own father. We stood face to face but seeing how angry I was he backed off, turned and walked through to the lounge, but he was still saying stuff. Incensed, I went after him. He shut the door on me so I literally kicked it open in anger. I thought we would surely come to blows but again he backed off and I could see he was startled and taken aback. Things calmed down and he shut up and didn't say any more. Amazingly, the next day the wedding all went ahead as if nothing had happened the night before.

Dad always did this. I cannot remember him ever apologising to any of us for anything he said or did. The atmosphere therefore was never cleared and so was not healthy. By the time the wedding came Mum and Dad both had a good drink aboard. This time I think it was Dutch courage as they both were never comfortable with being the centre of attention. I think Dad had a massive complex about walking my sister up the aisle. I didn't think that much of it at the time because alcohol and drinking had become such a big part of their lives. When I look back on it all, I think it must've been terrible for Jill to have had all this going on the night before her wedding. What a terrible pity for her on what should have been a very happy family celebration. I remember vividly as well when she and Graeme came back from their honeymoon. They had gone off for a two-week honeymoon holiday to Bermuda. Upon their return Dad couldn't even ask if she'd had a nice time. All she got was a whole bunch of crap about how badly she had left things in the business before she had gone away. However, these times were not much fun for any of us.

I believe alcohol was originally Mum's coping mechanism, but it had got steadily worse over the years. We knew she was a secret drinker too because we used to find half-empty whisky tumblers all over the house. The piano stool was one of her favourite places. The pantry in the kitchen was another, along with the book cupboard in the lounge and the cupboard in the hall. Much of the time we could smell it off her too. She would eat mints and Tunes incessantly to try and keep Dad from smelling it off her. Mum had become a serial drinker and, although she tried, was unsuccessful at hiding it.

The thing about alcoholics is that they deny everything and admit nothing. Most nights Mum would just crash out on the settee and it could be virtually impossible to wake her up. If you did manage to wake her, she'd sometimes be incoherent and would talk nonsense. She was just blotting it all out and numbing down the pain. Occasionally when Dad came home from the pub drunk, his line of attack would be to blame Mum for Douglas's death. In his drunken mind it was because she was a smoker or it was her punishment for not particularly wanting to have a third child. This was of course very hurtful and simply not true. The next day, however, it would be almost as if nothing had been said and, as per usual, no apologies. I never once ever heard my father apologise for anything.

My Aunt Margaret, Mum's sister, and her husband Uncle Bob, owned Cookston Farm, Eassie, near Forfar. The farm is now run by her son Davie, my cousin, and his wife Fiona. Tragically, Aunt Margaret's eldest son George, himself a Rangers fanatic, died in his early forties of heart failure. Aunt Margaret was a pillar of support to our family during Douglas's illness and after he died.

At one time Dad owned the shooting rights to Cookston Farm. This was where he taught me how to rough shoot for game, wildfowl and vermin when I was no more than thirteen years old. Dad had a collection of shotguns and I learned how to look after them for him. I had a proper gun-cleaning kit and in his office, which later became the 'wee sitting room', I'd strip the guns down after use, oil them and put them back together again. My first shotgun was a JR Gow 12 gauge. It was of course Dad's gun but he gave me it to use any time I wanted.

Often in the wintertime when we knew where and when the wild Greylags or Pink Feet were feeding, we'd go on reconnaissance a day or two before, to build a hide and prepare. At roughly 4.30am the next morning he'd get me out of bed. More often than not, Gavin would be involved too, so he stayed over when we were hunting. Of course it would also involve a day off school! I'd come downstairs and get all the guns and equipment ready. The dogs by now were excited, as they knew what was happening. Dad would be at the cooker boiling milk to add to his OVD Rum flask. This was his way of staying warm in the hide. We'd also have flasks of soup, typically homemade broth and filled rolls to keep us going for the day.

We'd set off, laden to the gunnels in his old mini-van. It took about half an hour to drive from Errol to Cookston. We'd get to the hide just before dawn, which is the time when the Greylags begin to fly from roost to feed. By this time we were lying in wait. Often it was bitterly cold and even with mitts on sometimes the tips of my fingers would be numb. You would then begin to hear the distinct noise of the stirring of the wild geese in the distance. Then the action would start.

The hardest thing about learning how to shoot a wild goose in flight is the temptation to shoot when you think it's in range. It's such a deceptively big target. Dad taught me to wait until it circles in, until it's no more than about twenty yards away. The problem with that is the geese are very wily and unless you have got perfect camouflage they can detect you and fly off. They are very intelligent and have great instinct. Often initially I'd fire too soon, only for the pellets to rattle off the dense plumage and the goose would fly on unharmed.

In one of Dad's earlier goose adventures, which he named 'revenge of the Pink Foot', he had been with a group who had decided that, due to lack of cover, the only way to hide from the geese would be to lie still, flat on their backs in the middle of the field! As the geese came in they circled round and round until someone shouted, 'Open fire!' Around five or six guns all started blasting away. All at once four or five geese fell out of the sky from around twenty to thirty yards up.

Unfortunately, one unsuspecting huntsman got taken out by a kamikaze goose that decided to land full pelt on his stomach! Bearing in mind a goose can easily weigh up to seven or eight pounds, it was therefore no surprise when the poor guy was carted off to hospital with internal bleeding. Thankfully, he was okay.

At the time for me shooting was an exciting sport or hobby. Nowadays, I have too much admiration for all wildlife and wouldn't lift a gun to anything. A typical shooting day would start with a goose flight at first light in the morning. We'd have our filled rolls for breakfast. Dad, of course, would have his flask of hot milk and rum! We'd then move on to hunting pheasants in rough cover. This was where the Spaniels would come into their own. By the end of the day we'd walked through or over several miles of cover, but whatever we'd travelled the dogs would've covered a hundred times more ground than us! Spaniels are also very soft-mouthed so if you shot a bird they would pick it up and bring it to you without harming the flesh.

That way it would still be perfect for going in the pot for a good dinner.

Not much game was wasted. Mum knew how to prepare anything we shot. There was also a market for selling game so if we had surplus then we could sell it to some of the game butchers.

Tommy Gemmell was also a very keen shot and also used to enjoy days out at Cookston with Dad. I think this was his reward for agreeing to be head coach of Errol Rovers! He seemed to have become good friends with Dad, anyway. It was Dad who also taught Gavin the rudiments of shooting.

I was always made aware of the dangers of the sport, as Dad had all the safety aspects drilled into me from day one. Ironically, being such a stickler for gun safety, he took a lot more risks after the shoots than during them! On one occasion, which I remember vividly, we'd typically stopped off at the Alyth Junction Hotel/Bar on the way home. It was a regular pit stop. One this particular day Dad had recruited a farm employee as his driver – no doubt so as he could have even more to drink 'après shoot' than usual. This was the only part of the day I didn't enjoy because it normally meant sitting watching Dad and whoever was with him drink one whisky after another. It was always a very long day. Gavin, as more often than not, was also in the squad that day. He was none too pleased. So at least I wasn't on my own. We would frown upon the drinking and maintain that we would never drink when we were older! Pity we couldn't have stuck to that! We did, however, manage to down some cheese and ham toasties along with a few Cokes, so at least we didn't starve. The grown-ups were downing 'nips' like there was no tomorrow and, funnily enough, there very nearly was no tomorrow for us all later that evening! Not only had Dad and his guest been going for it but Dad started plying our driver with drink too! By the time we left Alyth, they were all well and truly up the Junction!

Coming over the hill from Alyth to Errol we hit the dual carriageway in Dad's old mini-van at Invergowrie, just outside Dundee. Gavin and I were cramped in the back of the van with all the guns, dogs and dead game! The weather was really bad, it had started raining heavily and visibility was very poor – never mind through the fog of alcohol! As we crawled up the carriageway towards the Errol turn-off there were quite a lot of roadworks and as we neared Dad's farm Middlebank, which lies just off the main dual carriageway, there appeared to be lane closures. So we were down to just two single lanes with only cones separating them. The driver was so drunk that he'd begun to nod off. Dad was oblivious too. I felt a bump and noticed the driver had taken out a couple of cones and had wandered onto the on-coming lane. All I could now see was headlights coming straight towards us. I dived forward, grabbed the steering wheel and the van lurched back into the correct lane. The driver suddenly startled and woke up from his temporary coma! It had been a very close call indeed. Very close to a head-on collision.

Another time Dad came home very drunk and decided he wanted to go shooting wild geese in the moonlight. Mum on this night grabbed his keys to stop him going. They had a real barney and it ended with Mum thumping him on the head with a pillow! Eventually Dad got the message, gave up and fell asleep.

The drink was just to numb the pain and all the shooting I think may have been his way of getting rid of some of the anger he must've felt. Again, although never physically violent to any of his family, Dad still had a ferocious temper. He had little or no patience for anything or anyone during this time. His gun dogs used to get the brunt of his anger sometimes and once, when

Gavin and I were out with him, Judy, his main working Spaniel, had run too far ahead and was flushing out birds that were hence miles out of range. Dad was furious and began bawling at her to come back. Eventually when she did, she knew what was coming and within a few yards of his reach was already crawling on her belly.

'Come heeeeere!' he would say in a very threatening, menacing tone.

But what happened next left Gavin and I just standing with our mouths open in shock. Poor Judy knew she was in for a hammering when Dad got a hold of her. But he picked her up by the ears and thumped her onto the ground. Suffice to say his dog got the message and she did as was told for the rest of the day. Dad's anger in those days was never far from the surface. It could be very scary.

For me the real tragedy of my father was that, if it weren't for what happened in those extremely painful years, I'm sure he would've gone on to build a real business empire. One that would've really justified all the 'poor little rich kid' comments I used to have to put up with during most of my career. He was an extremely sharp, intelligent, hard-working businessman. His mental arithmetic was incredible and he would get frustrated with me because I was always hopeless at counting numbers in my head – by comparison to him, I might add! Looking back, I can understand and appreciate what his mind must've been going through.

Latterly in his life, as I had done by my late twenties to early thirties, Dad more or less gave up shooting. I think he was just done with all the anger and, again like myself, became much more appreciative of all the beautiful wildlife. He would much rather go and enjoy the therapeutic aspects of salmon fishing on his Newtyle stretch of the Tay that he had jointly acquired with a partner, Gordon Mitchell, a chicken farmer from Letham in Angus. Gone were huge catches. Now it was much more about relaxing and enjoying the countryside and the company of some of his closest fishing pals, like Geordie McInnes and George Todd, and even more latterly my father-in-law, Luigi Tortolano.

Now I have always been a dog lover. Seldom in my life have I ever been without at least one. From the early days of my teenage years when I learned how to train them to the gun, to today where my dogs are just house pets. The most satisfaction I always got from shooting was seeing the dogs working. Especially my Springer Spaniels. First there was Skipper, who I had from when he was a puppy, then Monty, who was son of! Spaniels have such a zest for life and are constantly on the move. They just live for hunting out game and seldom if ever are their noses off duty! We once very untypically had a toy poodle. I think it was Mum's dog, as she was given it as a present from her own mother. I will never forget the day we were up at the river at Newtyle when I insisted on taking it shooting with me and the working dogs. Mum was dead against it but I told her not to worry. It would be fine and I'd look after Kim, as he was called! What he lacked in size he more than made up for in spirit.

Anyway, we set off over the river in the boat. Skipper, as usual, jumped out halfway across because he loved the water. Incidentally, he used to take himself down to the bottom of the garden and go into the pool for a swim. I had taught him to use the steps so he knew how to get back out. He would swim around till he was done then take himself out, as taught. Only thing he didn't do was towel himself down! Anyway, on the other side of the river Dad, along with his partner, owned approximately thirty acres that was Newtyle Farm. It was not really very good for arable farming because the land was very hilly. However, it was good for rough shooting with good strips of cover woodland and ideal for pheasants, as there was lots of kale around and pheasants love to feed on that. As I set off through all the rough cover and fields, I got totally engrossed in the shoot and completely forgot about Kim the toy poodle. It wasn't till much later on in the day I realised he was missing. After promising Mum that he'd be fine, I had to go back over the river to the fishing lodge where she had been relaxing with some friends and inform her I'd lost Kim! Consequently, I was sent back across the river to find the missing poodle. I got back in the boat and headed back over the river, taking with me Skipper and Judy. They were hopeless because they were only interested in finding rabbits and pheasants. I was on my own with this one!

The search was to no avail. I had no recollection of when and where the dog had gone missing. It was a needle in a haystack job! Mum's dog was gone and I was responsible. At the time we'd been staying in a holiday cottage at Dunkeld. So we put an ad in the local press, giving a description of the missing dog. Realistically we were thinking we'd never see it again! I mean, it was so small a rat would've given it a run for its money! Three days later, however, we got a response to the ad. Someone had found the dog wandering on the main roads not far outside Dunkeld. They'd thought it was unusual to see a toy poodle wandering aimlessly in the countryside, so had stopped and managed to pick it up. Miraculously, and most thankfully for me, Kim came home safe and sound!

Whilst I was still at Perth High School, every year about four or five weeks in June/July meant only one thing – berry time! Dad was one of the first farmers in the Carse of Gowrie to grow soft fruit in large acreages. He had cultivated about forty acres at Middlebank Farm. There was very good money in growing strawberries and Dad had got in at just the right time. He was such an innovator and always seemed to be a step ahead of the game. During berry

46

time I always had to be up and on the fields by 7am until four or five in the afternoon. I learned to do all sorts of jobs on the farm. One day I would be weighing and paying. The next I'd be working in the wash plant. By my early teens I was proficient with all the farm vehicles and thought nothing of reversing a tractor and trailer with a huge load of fruit on it. In fact, I was so proficient I thought nothing of taking Dad's van or a tractor out onto the main road and up the dual carriageway between Errol and Inchture. Quite often I'd also have my shotguns, as I would be off decoying pigeons feeding on a field of grain. Pigeons were pretty much seen as vermin by farmers and there were few who would object to them being thinned out a bit. Not that I exactly made a dent on the local population! I knew how to build a proper hide, set up decoys in the right place and wait for them to come and feed. It was always best to gauge where the flight line was to give you an indication of where they would come from and at what part of the field they would most likely feed on.

I admit I could be a bit of a jack the lad at times but in comparison we could have some real villains working on the farm at this time of the year. One in particular I remember well because I worked with him on the weigh-and-pay bank. A young girl, not too many years younger than me, had been tragically murdered in Perth. It was big news all over the local press. A few days later Perth CID arrested the guy who worked beside me and charged him with her murder. Apparently the victim had been the daughter of his live-in girlfriend. Supposedly he'd killed her in a fit of rage. In any case, he was found guilty and given a life sentence to serve in Perth Prison. It was unbelievable to me because I thought he just seemed like an ordinary guy. He wasn't a full-time employee and only came to the farm during the berry harvest.

To get the berry squads out to the farm Dad sent in some old second-hand double-decker buses he'd acquired, to pick them up at designated points in the council schemes of Perth and Dundee. The buses would return laden with berry pickers. They were so crammed full of bodies the only available breathing space was quite literally on the roof! In those days getting pickers or labourers for farm work was never a problem. It was good money too for those that grafted.

We had another worker who had been a bit of a drifter but came to work for us one year and ended up staying on the farm for virtually the whole of his working life. Dad was a good boss and as far as I was aware, he looked after his workers as well as could reasonably be expected. One very memorable day, however, this guy nearly put the Redford family out of business for life. He'd been on a tractor going from Middlebank Farm over to the poultry farm at the Grange. To get there he had to cross the railway line further along from Errol Station. The Grange crossing had automatic electronic barriers and as he approached the crossing the barriers came down. Being in a rush, I think he got out to see where the train was. He looked left, up the line towards Dundee, and right, down the line towards Perth. Whatever happened he must've thought he was in the clear. So he got back onto the tractor with the trailer and decided to skip round the barriers, even though they were still down and the lights were flashing, indicating a train was coming. Just as he got the nose of the tractor onto the line, a train came out of nowhere and literally cut the tractor in half, leaving him sitting there holding practically nothing but the steering wheel. The train severed the front of the tractor as clean as a knife would cut a slice of bread. Miraculously, he was not even injured and, even more so, the train did not derail. If it had, there were three cottages right beside the level crossing and it would've almost certainly hit them, causing a major disaster! Fortunately he had a full driving licence and, from memory, got away with a severe fine and ban. Had any lives been lost he would've gone to jail and Dad would probably have been sued and put out of business for good! There were other workers though, who from time to time took tractors, and other vehicles for that matter, out on the main roads and who didn't have any licence – not mentioning any names!

Another family used to come out in a big old wreck of a car from Dundee. Every morning they were on the fruit field at virtually first light and would be picking even before I'd set up the weighing scales, which was normally around 7am. The father of this family would make all his kids graft all day and he belted them if they didn't. Then at the end of the day he'd take all they'd earned off them and put it in his own pocket. Then go drink it all away in the pub at night. This would go on day after day. It was heartbreaking.

In another episode, I had to help separate two women who had started fighting at the bottom of one of the drills. One was a local from the village, the other had been an alleged prostitute from Dundee or Perth. The verbals had started and before long they were trying to tear the eyes out of each other! Me and a couple of other helpers had to race down the field to separate them and get things cooled down!

During the summer Dad was very much a sun worshipper. Not in the sense that he ever gave himself the time to lie down and sunbathe, but more from the point he would go around with only his string vest on, like Rab C. Nesbitt! Dad was of the opinion that you had to burn first to get a good tan. He literally would not let me keep my shirt on when it was really hot. Consequently, I got some really bad sunburns and my skin used to peel often. I couldn't wait to get home from the farm after a day on the berry fields and get into the pool for a cool-off. Fruit picking is back-breaking work, especially strawberry picking. You are on your knees and bent over double nearly all the time. Some of the pickers knew if they grafted they could make good money but I'm not so sure too many people today would be willing to spend a whole day on the berry fields.

After a few years of doing well at the fruit Dad found, as in all farming since joining the EU, that competition was much more widespread and as a result margins became more and more squeezed, making it more difficult. He was not one for rules and regulations either, and I don't think would've fared too well with all the PC bureaucracy that is prevalent today. Too many rules and regulations. Compliance was coming and compliance was something that Dad just didn't do.

For me becoming a professional footballer was my escape from the berry fields of Middlebank! At sixteen years old I was earning my own money, even though I'm sure there were plenty of berry pickers who would've had more cash in their pockets by the end of the week than me as an apprentice footballer. Dad had always said to me to give up football anytime I wanted and come back and work on the farm. I knew this would never be an option because I would not have lasted any more than ten minutes working for or with him.

Ten minutes was about the time it took for us to fall out big time when he tried to teach me how to plough a straight furrow in a field up at Middlebank one day. Having shown me what to do, he watched me take control of the tractor and copy, but within seconds he was on my back ranting, 'No, that's useless. What do you think you're trying to do? Look at the mess you're making!'

That was it. I'd had it. I jumped out of the tractor cab and stormed up the field in a massive huff, leaving Dad shouting and bawling at me. What he just didn't know was how uptight he made me feel. I could never relax with him breathing down my neck, so more often than not I would make a hash of things in front of him. However, Jim West, one of Dad's longest-serving farm employees, had witnessed what had happened and when Dad left, he took me aside and showed me what to do. Within minutes I was ploughing the field perfectly!

In 1973 on an autumn Sunday afternoon, Davie White, who was then the manager of Dundee FC, and former manager of Glasgow Rangers, came specifically to watch both Gavin and me play in a home league match for the Rovers. His chief scout, Tom Arnott, had been alerted and had been watching us for weeks. Tommy Gemmell I think had also been making Davie White aware of our progress. After the match, I remember Davie spoke to both of us and asked if we'd like to sign for Dundee on a schoolboy form, or S-form, and we were happy to agree.

S-forms were the only way that a club could get control over you over any other club. Signing an S-form was pretty official. It meant you could not represent any other professional club until you had left school. The form also required the signature of the headmaster of your school, because school football still took precedence over all others. This ruling, or regulation if you like, almost got me into very hot water with the authorities because Dundee FC asked me to play in a reserve game when I was only fifteen and still officially at school and I had not asked my head-master for permission.

I remember on the morning of the match I told Mum and Dad that we needed to inform the school and get their permission first. Dad in particular told me not to bother with it, and who were they to tell me what I could and couldn't do? This was typical of him! He was always very anti-bureaucracy. It never occurred to him in this instance this rule was potentially more of a protective measure against some of the more unscrupulous methods used by some professional clubs. For example, it was known for some clubs to blanket-sign a whole load of players in the hope that maybe one or two would make it. The players got no compensation at all and the vast majority were simply rejected at sixteen – not a great time in your life to be told you're not good enough! At least with the school having a say in some instances it could prevent this type of thing from happening.

Although it was such a thrill for me to get this chance, I knew there would be repercussions if they found out. Which, of course, they did! I was called into the head's office and asked to explain my actions. Recognising that his threat to ban me from playing any and all organised football, including playing for Errol Rovers, was real, unless I apologised. I therefore told him I was sorry and would ask his permission the next time. Perth High School normally would never have tried to stop me from playing football. They just wanted to be given their place. I couldn't see what the big deal was about telling them!

There was no doubt Tommy Gemmell's influence on me as inspiration and coach of Errol Rovers played a big part in me getting signed initially by Dundee FC. Tam also undoubtedly became a friend of the family. He and his wife at the time, Anne, bought the Commercial Hotel in Errol and so moved into the area whilst he was still playing for Dundee. When it came to drinking, though, he'd met his match with my dad, and the two would have regular sessions in his pub in the village. I remember Dad recalling one night when between them, he reckoned they'd downed a good few bottles of wine, then he had to go out and play the next day!

By the age of fifteen, going on sixteen, I couldn't wait to leave school. The one thing that kept me going was playing for the senior football team. The older guys were great and used to give me lots of encouragement. By this time I was all left foot, fast and very skilful, and was beginning to become really outstanding at this level. The other players used to give me the ball and let me do the rest. I did become a target though, and sometimes would take some real kickings in matches from those that were older, stronger and quick enough to get anywhere near me. Paradoxically, my self-esteem was not very high. Football, however, seemed to be my way of being able to express myself. Without it, I really don't know what would've happened to me. I had graduated to the senior team in my last year at Perth High School, having played for the Junior High School teams all the way up from first year. It was evident that Gavin and I were both outstanding for the school. Our school junior football team manager was an economics teacher, Joe Leishman. Sometimes he was very uncomplimentary and that didn't help, as I didn't have a strong level of self-belief and was sensitive to any criticism.

'That's feeble, Redford,' he would often say.

Whilst at school I was very poor in class and would regularly skip lessons. Sometimes I would skip entire days! In the morning I'd sometimes deliberately miss the school bus outside our house and say to Mum that I would just take the train to Perth. I'd then wander round to the platform next door at Errol Station and instead get on the train to Dundee! Sometimes I would just wander around Dundee on my own for whole days, maybe going to the pictures. My favourite movies at the time were James Bond, and in particular I remember going to see *The Man with the Golden Gun* several times! Also when possible I'd head up to Dens Park and join in with the reserve team training sessions. I loved being able to do that. At that time I loved the atmosphere of a professional football club and really wanted to become a part of it.

For some subjects I was actually put into a separate class for disruptive, low achievers, especially for Maths. My teachers either didn't know what was going on in my life or didn't realise that I was in fact completely deaf in one ear and not capable of processing information as efficiently as someone with normal hearing. My records must have shown that I was partially deaf. It is apparently a statistical fact that even if you are partially deaf, as I at least was at the time, you are 35 per cent more likely to fail your exams. My maths teacher would get so exasperated with me. One day she pulled me out of class, saying she couldn't understand why I was doing so poorly when it was obvious to her that I wasn't stupid. Today I think they probably would've found some label to pin on me. At the very least I should've been made to sit right at the front of the class in order to be able to hear the teacher better. Me being me, however, I would always try to sit anonymously right at the back of the class if possible.

The best way I can describe the difference between partial deafness and normal hearing is like the difference between reading text in small faint print as opposed to reading it in large bold print. In large bold print it's far easier and much less of an effort to absorb. The word 'absorb' is the key here, because although you can see and hear something to a certain extent, it doesn't mean your brain has processed or absorbed the information. Possibly without realising it, I would just switch off in classes entirely because I was simply not processing the information in the same way kids with normal hearing were. Another factor for me was that I didn't wear adequate noise protection on my good ear when I was shooting. Subsequently, I believe this has cost me dearly in terms of hearing quality in my good ear. Mum and Dad never seemed to bother or realise I could be harming my good ear by shooting. They also showed little interest in my academic results. That suited me fine though, as I was just not interested in anything at school apart from sports.

In French one day, my teacher pulled me out to the front of the class after I had been acting the clown. He asked me in a very mocking manner: 'Redford,' he said, 'just what on earth do you think you are going to do with your life?'

'Well, sir,' I replied, 'I'm going to be a professional footballer.'

He started laughing in my face and said something along the lines of, 'And just how do you intend to do that?'

'Well, sir,' I told him, 'I am already signed for Dundee FC and will be playing for them full-time next season.'

His face went red and there were a few sniggers from the rest of the class, then he told me to get out of his sight!

The last day I ever attended Perth High School was on sports day and I became sports champion, setting new records in nearly every event, including 100 metres, 200 metres, 400 metres, high jump, long jump, shot putt. I was also chosen to represent Perth High School in an inter-county athletics meeting. I used to love doing the high jump and used the old Fosbury Flop technique, which I had basically more or less taught myself. These records stood for many years until broken by Graham Farquharson, younger brother of Kenny and Lynn (who married Sean Lineen, the famous rugby player). The Farquharsons were very well known and respected farmers in the Carse of Gowrie. They owned and ran The Horn Milk Bar. I remember Graham bumped into me one day, years later, and told me that he had been the one that took out all my records. He was a good athlete and I think he ran and competed at county level.

I remember being surprised at doing so well that day. Again I had not seen myself having this potential in athletics. On the day something just seemed to click and I seemed able to lift things to another level altogether when I needed to. I had certainly never shown this winning potential in any of the heats. But on the day I just managed to do it all exactly when it mattered. Looking back, this kind of thing can be typical of me when I have little or no time to allow my mind to get in the way! That's why I really like the Nike slogan 'Just do it'. Very clever and so very true!

I actually felt really proud of myself that day, to be leaving school as senior sports champion. However, when I got home and told Mum and Dad what I had just done they just didn't seem interested at all. It was strange. It was like they didn't care about what I had achieved that day. Yet if it was anything to do with playing with Errol Rovers, it seemed to be an entirely different matter. Thinking back, Dad did become funny about me playing for the school football team. I wonder now if it possibly may have had something to do with the fact that it simply reminded him of the day when he got the call to go home and to the hospital the day Douglas died.

Having become senior sports champion of Perth High School, I didn't show up for the presentation. This is something I really regret. I felt shy, awkward and uncomfortable to be the centre of attention, unless it was on a football pitch. I should've been made to go or made myself go to collect my prize. For years after I had turned pro as a footballer I used to get an invite from PHS rector Ian Agnew to go to the annual prize-giving day and present the awards, but I always seemed to make up an excuse not to go. For years I felt bad about that, because I think Mr Agnew was genuinely understanding of me and proud of the fact that a pupil from Perth High School had gone on to play for Glasgow Rangers and had become the most expensive player in Scotland.

As a parent I have always been so proud when my kids do something well, and over the years they have both given me so much to be proud of. Ian Junior, with his success as an up-and-coming young golfer and Natalie, with her drive and ambition gained a first-class honours degree at Edinburgh University studying the art of photography. I can't imagine ever being any different with them no matter what the circumstances. I always make a point of telling them to try and do things without fear of failure. Success rarely comes to those in an instant. Success tends to come those who have constantly failed but keep learning and more importantly trying.

It's taken me a long, long time to realise that actually failure and success only really exist in your head relative to how you think and feel about yourself. It's always the doing part that is the best bit and without a doubt that's the bit you always look back on and remember most. I try not to over compensate with Natalie and Ian though, and like to think we keep things in perspective. Both good and bad! It's about balance.

The year I left Perth High School, 1976, was also the last year I played for Errol Rovers at Under-16s. The club did continue, and although a younger generation came through, there was never another Errol team that produced the same calibre of player as the one I played in. Playing for Errol Rovers had given me a great grounding because the Dundee Sunday Boys league was a very competitive league. Many of the top players that came out of Dundee had been brought up playing this league. Players like David Narey, Ralph Milne, Davie Dodds and John Holt, all out-and-out Dundonians.

In all I think I must've played Juvenile football for Errol Rovers for about five years. However, now aged sixteen, I was ready to graduate and become a professional footballer.

One thing I have mentioned in this chapter was the rivalry between the top Dundee Juvenile clubs and Errol Rovers. I have spoken of the perceived jealousy that seemed to exist. There is one thing that put it all into perspective for me. When my brother died we got much genuine sympathy from all the other clubs in the league, including all the committee members. All the petty grievances, whatever they were and however they had existed, were literally washed away by the very kind and sympathetic human reactions of ordinary people. I know Mum and Dad appreciated that and I also never forgot it. Funny how the most meaningful and genuine things seem to stick in your mind. It showed that although we were the outsiders from the country-side when it came down to the things that really mattered there were no differences at all. I think this could explain why I have always felt Dundee and Tayside is more of a spiritual home to me than any other place. All of my best football memories seem to be related in one way or another to Dundee.

3

DUNDEE FC

In 1976, approximately three years after signing S-forms for Dundee, the club offered me my first full-time professional contract. Having left school at the age of sixteen with virtually no academic qualifications, I had achieved my ambition of becoming a professional footballer. At the time Dundee were without doubt the right club for me. I was by now very familiar with the surroundings and environment of the club. I knew Dundee manager Davie White would not be afraid to give me my chance to make the breakthrough early if I was good enough. In any case, I had already made good progress for my age, because at only aged fifteen I had already made more than a few appearances for the reserves. I was happy to be joining a professional club with the stature and reputation of Dundee FC. Over the years some very good players, and one or two great players, had played in the famous dark blue jersey. Players like Billy Steel, Charlie Cook, Alan Gilzean, Alex Hamilton, Ian Ure. Dundee FC had also at the time recently sold John Duncan to Tottenham Hotspur.

In that era, for a young player like myself, playing for the reserves was fantastic! You always played on a Saturday at 3pm or occasionally in midweek but the matches were never played on practice grounds or Junior parks. They were always played in the main stadiums. When coming up against the bigger clubs there were also usually some big-name players on the team sheet who were either coming back from injury or had been dropped and temporarily, or even permanently, out of favour!

In my very first game for Dundee reserves at the age of fifteen I played against Ayr United at Dens Park. Playing in the team alongside me that day was my mentor at the time, ex-Lisbon Lion and Celtic legend, Big Tam Gemmell. By this time his legs had gone but he had a great football brain and was an influential character in the dressing room. For me at that young age it was a thrill to be on the same park as him. In one reserve match round about the same time, I remember playing at Parkhead one night against Celtic. They had guys like Alfie Conn, Harry Hood and Bobby Lennox in the team. It was a dream come true for me to be lining up against such football legends, players that I had only ever previously watched from the old wooden stands of Muirton Park and Dens. From such an early age to get this opportunity I reckon was an incredible and invaluable experience in my early development. Rubbing shoulders with these guys at my age helped me enormously to realise my own game had nothing to fear in this type of company. As good as some of these greats were, they were not superhuman or untouchable. Consequently, I got over the star-struck teenager phase quickly and didn't spend too much time being over-awed on the pitch. In any case, I was just enjoying the whole experience too much!

Looking back, playing football was my escape. It was the only thing I did that made me feel any good about myself. When playing football I got lost in the moment. As a child I had practised for this time so much. My skills developed and I became good technically. It also seemed the better I became the better I felt about me. I was, however, very one-footed. I'm not really sure why but some of the best players in the world are very one-footed. I could strike a ball on the volley or first time with my right but my touch and control with it were non-existent from a professional standards point of view. Looking back, maybe I should've put more work into cultivating my right side but if it was good enough for the likes of Jim Baxter or Davie Cooper, then it was certainly good enough for me.

In 1972 Davie White, formerly of Clyde, assistant to Scott Symon at Rangers and former manager of Rangers, became manager of Dundee FC. As early as the following season, 1973/74, he delivered a major trophy, when Dundee beat Celtic 1–0 in the League Cup final at Hampden Park. This I remember was the first major Cup final I had ever been to.

Dundee had a very good team at the time and had players of real quality, with the likes of John Duncan, Gordon Wallace, Bobby Ford, Thomson Allan, Iain Phillip and, of course, ex-Celtic legend Big Tam, whom Davie White brought to the club. It was obvious they weren't as big a club as Rangers or Celtic but they were perfect for me at the time. However, within only a few seasons of that famous League Cup win, the new Scottish Premier League was formed in 1975/76. With just ten teams set to be playing in the new top-flight league, there was a lot of pressure on clubs such as Dundee to stay in that elite top ten. Unfortunately, Dundee did not earn the right to be in the Premier League structure, as they had failed to finish in the top ten the season before the new league commenced. Consequently, the club found themselves in the newly formed second tier, which was to be the new First Division. With a huge full-time staff to pay, this was a crippling blow financially to the club because of a massive reduction in revenues due to lack of games against the big clubs. The new top ten structure also meant that teams would play each other four times. Missing out on a guaranteed four games against the Old Firm of Rangers and Celtic was devastating. By the time I had signed a full professional contract in 1976, Davie White was already under increasing pressure to get the team back up into the top ten or Premier League.

Looking back at that first season as a pro, I didn't realise just how much standards were well below levels of what you would expect from a top professional club in Scotland. Being a youngster of only sixteen, I just didn't really know any better, as I had never experienced life inside the core of a full-time professional football club. In hindsight, during this time, things were very poorly run and disorganised. On a Monday morning we'd come in to the stadium and get our training gear for the week but no matter what the weather conditions, your training kit was not washed again until the Friday. Every day after training you would simply hang all your used kit on a hanger and stick it in the big drying cupboard, situated just outside the home and away dressing rooms. By the end of the week the training kit would be absolutely filthy and foul-smelling. By Wednesday my socks were stinking and by Friday they were standing to attention like a couple of bits of cardboard! The tracksuits and training tops were mostly cotton. They too were rigid by the end of the week. It was actually better when it was raining because the water would soften the material! Some players ended up taping some of the ripped gear with duct tape to hold it together. Thinking back, it was a total shambles!

As a young apprentice, I wasn't given much else to do apart from mop out the dressing rooms after training was done. I have to say, I am not a great believer in young players being treated like skivvies and having to run around after older players. If you are a professional footballer then your time should be devoted 100 per cent to becoming as good a player as you possibly can. Time is critical and each day you have is valuable in your progression as a player. You don't become a good player by spending hours cleaning boots or working on all sorts of other menial tasks. However, I'm not suggesting for a minute young players should be pampered. What I am saying is that I believe 100 per cent of time and effort should go into improving themselves as footballers.

In those days at Dens Park, more often than not the younger players would get their kit blagged or nicked by some of the older players. It was like a free-for-all in the lockers when it came to training kit and towels. It was dog eat dog! The overall kit situation for a professional club of such status was a joke. It got to the desperate stage where I was even prepared to nick some gear for myself, but one morning I sure as hell got my timing and selection very wrong indeed. On this day I decided to help myself to a towel that was on a hanger in the dryer but at the precise moment two things were very much not in my favour. The first thing was that the person whose towel I was helping myself to just happened to be standing right behind me. Secondly, that person was our goalkeeper, Ally Donaldson, a giant of a man and probably the very last person at the club you would want to fall out with. Ally was none too pleased that a sixteen-year-old whippersnapper was helping himself to his towel. I thought I was going to get a hiding, but luckily I got away with a stern lecture, as Ally was one of the more civilised and educated characters within the squad! Thankfully, lesson learned, I remained unscathed but the fright alone was enough to ensure I never did it again!

Monday mornings were the worst in the first year because I was mainly playing in the reserves and reserve coach George Blues, aka 'the Blue Max', just loved to get his players on the track and run them till some were on their knees throwing up. I would come in to the stadium on a Monday and look out over the pitch. There would be the Blue Max, pacing out yardages on the track and marking them out with his cones. It was like cone city! Among George's favourite exercises was the 'coffin'. It was a routine where you would run one leg, jog the next three, run two legs, then jog two, run three legs, then jog one. Finally, you would run all four legs. After approximately two or three minutes you'd do it all again and again.

There were other gems, like the forties and eighties, where you would run forty yards and back three times then walk to the eighty-yard line, where you would run eighty yards and back three times. It didn't seem like football training to me. It was more like army training or punishment for a poor performance on the previous Saturday.

One thing it did, though, was get me really fit. George Blues just made you run till the blood was coming out of your eyes! He had this maniacal grin and his eyes lit up when he knew he was pounding you on the track! I think he must've spent too much time on the sand dunes with Big Jock Wallace! George could actually be a very funny guy and was a good fitness coach. I remember he had this old beat-up brown Triumph Herald that he used to cruise in back and forth from training. On a Monday morning, though, he could become the most hated man at Dens Park! As a first-team player, the thought of dropping back down into George's squad was motivation enough to scare you into playing well and keeping out of the reserves, or the 'stiffs'!

Most clubs during that era had a big communal bath and at Dens Park there was one in both dressing rooms. There was a shower and slip bath in both too, but most players just seemed to bypass them and jump straight into the communal bath! In retrospect, it was so unhygienic. Yuck – when I think about it now! There was usually a film of scum and hair on the murky water's surface. Players also just washed their hair in the communal bath. Today the environmental health department

64

would've slammed a condemned order on the place and shut it down. It had to be germ city! When one member of that squad, who'll remain nameless, came in one morning and announced he had a dose of the crabs, bath time at Dens took on a whole new meaning and became a bit like playing Russian roulette! How no one picked up a serious infection or disease from that cesspool we bathed in daily I will never know.

The treatment room at Dens was adjacent to the first-team dressing room and was never busier than on a Monday morning when all the 'skivers' would come in, nursing hangovers and with 'injuries' from Saturday's game – especially if the result had been a bad one, or when George Blues could be seen pacing up and down the track with his cones! Club physiotherapist Eric Ferguson, who was also a physio for the national squads, was such a likeable guy but he could be a bit of a soft touch. There were two treatment tables in the physio room, which was adjacent to the home or first-team dressing room. When it was your turn you'd hobble up onto a table or bench. Eric would usually wrap the injury in an old worn towel then put a pair of old heat padded electrodes on top and tie them on with a crepe bandage. After the initial blast of microwaved heat, and depending on the extent of the damage of course, Eric would get out the Johnson's Baby Powder and massage the injury for a few minutes. After a break you'd then get a session with the ultrasound machine. I think Dundee were actually one of the first clubs in Scotland to have one of these machines. Nowadays they are very common-place and one of the most efficient methods of getting rid of swelling from the damaged tissue area. I know they are much more sophisticated now, but originally the machine looked a bit like an old wireless transmitter with a metallic nodule attached that he would apply on the injured part. The principle was, of course, the transmission of sound waves to the injured area, which were supposed to break up and disperse the swollen and/or bruised tissue.

When the treatment was done you were finished until after lunchtime. In the afternoon you would be called back in for a repeat session. There was very little by way of a gym or equipment at Dens so not many seemed to bother doing much by way of circuit training or weights in those days. There was also little to no catering at the club and so after a really hard training session there was nothing to eat or drink, except for a cup of sweet tea. Most players who were back in the afternoons – which was rare – were more likely to go for a pub lunch somewhere in a bar near the stadium.

We often used to train on the grounds of the old Strathmartine Hospital. So in the mornings most would pile into their cars or grab a seat on the only existing club mini-bus and would head there with all the balls, bibs and cones. Strathmartine Hosptial was at that time a mental hospital and it was not uncommon for some of the inmates to come wandering down to watch training. There were some poor-looking souls among them but we had a laugh with one or two who were keen to get involved in training.

It was just like a scene from the movie *One Flew Over the Cuckoo's Nest*. The Blue Max one day pointed over to one poor but very harmless-looking soul that used to just wander around repeating himself all the time saying, 'Am gonna get a cup of tea with nae sugar.' He just kept saying this over and over again.

George would then say, 'Look at that poor guy. Did you know he used to be a football coach? That's what too many years in this business does to you.'

During the Seventies and early Eighties there was a real drinking culture within Scottish football and Dundee was no different to most other clubs, except possibly our biggest rivals, Dundee United – Ralph Milne excepted, as he would've fitted in admirably at Dens Park! United's manager Jim McLean more or less forbade drinking completely and would fine players heavily if he caught them at it. The young up-and-coming Alex Ferguson was also a very strict disciplinarian when it came to that sort of thing. His reputation was quickly gaining ground as a manager no player would dare cross.

In my era at Dens we had guys that would've been capped for Scotland at drinking. The Three Barrels pub, situated at the top of Lochee, was just a minutes' drive from the stadium and was where the Dundee players did most of their lunchtime 'swallying'. It was really frowned upon within the hierarchy of the dressing room if you didn't drink when out with the lads. Binge drinking was just the done thing in football and for a period in the younger part of my career I was no exception. I reckon it must have cost me though in terms of consistency of performance. I remember some of the older players saying to me, when I was still a youngster in the reserves, 'Aye, son, ye'll never be a player until you can take a good bevvy.'

In the beginning, being underage, I would sometimes still go to the pub. Unfortunately I often relied on Big Tam to give me a lift to and from training. When he and some others went to the pub after training for a 'few' I would simply have to sit and wait till they were finished. Alternatively, sometimes I walked down the town to the bus station to get a bus home. On other occasions I would stay on and do some extra training myself. During all my time at Dundee it was very rare that we were collectively back in the afternoons for extra training. If we were it was only ever seen by players as a punishment. In hindsight, this was totally ridiculous! Often I'd go back alone in the afternoons, kicking a ball off a wall under the stadium. Sometimes I'd be allowed to practise corners or free kicks on the pitch, but that was rare.

Head groundskeeper George Hynd treated the pitch like

sacred turf. Very rarely were you ever allowed on it with studs, unless for official match duty. There was literally nowhere proper to go if I wanted to do some specific ball work. The only grass area was a small bit behind the goals. I would grab some of George Blues' cones and practise dribbling round them. You just had to make the best of it.

Most Scottish footballers in the early 1970s expected to work only two or three hours in the morning till lunchtime. This paved the way for all the swally merchants in the afternoon, some of which also enjoyed a gamble on the horses. This was not a very healthy lifestyle. I knew of some players who drank all afternoon, went home and had a nap, then something to eat and were back out again in the evening. Then they'd come back in the next morning and supposedly be fit for training! This was quite literally the way some players lived!

Guys like Dundee's legendary goal scorer Billy Pirie were unreal. Billy, or BP, was one of the best finishers I ever saw and was my main striking partner along with the big, rugged Eric Sinclair, who lacked pace but was brilliant at holding the ball up for midfield players, when I first broke through from the reserves into the first team. BP at the time could down pints like most kids could eat a packet of Smarties! However come Saturday, if you put the ball in front of him with a chance of a goal, it was in the net almost every time. What a finisher he was, on and off the park!

Training facilities generally in Scotland during this time were little short of pathetic, considering it was supposed to be professional football. The word 'professional' was a very loose term indeed when applied to Scottish football at that time. Things slowly did begin to change in the Eighties but generally still fell a mile short of the total professionalism of most other European countries. New managers like Jim McLean and Alex Ferguson

68

were the main pioneers for a new breed of management that was much more conscious and demanding of dedication, health and fitness. To play professional football to a consistently high standard, you have to be an athlete. Some of us just didn't get it!

In the early years my cousin Gavin, now also with Dundee, and I both succumbed to the drinking culture that existed within the professional game. To be honest, we both sometimes took it to ridiculous and very dangerous levels. On one very bad occasion it very nearly cost us our careers and quite literally our lives. One night whilst still only sixteen years old we'd been to a party in Perth and had come back to Gavin's home via bus. Somehow we decided we wanted to go back out again but as the bus we caught was the last bus, we had no legal means of transport. In a moment of alcohol-induced madness we decided to take Uncle Phil,s works van as our mode of transport. Drunk and unlicensed, we set off for the bright lights of Perth, the 'Fair City', fifteen miles away at about 1am. I was co-pilot as Gavin drove. Remarkably, we got to Perth without incident and drove around the town, trying to find some nightlife in the early hours of the morning.

At a set of traffic lights we pulled up alongside Gavin's older brother Phillip, who was licensed to drive! He went nuts and told us to get the hell out of town before we got ourselves arrested. We decided then that enough was enough and headed off home. It was, however, wintertime and had begun to snow. The roads had also begun to freeze as we set off out of town towards the dual carriageway back to Errol. Just as we were coming out of Perth, Gavin accelerated into quite a sharp bend. The last thing I remember saying to him before all hell let loose was, 'You'd better slow down here a bit.'

It was too late; we'd lost control of the van and it began spinning on black ice. I think we were doing approximately fifty to sixty miles per hour. Neither of us were wearing seatbelts and in the back of Uncle Phil's works van there were lots of old bits and pieces of scrap metal and heavy tools. As the van spun out of control, I just shut my eyes and prayed. We were both suddenly in a tumble dryer going full pelt along with all the other bits and pieces that were being thrashed around inside the vehicle. I was just waiting for the lights to go out as I thought, This is it I'm a gonner! The thrashing, crashing and bashing seemed like it was never going to stop but eventually when it did we came to a standstill with the van completely upside down and smashed to bits. When the whole nightmare came to a halt I looked round to see how Gavin was. For a split second I was in fear that he'd been killed. Miraculously we were both relatively unscathed apart from minor cuts and grazes.

We decided to make a run for it and get as far away from the vehicle as we possibly could. Scrambling out of the van, we got to our feet and headed off on foot in the direction of Errol, which was at least a good ten miles away – bearing in mind we had no coats or jackets on and it was absolutely freezing cold. We were like a couple of escaped convicts as we hirpled off into the snowbound night. All that was missing was a helicopter above, hooters and sniffer dogs on our trail. I knew we would need help because I could see Gavin's face was bleeding, even though it probably looked worse than it was. I was fine, apart from a cut on my face. Unfortunately, I still have the scar! Possibly we may also both have had slight concussions.

Eventually we came to a house not far away, situated off the main road. It would be around 2am as we rang the doorbell. We didn't get any joy and were shouted at and told to move.

Not much further down the road we came to another house, where fortunately we were allowed in and given permission to make a phone call. The poor couple must've thought we were a couple of escapees from Perth prison, but I suppose if they had they wouldn't have allowed us in either!

The dreaded phone call home was made and within about half an hour Gavin's mum, Auntie Isla, appeared along with Dad. I think they were too much in shock at what had just happened to give us the major rocket I had been expecting. Instead they took us directly to PRI [Perth Royal Infirmary] where we both received stitches for our various cuts. To have both survived what we had that night without major injury or even loss of life was truly nothing short of a miracle.

Of course, it wasn't long before the police had cottoned on to the fact there was a vehicle lying upside down at the side of the road just outside Perth, with no report of an incident or accident. Unfortunately we had not been able to get the vehicle towed away quick enough. Naturally, they had checked the local hospitals to see who had been treated the night before for injury. Inevitably a couple of days later they came knocking at the door. Uncle Phil decided to tell the police it had been he who had crashed his own van and, as there were no other parties involved, it seemed logical to retrieve the vehicle the following day and not report the incident.

The police, of course, would know the real story. I think maybe Uncle Phil got a reprimand for not reporting an accident but, apart from that, amazingly no further action was taken. How stupid we had been to do such a thing and how lucky we were that night in more ways than one. The accident had happened on a Friday night, as there was no reserve game the following day due to the weather. On Monday morning Gavin and I were back at training again, trying to best explain all the cuts and bruises!

During those teenage years I could be a very determined individual but I was also a very angry, mixed-up and reckless teenager – possibly even with a death wish. When I look back on some of the crazy things I have done I can scarcely believe I had the nerve to do even half of them. I was definitely a very angry young boy, racked with fears, insecurities and heavily burdened with guilt; or rather, false guilt. Football I reckon was not only a good outlet for me; it was more like my total salvation! To a certain extent playing football enabled me to keep the demons at bay, as sometimes they were harder to live with than others. Maybe I should've been a boxer, as during this time I had no fear of physical confrontation at all. Sometimes I would even put my head where others would've thought twice before putting their boot.

One time during a youth tournament in Holland whilst playing for Dundee, I won best player of the competition. I went for a ball with my head in a fifty/fifty challenge with the opposing Dutch goalkeeper directly from a corner kick. He tried to punch it as I tried to head it. We hit each other full-on. Both the ball and the goalkeeper ended up in the back of the net for a goal! He was stretchered off semi-conscious and I was very dazed. I could've so easily broken my neck but the point I'm making is that I just did not see or feel danger. The Dutch home fans were incensed with me and I was booed every time I touched the ball from then on. It was typical of the reckless type of action I would take on the field of play. I just had no regard for my own safety. I wasn't always this way though and after a few seasons of painful knocks and a bit more maturity I slowly and thankfully began to get the message!

By 1977/78 Davie White was gone. He was replaced by Tommy Gemmell. This was no real surprise to all at the club, as things had been slowly but surely going downhill for a while. I really liked Davie White both as a person and as a manager. Some of his half-time/full-time dressing room quotes were memorable: 'That performance of yours was so bad, son, it would put hairs on a grape!' I do remember him bawling and yelling at me when I was only about fifteen years old and part of a Dundee youth team that went to play in another competition in Amsterdam. I thought he was scary!

It may be the case that his teams had too many older players needing replaced and maybe he just wasn't able to do that successfully enough. I'll always be thankful to Davie White. He gave me my full first-team debut for Dundee in 1977 whilst I was still just aged sixteen. Many years later, I used to see Davie at Gleneagles where we were both members. He was always up for a chat about football and his enthusiasm for the game was still very evident.

By the beginning of the next season it was Tommy Gemmell who had the task of getting the club back up into the Premier League. Tam made a few signings to strengthen the squad. The most notable being Jimmy 'Jinky' Johnstone, his ex-Lisbon Lion teammate. I got to know him well because Jinky stayed with Tam and Anne in their hotel/pub in Errol. Gavin and I would sometimes pick him up and take him to training in the morning. Often he would be reeking of booze. Some of his touches with the ball on the training ground were almost god-like but it was plain to see he was not going to be one who could be relied upon to make a major contribution. In the end, after Tam slapped a curfew on him he would sneak out of Tam's pub, which was the Commercial Hotel and head up to the only other pub in the village, the Central Bar. It seemed Jinky was another who was determined to drink. I was the wiser and the better for knowing him though – even if it was only temporary. It was a treat to watch a master craftsman at close quarters on the training ground. The late Jimmy Johnstone was one of the few genuine greats of Scottish football. Simply a world-class talent!

By the start of my second full season, 1977/78, I really began to come out of my shell and had begun to make some real progress. In all honesty, though, I did find it very difficult to express myself and was self-conscious in the dressing room. I was too shy for my own good. Some of the older players gave me stick about my so-called silver spoon upbringing and coming from a so-called wealthy family. I was even nicknamed 'greenbacks'. Footballers were not paid much during that time. There were a few with chips on their shoulders, who never missed an opportunity to try and knock my confidence. Also due to the nerve damage which caused my hearing loss, as I mentioned earlier, I tend to speak a bit out of one side of my mouth. Growing up I thought nothing of it but when I was younger I became self-conscious about it because of the mickey-taking.

Some of the older players could be very cutting and sarcastic. It's not really my idea of humour, never has been and never will be. Nowadays I realise this type of stuff says more about the insecurities of those who dish it out than those who are on the receiving end. Being partially deaf and lacking in confidence, I wasn't great at holding my own verbally in that type of environment.

Gordon Strachan was an outstanding prospect at Dundee but I think Big Tam for some reason possibly saw him as a luxury he couldn't afford in the First Division. When I broke through into the team Strachan was spending more time on the bench. Big Tam had changed the style of play and Strachan, who was a very skilful, creative player, didn't seem to be fitting in with Big Tam. It was also known in the dressing room that Big Tam was chummy with my dad. I'm sure that also fostered some jealousy, as I was probably seen in some quarters as being the manager's 'favourite'. This was rubbish. Tam treated me just as he treated any other player. All I wanted to do was play football and avoid the bitching.

Strachan was too good really for the Scottish First Division, and when Billy McNeill took him to Aberdeen in 1978, it was the best thing that could've happened to him. His career really began to take off with up-and-coming Aberdeen. Eventually, of course, he went on to establish himself with Man United and Scotland. Strachan indeed was one of the top Scottish players of his generation. I did regret that we weren't teammates for longer. You could only learn from playing with and against players of his quality.

I remember the day in training when I finally came out of my shell as a person and as a player at Dundee FC. I got smacked in the face full on with the ball and it felt like when you hit yourself on the head accidentally by bumping into something. My instant rage seemed to release a lot of pent-up anger and frustration. Suddenly I felt like I had real clarity and I was no longer time travelling in fear or anticipation. It was as though for the first time as a professional player I was able to just be me in the moment. Call it expression or confidence or whatever, it's basically all the same thing. The individual flair and talent I had shown as a juvenile and schoolboy, I was now expressing fully on the training pitch as a professional footballer. Any athlete or sportsperson will tell you that when they break free of the shackles of doubt, fear and anxiety and feel confidence begin to flow through their veins, it's just about the best feeling in the world. I'm sure the greatest achievers in sport are the ones who know how to tap into it through instinct or intuition. I knew I had it. It was there but it only seemed to come in bursts with me. I just didn't know or understand how to trigger it in myself. Maybe I just needed someone to kick a ball in my face every now and again!

There was a large part of my personality that was still far too accommodating and self-conscious. As a young player I was always too willing to accept blame for someone else's mistake. I hated the mickey-taking about my family's so-called wealth, when, in fact, for the most of my teenage years I was totally heartbroken and miserable. No amount of money would've changed that.

I'm convinced that the majority of the greatest sporting moments have been achieved when the conscious mind is metaphorically simply sitting on the bench. In other words, it's not actively telling you what to do or how to do it, because you are just doing it regardless and without any thought. When you are consciously thinking about how to do something and maybe also allowing your mind to stray onto the outcome portion of things when under pressure then you are simply getting in the way of expressing your skillset freely. When someone passed a ball to me and if I was thinking or worrying about how I was going to control it then chances were my touch would be clumsy, in contrast to if my mind was totally present or in the 'zone', where the ball would be instantly under my control.

You hear people talk a lot of being in the 'zone' or being 'focused'. Literally all this means is you are present in time. If someone asks you to pass the ketchup, you don't wonder or deliberate over it because there is no consequence of outcome. You don't have to think about what you need to do to pick up and pass a bottle of ketchup. You just do it! Young kids play without fear or thought but as adults we think, we doubt, then we try to play. You don't see many kids playing who are worrying about the outcome of what they are doing. Ask yourself: do you think kids need to learn to be professionals as much as professionals need to learn how to become kids again? As we get older and enter adulthood our minds get so jammed full of people telling us what to do, when to do it, how to do it. Bad coaches and bad managers spread fear like wildfire and it rages through a dressing room. Not many managers are good at hiding their own fears and are prepared to take it all on their own shoulders for the benefit of allowing the team to play in an expressive fashion. Only the good ones know how to positively affect a negative mind and only the bad ones know how to negatively affect a positive mind. When playing without confidence, suddenly you find yourself thinking twice before taking on that defender: what if I lose the ball and they break up the park and score? If you are playing out these scenarios then your mind is not in the present, which is where it needs to be.

Soon after breaking into the first team, I managed to establish myself in the Scotland youth team Under-18s and also made my debut for the Scottish league. At seventeen years of age I became one of the youngest ever to have played for Scotland at this level. Scotland manager at the time, Ally MacLeod, raved about me after a match in which I had played against Denmark. He described me as 'fantastic', labelling me at the time as another potential, Joe Jordan. Mind you, he did also say we were going to win the World Cup in Argentina! Well I was left-footed, very brave, was good in the air, mobile and was scoring goals regularly. There was no doubt at the time the potential was there. Even to be mentioned in the same breath as a great like Joe Jordan was a huge compliment to me.

In our last game of Big Tam's first full season as manager, a victory against Morton at Cappielow would still gave us a chance of promotion. However, disaster struck for both the club and myself. We did what we had to do and that was win the match, the score being 3–2, but our big rivals in the league, Hearts, had scored late on in their match and because they held their destiny in their own hands got the promotion slot just ahead of us. It was disaster for me because, after scoring early on, I was carried off in the first half, having gone totally committed into a fifty/

fifty challenge with Morton's veteran defender George Anderson. In my naivety and recklessness I had gone straight for the ball, but wily George arrived late. He hit me with a straight-leg tackle that left my ankle feeling like it was hanging by a thread. It was my left one too. I was in absolute agony – the pain was just incredible! I seriously thought my ankle was broken but, in fact, the ligaments had been badly torn and I was to be out for weeks. This couldn't have happened at a worse time for me and it was a massive blow to the club missing out on promotion once again.

So now not only was I ruled out of the Scotland squad for the pending European Youth Championships in Poland, I was also now struggling to be fit for Dundee's scheduled end-of-season tour to Australia and New Zealand. Scotland youth team coach, Andy Roxburgh, was disappointed, as he'd told me previously he was relying on me as one of his key players. But Big Tam persuaded me to go on the Dundee tour. He said to treat it like a holiday and told me there would be no pressure on me to play. It was all about recuperation and getting back to full fitness.

On that basis and having just turned eighteen years of age, I thought it would be a fantastic chance to see another part of the world. I was excited by the prospect and it more than made up for me missing out on playing for Scotland in the European Youth Championships. I felt bad about letting Andy Roxburgh down, though, because he had given me some real responsibility in that Scotland team. He made me feel that I was a key player for him. Andy was a good motivator of young players. He would make you feel real pride in wearing the Scotland jersey and he used to go round the dressing room right before the kick-off, personally handing out your own team jersey with your name and number on it. Believe me, by the time you put it on your back you had no fear at all, only a real eagerness to get out on the park and play for your country. I think Andy's ability in this department was underestimated and I know when he eventually graduated to the senior national squad as coach there were some who scoffed at his lack of experience in top-level football.

The Australian tour was a marvellous experience for me, but as a result, I was beginning to see my manager Tommy Gemmell in a whole new light. He had been like an idol to me when I was only thirteen and was a very big influence in those early stages of my career. Instead of allowing me to recuperate, though, I felt as though he got me to play in certain games when the ankle was nowhere near right.

Tam was a bit of an extrovert, a showman as a player. He liked to play to the gallery. However I never saw him so down as he was the morning after a defeat by Celtic at Dens Park in the League Cup. Dundee I think had been winning 1–0 with only seconds to go. They had played a very strong Celtic team off the park. Ex-Celt Big Tam of course was loving this, but he was time travelling and got ahead of himself. And just as he was starting to really enjoy it – some might say showboating – it all went wrong when he was caught in possession. Celtic immediately took advantage and Harry Hood, I think it was, scored the equaliser with virtually the last kick of the game. You only ever got one chance against the Old Firm in those days. Naturally, when it went to extra-time there was only ever going to be one winner! Tam didn't need anyone to tell him. I'm sure he felt as though he had let everyone at the club down that night. The next morning he appeared in our kitchen, probably for a dram. I saw how hurt and remorseful he was. He looked genuinely depressed about it, and I'm sure he was. Big Tam was very much a man's man. He played hard, he lived hard. His drinking exploits along with my old man and some others were legendary in Errol. Tam was very much a fun-loving guy but he was also no mug. However, now as a manager the stresses and strains of the game were possibly already beginning to show. Dundee were a big club playing in a lower league and expectation levels were high. I think the pressure was beginning to get to Tam in his new role as manager. He knew he simply had to get promotion or it would be game over.

The following season, 1978/79, would be Big Tam's year. At Dens Park on 10 May 1979 we needed only a draw against Ayr United to win the league, thus ensuring promotion back to the Premiership. We duly did by drawing 2–2, in a match in which I scored both our goals with headers. I probably scored more headed goals on average than most strikers. I had been on occasion compared to the great Alan Gilzean but I never saw myself as being as good as him with my head. The clinching goal finally came with only eight minutes to go. Crucially, in the last two games of that critical league campaign the team scored four goals, with me scoring three and assisting in the other. In the run-in to that league campaign I had never felt more tension than I did in those last few games of that successful season. After it was all over it was such a relief to have at long last delivered something tangible to our very loyal Dundee fans. It's sometimes hard to relax and enjoy playing football quite as much when under the huge pressure of expectation.

In the days and hours in the lead-up to these crucial games I'd spent a lot of time doing nothing but resting and thinking about what was needed to be done to get us over the line. The tension and anxiety was palpable. No wonder professional sportsmen, or women for that matter, sometimes go off the rails! There is just so much pressure of expectation condensed into such a small timeframe when the big game comes. When it comes to the crunch of doing it when it really matters, there are not too many that are able to produce what's required. That's what makes professional sport difficult and why the ones who can perform constantly to the highest levels are in such demand. If it were easy, we'd all be doing it!

Possibly, in some respects, I think I would've been better suited to being a golfer, from the point of view that as a footballer or team player I wasted too much tension and energy worrying about letting people down. In hindsight though, the letting-down aspect was mainly to do with my father. All things considered, I think I was coping well with the pressures of being a key player for Dundee. Much like the Glasgow Rangers of the First Division, we were the club the majority wanted to beat because we were expected to be back in the Premier League.

Before games I could become very tense, nervous and anxious. There were spells where I would be just lounging around the house, resting in preparation for a match. It's an uncomfortable feeling to constantly have inside you. Winning a league title is the hardest thing to do in football because it demands the most from everyone at the club, over a long period of time. Being tense and anxious before games is part and parcel of it. Good players have their own coping mechanisms but without doubt all players feel an enormous sense of relief at the release of tension when a big event is over. A season lasts not far short of ten months, during which time every aspect of the club and its players will at some stage be under the microscope – from boardroom to management, right through to the dressing rooms and the backroom staff. All will have played their part at some point along the way. For sure. When a team wins a league title they have really deserved it by virtue of the fact that they have done things better than anyone else over the length of the season.

After that final game that night in the home dressing room at Dens Park I must've drunk a whole bottle of champagne by myself in one go! The relief when it came gave me the most incredible high. Winning the First Division with Dundee FC that season was my first taste of success as a professional footballer. I don't think Big Tam would've survived another season in the First Division.

Season 1979/80 was to be my last for Dundee. My name and reputation was growing within the game in Scotland, even though I had only been playing with Dundee in the First Division. Being ambitious, I really wanted to be playing at the highest levels, and playing in the Scottish Premier League gave me a greater chance to prove I could live up to my ever-growing reputation as a player. More and more clubs began coming to watch me. As always, there was lots of speculation.

It was a very exciting time for me. If truth be told, I really wanted to go and play in England for Arsenal or Tottenham. It was such a thrill for me when I learned that Spurs had sent Bill Nicholson to watch me play at Ibrox against the mighty Glasgow Rangers. My manager and I by this time had not really been seeing eye to eye. He had started to play me more as a wide-left midfield player. All I wanted to do was get forward and score goals.

Early on in that first season back in the new Premier set-up we played against St Mirren in the league at home and, playing on the left side of a four-man midfield, I scored all four goals in our 4–1 victory. It was described in some quarters as one of the best individual performances ever seen by a Dundee player on Dens Park. I remember lying on the physio table feeling very tense before the game. We were not long back in the Premier League and the pressure was already on to begin picking up points. I was, as usual, feeling some pre-match nerves. Big Tam came in and this time was reassuring. He told me just to go out and show them what I could do.

I got my first goal early on and that felt like a weight lifted off my shoulders. It all just started to flow again from there. After I had got the fourth I remember feeling so confident and capable that I felt like I could take on the whole St Mirren defence singlehandedly. After the match I remember receiving a standing ovation from the fans. I don't profess to make any claims about how good I was in comparison to some of the great Dundee players over the years. What I will say, though, is there will not have been many better one-off individual performances at Dens Park from a Dundee player than the one I gave that afternoon. A Dundee supporter on an online fans chat forum recently described me, in my early years, as having the most energy he had ever seen from a Dundee player in fifty-five years of watching the club.

When I got back home after the match I remember parking my car in the drive at Holmlea and seeing Mum and Dad just standing there. They were both in tears and this outward show of emotion from them really took me very much by surprise and I wasn't sure how to handle it. This was not something I had seen from either of them towards me for a long time. Throughout the years I had grown unaccustomed to any outward show of emotion from my parents. I realise they must've been proud of me that day but it just made me feel uncomfortable, which was sad. When I see the way in which my own kids will hug both their mum and me, it all seems so easy and natural. Ian gives his mum a hug or a kiss at least once a day and he's twenty, a year older than I was when I scored all those goals on that day.

It had just been one of these rare days for me when it all just began flowing. There were no doubts and no thoughts. My skillset had been released by the early goal and it allowed me to do what I was capable of doing. I scored a volley with my left foot, a penalty kick, a header, then another volley with my left foot. I honestly felt as if no one could've stopped me that day. Nearly all the national newspapers were full of my performance. Some said I had arrived as one the new personality players of the Premier League. Big Tam, though, was more intent on keeping a lid on things – rightly or wrongly! He let the press know that he thought my defensive qualities were lacking, meaning I didn't track back enough and was a bit selfish. In hindsight, it was all true. It was funny because in the first half he kept jumping out of the dugout and screaming at me to get back! However, when the goals started going in he shut up. I can look back and honestly see Tam's point of view because I was still very young. He was really only trying to make me more of an all-round team player and a bit less of an individual. I could be stubborn when I got things in my head and if I decided it was best to stay up and play my way then I would do it. Even though I didn't want to let my teammates down, in my own mind this was my way of doing the best job for myself and the club.

Things came to a head, though, when Tam dropped me from the team after that famous St Mirren victory. It was a League Cup game at home against lowly Cowdenbeath and, fine, he knew the team would win easily without me. From my point of view I'd seen it as a great chance to add another barrow-load of goals to my ever-growing tally. My confidence was sky high and, after the previous Saturday, it had every right to be. My manager was trying to teach me a lesson but I'm afraid I have never been a very good pupil. In truth, I rarely ever reacted well to this type of man-management. It was maybe something to do with my rebelliousness against my father's dictatorial attitude towards me. Anyway, as yet unknowing, I arrived at the stadium for the match against Cowdenbeath and fully expected to play. As usual the team were assembled in the home dressing room and waiting for Tam to pin the starting line-up on the notice board. He came in, pinned it up without saying a word, and then disappeared. When I went over to read the list it took me some time to realise I was down as being a substitute! First I was confused, then confusion turned to anger. I was incensed at being left out with no explanation. Instinctively I simply walked back over to my peg, put my jacket on, walked out of the stadium, across the street on Dens Road, got into my car and drove home, without saying a word to anyone. By this time there were some bewildered fans wondering why I could be seen looking not too happy, jumping into my car and heading away from the stadium. I should've been pulling on my Dundee jersey going out and banging in a few more goals. That's how confident I was feeling. The word had spread quickly and apparently Tam had been seen at the main door looking for me. By which time I was long gone!

Again in retrospect my actions were very wrong and immature. This, however, was just in my make-up. It was the way I was. I had become a very strong-willed individual but I also had lots of demons and lacked any real guidance. What I really needed was a football mentor. I don't look back so often these days but when I do I often wonder if having a proper mentor would've made a big difference to me. Someone I could really look up to and respect both on and off the park. Someone who could've taken me aside and told me how important it was to look after your health and fitness. That would've made a big difference to me. It was not that I couldn't be influenced – I could be, and easily so.

Dad was no use as a role model. Often he would just unwittingly and unknowingly wind me up. He was forever telling me not to listen to 'them' and tell them to 'stuff it' if I wasn't happy. However, I always knew I would be far more miserable working on the farm for Dad than I would ever have been playing for a manager I didn't get on with very well. In the end, however,

I suppose it was up to me as an individual to either choose to listen to him or not.

To walk out on Dundee that night had been a very stupid thing to do. At best it was immature and at worst it was petulant and selfish. I had my demons though and at times like this I could be my own worst enemy. No doubt Dad had wound me up but I was only prepared to think that Tam was deliberately trying to teach me a lesson by smacking me down a peg or two.

Whilst I agree in principle with what he was trying to do, I disagree with the way he went about it. I think his lack of communication with me was the problem. What he should've done was take me into his office, sit me down and explain to me what it was he thought I was lacking and needed to improve on. He knew me and he knew my family, and if he thought he could ever get the best out of me by dumping me out of the team under these very spurious circumstances then he just hadn't done his homework! There were faults on both sides and not much give in the middle.

Dundee FC director Graham Thomson, himself a successful businessman, eventually intervened by calling me up at home not long after the game had ended. He persuaded me to go back into the stadium to meet with the manager the following morning. The board did not want a situation lingering between me and my manager. In truth, I had become the club's biggest saleable asset and Dundee were very much a selling club – they had to be.

I will always remember Graham prepping me for my meeting with Tam. He told me to do something which I have never forgotten, and that is to always look people straight in the eye when you are talking to them. To be honest, I don't think the directors were too impressed with how Tam had been managing me. I know Graham Thomson wasn't happy about the way I was just left out after the St Mirren game without any explanation and with Tam seemingly only wanting to talk to the press about it and not to me. Our meeting was a strange affair because across the table from me was someone who I had known as a family friend and a teammate. It was a very awkward situation for me, as I was not used to dealing with this sort of thing. I could tell that Tam also was not happy. I think he had been told or ordered to sit down and talk to me. This would not have worn well with him, as he was very much his own man who liked to do things his own way.

After the meeting we'd managed to patch things up, at least on the surface. I was immediately reinstated for our next match against Sheffield United away in the old Anglo-Scottish Cup. It was all fair enough, but I think the damage had been done. I think overall what had disappointed me most was the way my manager had criticised me publicly. I had just given the performance of my career and fine everyone knew it. Yet much of the after-match comment was about Tam's criticisms of me.

After this it was never really the same for me at Dundee with Tam as manager. I had really enjoyed playing for the club I had been with since I was thirteen years old but my in mind I now only wanted to play for a move away from Dundee. I was playing really well and scoring goals and by the beginning of October that season I think I may have been top scorer in the Premier League.

Fate again, though, played a huge role in what happened next. We were playing our big city rivals, Dundee United, in the local derby at Dens. It was massive because it was the first time we'd played against each other in the new Premier League set-up. I always loved playing against Dundee United. They were a great football team and played the game the right way, thanks to the mercurial skills of up-and-coming Jim McLean. There was, I remember, a huge atmosphere that day, and I was totally absorbed in the whole thing. This is what I loved so much about playing football. Big games!

The match started really well for me and I felt as though I was right up for it and on form. Not long into the first half I picked up a loose ball inside my own half and went straight at United's defence at pace with the ball at my feet. I got clear of both Paul Hegarty and Dave Narey in the process, and that was no mean feat, as they were among the best in the business. I had wriggled clear and was now homing in on the United penalty box and getting ready to pull the trigger. I felt sure I was going to score a great opening goal when CRUNCH! United utility man Derek Stark made a rather clumsy last-ditch lunge from the side and caught me just as my weight was on my left foot. My ankle completely buckled again from the sheer weight of his challenge. It had not been an intentionally dirty foul but it put me out of the game for months and totally wrecked all the transfer momentum that had been beginning to build up around me. I was absolutely gutted and, in fact, I can remember sitting in my car in tears after the game. I knew I would be out for ages and I just hated being injured!

This was a real blow to me, and possibly to the club at that time too. They were more than happy to allow the ramped-up transfer speculation surrounding me to gain ground. It seemed every week my transfer fee was getting heavier and heavier! Interest in me had been growing and most of the big clubs in both England and Scotland had at the very least been keeping tabs on me. Both Rangers and rivals Celtic had been reported as being keen but now all transfer talk and speculation was over until I could get back to prove my fitness. Any professional footballer will tell you the worst and most depressing part of the job is being injured long-term. It's soul-destroying – especially when things have been going as well as they were for me at that time. In fact, they could not have been going any better. It may well be different today but a long-term injury meant spending a lot of time on your own. I would feel so empty and lonely on the Saturday just sitting there in the stand, when all I wanted to be is out there in the pitch. Your match fitness ebbs away quickly despite the fact you exercise as much as you can to keep your body in shape. Let's put it this way: for a long time after that injury Derek Stark was not exactly on my Christmas card list!

As always, and despite even the huge guaranteed salaries of today, most genuine players try to come back too early and end up setting themselves back in the process. I was no exception! I tried to do too much too soon after around six or seven weeks. I started to do some ball control work by dribbling round some cones at the side of the pitch. I felt something go *ping*. It was a tendon in my ankle. This set me back, I reckon, at least another two months! That season after the injury in early October I reckon I did not play again for the first team until late January of the New Year. I had missed almost half the season. Nightmare!

Virtually as soon as I came back, though, things began to hot up again. I scored one against Morton at Dens in a 1–0 win when still not feeling great fitness-wise. The last league game I remember playing for Dundee was against Aberdeen, on a very cold early February afternoon at a snowbound Dens Park. I scored our only goal in that game. I think we lost 3–1. I felt very sluggish and knew it would take me a good while longer to really get my fitness back to what it had been like at the start of the season. My ankle still felt very weak and had to be heavily strapped. The goal I scored against Aberdeen was a scrappy goal and it turned out to be my last league goal for Dundee. It was, however, enough to get the rumour mills grinding again as transfer speculation was back on the agenda. The papers were saying that Dundee had turned down an offer from Rangers. The press were saying Big Tam was insisting the offer of £200k was just not enough.

The following week, with all the transfer speculation in the newspapers and me being quoted in the press saying I wanted to leave, we played Newcastle United in a friendly at Dens on the Friday night. We lost 3–1 and for the first time the fans had really began to turn on me, and I was booed every time I touched the ball! It was a horrible way in which to play my last game at Dens for Dundee, as I previously had such a good rapport with them. They had originally nicknamed me 'the Sundance Kid' after my namesake Robert Redford's character in the famous movie *Butch Cassidy and the Sundance Kid*. I think they too were just sick of all the speculation. It was clear to them I was leaving but they didn't really know the real reasons why, in my eyes, it was time for me to move on.

With new legislation about to come in with regard to the rules and regulations governing the transfer of players. The new 'freedom of contract' laws meant that I could've waited till the end of the season when my contract was up and been able to dictate on my own terms as to what club I wanted to sign for. Had I in fact chosen to go abroad to an EU country then Dundee would have been lucky to get any more than £40,000 for me, as the formula within the EU for calculating transfer fees was largely based on ten times your gross salary – my gross salary being little more than £4,000k! It was rumoured there were some foreign clubs watching me, especially before I got my injury. There was also speculation Toronto Blizzards from the North American Soccer League had made a verbal offer of

£400k and it had also been turned down. This was an indication of what Dundee obviously thought they were going to get for me. They probably thought United got £400k for Raymond Stewart and he was a defender, so what price for teenage Ian Redford one of the leading scorers in the Premier League? One minute I was off to Arsenal as a replacement for Liam Brady, the next I was going to Tottenham. Jock Wallace, manager of Leicester City, had apparently also verbally offered £300k, Liverpool were watching, as were Celtic. I knew my form since coming back in late January was still a long way from what it had been at the start of the season. The weather had been terrible and getting proper match practice in the form of competitive league games was really difficult, but this was what I needed more than anything. That said, on 22 February 1980, on a Friday lunchtime, my career and life changed dramatically.

I really was walking out on Dundee FC and Big Tam – this time it was for good! Still the raw teenager, I had begun dating a local girl from Dundee who just happened to be twenty-six years of age. Jeanette Lamb was my first-ever real girlfriend. She was a very attractive blonde hairdresser from Dundee. Jeanette and I first met one night at a club in Dundee. We'd not been going out for very long at all and had arranged to meet for lunch on that fateful Friday. I was totally oblivious of what was going on when the big news came. How anyone knew where to find me that day, I'll never know! However, a message got to me that I was to report immediately to Dens Park. I still honestly did not know what it was all about but did as was asked and quickly got in my car, leaving Jeanette in the restaurant, and returned to the stadium.

When I walked in it was like a graveyard. There was nobody to be seen. As I went through to the dressing room I could hear a noise through in the adjacent home bathroom. I walked in and there was reserve coach, Hugh Robertson, lying in the single bath. I asked him not to get up!

'Hi, Hugh. Why have I been summoned? What's going on?'

Without causing a ripple he said, 'The club have accepted an offer from Rangers and John Greig wants to see you this afternoon.'

I was in shock. I could feel my heart pounding against my chest. It took me all my time to compose myself enough even to speak. I had only just got back playing again after being out for nearly four months and now Glasgow Rangers wanted to sign me. On the one hand, of course I was really excited, but on the other, I just never imagined I would be leaving Dundee FC so suddenly. I certainly imagined it would happen one day but just not in this way.

I don't know what I expected but there was literally no one else in the stadium to speak to me. I was disappointed not to get so much as a goodbye or best of luck from anyone at the club apart from perhaps ex-chairman Graham Thomson, who had also given me some good advice earlier in my career. I hadn't really expected much from my manager, as our mutual relationship was not great in the end. However, he had known me since I was around twelve or thirteen. He had played a huge part in the early formation of my career up to then and had also been a big family friend. We'd shared some good times out shooting together with Dad. It was understandable that he thought I'd made some things difficult for him as my manager. I for one would've very quickly buried any grudges and past history over a good-luck and a best-wishes handshake. Yes, in some ways maybe I was not the easiest person to handle but I had done a very good job for Dundee in a relatively short space of time. Especially considering how badly injured I was in my last season. They were about to receive a transfer fee that was bigger than any other Scottish club had ever received from another Scottish club, thus making my transfer to Rangers a new Scottish club record. Again disappointing, from my perspective, that no one from the club was there to wish me all the best.

What I also felt was bad, having earned such a large amount of money for me, was that I did not receive one penny of the transfer fee! It just didn't happen! I'm sure the fact that I was perceived as wealthy outside football also worked against me in these circumstances and in this era. 'Well, after all, he doesn't need the money, does he?' was a remark often made in reference to me.

Disappointingly, after reserve coach Hugh Robertson broke the news to me there was nothing more for me to do but to go and collect my boots. I was full of different emotions as I walked through from the home team dressing room to the boot room. I was disappointed, excited, afraid, elated, and sad and, if possible, all at the same time! I do not know how my brain managed to process any of what was going through my mind. I picked up my boots, walked back along past the reserve dressing room, the smelly old dryer, the home dressing room, and the physio room. I continued out into the foyer without seeing a soul. I walked out of Dens Park that day completely on my own for the last time as a Dundee player.

The news had somehow already spread to home. When I arrived back at Holmlea I thought Dad's face was going to explode, it just looked so red! I wanted to talk to him, I wanted to talk to Jeanette, I wanted to talk to anyone! Part of me was saying, 'Hey, a wait a minute, just slow down here. This is all happening a bit too fast.'

Dad couldn't get me in that car quick enough and on the road to Glasgow and Ibrox stadium. I'm sure this was what he'd wanted more than anything. Without doubt he'd had a dram or two, judging by his ruddy complexion. His long-time pal and fishing buddy, ex-CID big Geordie McInnes from Perth, drove us both through to Ibrox.

And that was it! I was on my way to Glasgow on that Friday afternoon to meet the manager of Glasgow Rangers, John Greig.

4

PLAYING FOR RANGERS:
THE JOHN GREIG ERA

That Friday afternoon in February of 1980 was one I will never forget.

The journey to Glasgow was a very tense and nervous one for me. I just did not know what to expect at the other end. All I knew was that Glasgow Rangers had just offered Dundee FC a Scottish record-breaking fee for my services, but I just couldn't get a handle on the fact that I was on my way to Glasgow to sign for Rangers. Big Geordie, himself a former footballer who had a spell with Aberdeen among other clubs, was doing a stellar job of calming down the old man, who looked like he was going to explode.

I sat very quietly in the back saying nothing, but contemplating everything. My mind was in utter turmoil. I wanted that car journey to last much longer than it did, to give me a chance to try and make some sense of what was going on. However, it seemed that in no time we were in Glasgow.

When we arrived at Ibrox stadium, we parked just outside the main door and I was the only one who got out. Taking a really deep breath, I walked in through the main doors and was immediately standing in the large reception area. Ahead of me, no more than a few yards away, was the first step of that famous marble staircase. I immediately sensed the stature of a massive football club. Glasgow Rangers, one of the biggest football institutions in the UK and in world terms too. Rather apologetically, I announced myself at reception and was told that Mr Greig was waiting for me upstairs in his office.

John was actually standing at the top of the stairs. He shouted hello and ushered me up to his office, which was situated left of the top of the staircase and not far along the corridor from the world-famous trophy room.

As I walked up that very famous staircase, looking down at me were some of the great legends of the past, adorned in all their glory, hanging portraits of the likes of Alan Morton and Bob McPhail. They were the players who began to carve and mould the place into what it became. I defy anyone to walk in through the doors of Ibrox and not feel they are within the boundaries of a very special football club. There was just an aura about the club which is hard for me to describe. There is a realisation within a short space of time that you have much to live up to, as you are surrounded by reminders of the club's great past and traditions. In front of me now and shaking my hand was another of the club's greatest-ever servants, Rangers manager John Greig. Former Scottish internationalist, former captain of Rangers, one of the club's biggest legends.

'Come on in, son. Take a seat. Is there anything I can get you?' he said.

I was so nervous I could hardly speak and he must've realised that.

Now, if truth be told, Glasgow Rangers were not where I imagined I'd be going when I made up my mind I wanted to leave Dundee. There had been much speculation about me going to England and truthfully I had originally really wanted to join my former Errol Rovers teammate Ray Stewart in the English

First Division (as the top league was known as back then). As I mentioned earlier, I imagined signing for either Arsenal or Tottenham, because I really liked the idea of living and playing my football in London. It wasn't anything to do with the so-called glamorous nightlife, it was more of a cultural thing that I felt I would like to experience. In truth, although Liverpool were watching me they were so strong I just couldn't have seen myself getting a game ahead of some of the great players that were in that team. Maybe further on down the line if my game developed. The injury, however, had set everything back and Rangers had taken the initiative and were the first to move for me since I made my comeback at Dundee. I had only played two games, which was not really giving anyone else a true chance to assess how I was looking after my long spell out.

Although initially all the speculation about going to England was exciting, it was becoming clear to me that Rangers were the only club who genuinely seemed to be prepared to make a real offer. Dundee had agreed the transfer fee with Rangers and, as far as they were concerned, that was it; I was on my way. In any case, my latterly strained relationship at Dundee, in particular with my manager, would've made it difficult for me to remain at the club had I decided to hold out for England. There would've been enormous pressure on me from all angles. Dundee had supposedly rejected an initial offer from Rangers of £200,000, but Rangers soon came back with an increased offer of £210,000, which was the offer that was finally accepted.

I can't swear on this, but I also have a feeling that Dad was somehow involved in what was going on. He knew people that knew directors at Ibrox and my feelings were there were conversations regarding my future going on behind my back. I know for certain Dad was desperate for me to sign for Rangers. One of his best friends for years had been Dave Symon, son of ex-Rangers manager Scot Symon. Often Dad and Dave Symon would travel to Ibrox together on a Saturday to watch them play.

As far as Dundee was concerned, they just wanted as much money as they could get for me, and their realisation was that with each day passing, the bird in the hand was looking much better than the two in bush! They say in life if you try telling God what your plans are for the future, you will just make him laugh. I think the whole transfer escapade between Dundee FC and myself was major lesson number one for me in mine!

The transfer negotiations, if you could even call them that, were as simple for John Greig as they possibly ever could have been. I was a complete novice who hadn't a clue what to do or say. From experience, I believe any good young player is right to have a good agent or representative negotiating on his behalf. As a young player you may only ever get one chance where a big club will do almost anything to get you. It is right, therefore, to get as much out of it as you can. Football careers are very precarious, and who knows what lies just round the corner? Most big clubs took advantage of the fact they knew most young players were totally overwhelmed, as I was. They would make you feel as if they were the ones who were doing you the big favour. I believe it should always be seen as a two-way thing. Agents were virtually unheard of in my day. So there I was, on my own, trying to stay as calm as I could under the circumstances. I mean, Rangers were giving me the chance to play for them, right? Don't get me wrong, of course it was a great honour to play for such a great club, but this was my livelihood, my bread and butter. Therefore to not consider all the financial aspects was at best naive and at worst plain stupid. Unfortunately, I was both!

I was completely taken in and blown away by the sheer

magnitude and size of the club. It was not long at all before I was drooling at the thought of pulling on that famous blue jersey and lining up alongside some of the biggest, most famous names in Scottish football: Jardine, Johnstone, Cooper, Russell, Jackson, Forsyth, McCloy. Yes, in the end I was without doubt thrilled to be signing for Rangers FC!

The transfer 'negotiation' went something like this:

JG: Okay, son. How much do you want?

Me: Em, well . . . I don't know what to ask for, Mr Greig.

JG: Call me John.

Me: Oh, okay. Well, em, I, err . . .

JG: Okay, son. How about we say six thousand pounds to sign on [taxed, of course, at approximately 40 per cent] and the basic wage is £150.00 per week? All first-team squad players earn the same wage here.

Me: That sounds fine to me . . . where do I sign on?

My basic wage at Dundee at the time was just over £100 per week, my starting basic as an apprentice at Dundee was £19 pounds per week, taxed! What I also hadn't realised, but assumed and didn't find out for another few weeks, was that I was not entitled to a penny of the transfer fee.

I went up to the office to ask the secretary, Campbell Ogilvie, when I could expect my share of the transfer fee they had paid to Dundee. Being so naive and stupid, I thought it was a mandatory 10 per cent and that it would've been deducted from the original £210,000 and paid to me. Without this, and taking the tax into consideration, I became Rangers' biggest ever signing at the time, for practically nothing! That was basically all the terms that were agreed for a four-year contract, subject to the medical, which I was dreading.

JG: Oh, by the way, bring your boots tomorrow. We're playing Morton in the league and you are starting on the left of a three-man midfield, you okay with that?

Me: Yes, fine, Mr Greig . . . err, John.

JG: Oh, and you'll need to bring your passport, as we are flying to London right after the game because we are off to Dubai and Kuwait for a short two-game tour next week.

At the time my name and reputation at Dundee had been built as a wide attacking left-sided player or striker. John Greig, however, wanted to change that and play me as a more orthodox midfield player. However I had rarely played in this position, if ever, at Dundee. But that wasn't all. There were so many things about my move to Rangers that weren't right for me at that particular time.

I should've stood up for myself more and put my foot down with both clubs, not to mention my father. I just didn't have a big enough shout for myself to do so at the time. Signing for Glasgow Rangers was a very intimidating prospect for a naive country boy with low self-esteem. Not for one minute would I accuse John Greig of deliberately taking advantage but he didn't need to. He just knew he had me over a barrel and that I was totally overawed by the whole thing. I should've had someone with me in that office, someone who would've looked at things a bit more objectively. Someone who would have got me a much better and fairer financial deal because Rangers desperately wanted to sign me.

A good deal is when all parties can walk away concluding they are happy enough with it. Well, my father was over the moon, as were Rangers, and Dundee FC had just made £210,000, the biggest transfer fee ever paid by a Scottish club to another Scottish club. In business terms, however, Ian Redford got virtually

100

nothing financially out of this historic deal. A good advisor acting in my interests would've got me at least a twenty-five thousand pound signing-on fee and at least 10 per cent of the transfer fee. Later on, in financial terms, I was left feeling like I'd lost out big time. Truth was I just hadn't a clue and had no one in my corner, but on the upside, I was now playing for Rangers.

On that fateful Friday, within in the space of three or four hours, I had gone from sitting in a pub in Dundee, enjoying lunch with my girlfriend, looking forward to playing for Dundee on the Saturday and probably going out for a few beers after the game in Dundee, to the realisation that instead I would be walking out onto the Ibrox Park turf as a Rangers player. It was totally mind-blowing, almost surreal! Not to mention the next day I would be on a plane bound for the Middle East to play in matches for my new club in Dubai and Kuwait. Talk about life changing!

What had I just done? With no time to think or even contemplate whether it really was the right move for me, I had just committed myself to Rangers for four years, but it wasn't the four-year contract or lack of money that was putting me off. The money at the time was irrelevant to me and my ambitions as a footballer. The reality was I knew this was a struggling Rangers team I was joining. They had not won in four matches, that for Rangers was totally unacceptable. The hardcore support were beginning to get on the players' backs and there were also rumblings of discontent in the dressing room. It was a time of great change at Ibrox, as it was the end of the treble-winning Jock Wallace era. Many players of that team were beginning to age in footballing terms.

The John Greig era was a new chapter. A time of transition and change. Rangers supporters though are bred on success. They were sometimes not the most patient of fans and the constant expectation and demand for trophies was beginning to be a burden this team was finding hard to carry – rightly or wrongly. What was nagging away at the back of my mind was the fact that, although I was delighted to be joining such a great football club, in reality they were a struggling team and I was still struggling too. I wasn't anywhere near fully recovered from my injury. I was only really two full games back from being out for practically four months. I was just not fit enough to do myself justice and to handle the immediate pressure I was under.

Dad was no help to me in all of this because all he wanted was to see me playing for Rangers. I think that was his dream. He didn't want me going to England. He was not advising me about what was best for me, he was advising what he wanted for me. He never once sat me down and asked me what I wanted to do. No, it was all too hurried and rushed. I wish I'd had someone to talk all these things through with before I grabbed the pen and signed. In the end I probably still would've signed, but I think I may have been better prepared mentally regarding what to expect from the reality of the situation. To be able to look back and say I played approximately 250 games for Glasgow Rangers gives me an enormous sense of pride. Anyone who has run out onto Ibrox in front of a large partisan Rangers support in a big game will tell you just how good that feels. It's just that the timing of my move was wrong. I think that was what the root of my concerns was and why the warning bells were going off in my head.

Having immediately put pen to paper, subject to the medical, the only thing remaining was for me to go down to the physio room to meet the club doctor. At this point I was crapping myself as I was terrified they'd discover I was deaf and the deal would fall through. However, the medical could not have been more straightforward. I told him about my ankle but he just accepted it was a typical ankle injury with no long-term implications.

By late afternoon I was emotionally and physically exhausted and just wanted to go home and sleep in preparation for my debut the next day. John Greig had other ideas, as he wanted to introduce his latest club-record signing to the press! It seemed like within minutes of him making a phone call there was a posse of them at the stadium. My first ever press conference was conducted in the splendour of the magnificent Ibrox trophy room. It is simply a must for anyone who gets the chance to visit Ibrox. For the very first time I felt what it was like to be scrutinised by the national press. Brian Scott of the *Daily Mail*, who I got to know a bit over the years, seemed intrigued about where I had been at the time the news broke. I wonder, was he was possibly probing that I was in a pub drinking on Friday lunchtime before a game! In the main, though, it all seemed light-hearted to me and initially the national press were pretty good to me. After all I suppose I was big news being Rangers' newest and most expensive signing.

I eventually left Ibrox very late that afternoon. We stopped off on the way home for something to eat at the Crowwood Hotel, as it was now around six o'clock. I knew I needed food but had no appetite, as my stomach was a total knot. As we went upstairs to the lounge the Scottish news was on TV, and guess who was star billing? I remember Dad transfixed on the telly. He just stood staring at it, as if he couldn't quite believe what was going on.

When we got home Mum looked as though she'd had more than a few to calm the nerves! I knew I just had to get to bed and try to get some rest before what was about to unfold the next day!

I didn't really sleep much on the Friday night. I just could not believe I was playing for Rangers the next day. How could I possibly sleep with all this going on in my mind? Next morning my legs were feeling like I had a pair of deep-sea divers' boots on!

I don't think under the circumstances I should've played the next day. It was the worst possible preparation for making my debut. John Greig was keen to offer the frustrated fans something to give the place a lift and I think this was why he was so keen to get me on the park the next day.

I was very uptight and nervous that Saturday morning as I set off for Ibrox on my own in my car from Errol around midday. As soon as I arrived and parked my car, I knew this was another level altogether, as my car was surrounded by fans all wanting my autograph. There was just never the same intensity or volume of people at Dundee. Not saying the Dundee fans were not passionate, they were, but it was like everything was just magnified so much more. I was escorted by stewards from my car for the short walk across the road to the main entrance of the stadium. I was greeted at reception and ushered through to the dressing room, where I was met by my new manager John Greig, who then took me into the home dressing room to introduce me to my new teammates.

Suddenly there I was in the same dressing room as Jardine, Jackson, McCloy, Forsyth, Johnstone, Cooper, Russell. All household names, Rangers legends all of them, who had made big contributions to the Jock Wallace treble-winning era. It was pretty overwhelming for a young teenage country boy from Tayside. Like everything else in the stadium, the dressing room was old and traditional with wooden benches and panelling round the dressing room walls. It was massive, much bigger than the home dressing room at Dens Park. I remember there was a TV situated in the middle and some of the players were watching some of the traditional Saturday lunchtime sport. It was all surreal to me, like a dream.

It was TV off though when John eventually got down to doing the usual pre-match team talk. He read out the team and gave out some basic instructions regarding picking up at set pieces, corners free kicks, etc. He didn't really say very much to me, apart from wishing me all the best. At the time there was a warm-up area we called the tunnel which was under the main stand. It was where all the players went to properly warm up before going out onto the pitch.

All my new teammates had by now wished me all the best as we approached the bell with about five minutes to go to before kick-off. The referee came in and went round to check that all the studs were legal. Then big Tam Forsyth would take his boots off and go and put on the ones that had spikes instead of studs! Ha ha – only joking! My adrenalin had kicked in now and I was getting up for what lay ahead. The bell went and it was time to go. We were all on our feet and lined up at the door. Some players got really animated at this point. It's all nervous energy.

We were ready to take the short walk through the corridor and out into the area below the main stand, then out of the tunnel and onto the pitch. It was an awesome feeling to suddenly find myself standing in line with so many legendary Scottish football giants.

As you walk into the tunnel, the fans opposite see you immediately and the noise level begins to rise throughout the stadium. By the time you take to the field, it's at fever pitch. As I strode out onto the park to be greeted by approximately 30,000 passionate Rangers fans, it gave me a feeling that I have never forgotten to this day. The welcome I got practically brought tears to my eyes. Now I understood why I had so easily signed for this club!

Our opponents that day were Morton in a league match. I knew there was an edge to the match because Rangers had been in very poor form, having not won any of their last four league games, and the pressure was mounting. When the game started I was still very uptight but managed to get a couple of decent early touches. Bobby Russell, a genius of a creative midfield player, alleviated the pressure early by scoring a great goal to put us in front and that, together with the buzz of my introduction, gave the whole place a massive lift. We went on to win comfortably 3–1. I hit the bar with a header and almost scored another couple of times. Generally, though, I had a quiet debut but showed some decent touches considering these last twenty-four hours had almost been the most emotionally, physically and mentally demanding of my life. There was no time for relaxation or rest, though, because immediately after the game we were off to the Middle East, as John had said.

We flew to London on the Saturday night and then headed out to Dubai early on the Sunday morning. I was completely knackered. The trip itself was fine but to have two matches wedged in between two league games at such a crucial stage of the season was just plain crazy. On the plus side, it provided a good chance for me to get to know some of my new teammates. In Dubai I actually scored my first goal for Rangers and I also played in the next match in Kuwait. By the time I got back from the trip it was late on Friday. In the space of seven days I felt like my feet had not even touched the ground. The next day, however, we had another big pressure situation: Hibs at home.

The really big games always take care of themselves but I always felt more pressure existed against stuffy, difficult opposition that the fans expected you to beat comfortably. Playing for Hibs that day in my second league match at Ibrox was George Best, a hero of mine and one of the greatest players of all time. John again played me on the left of a three-man midfield. Not surprisingly given our schedule of the last seven days, we were awful. The fans were unforgiving and were quite rightly demanding better. With both my fitness and confidence low and feeling so tired and lethargic, I couldn't raise a jog, never mind a gallop. In truth, I was awful. The fans must've been wondering what on earth the club had just paid all that money for! I will never forget that match, more for the fact that it was the one and only time I ever shared a football pitch with George Best. Sadly, 'Bestie' was a pale shadow of what he used to be and I reckon he touched to ball in the first half about as many times as I did, and that was not often. The game just completely passed me by. George at least had a good excuse as it was alleged he had downed a few lunchtime pints before taking the field! George was subsequently removed from the park at half-time. To be honest, I should've been too. It was sad for me to see such a decline in such a great footballing talent. I didn't have time to dwell on it, though, because I had enough problems of my own.

To his credit, John Greig kept faith – well, he had to really, having just broken the Scottish transfer record for me. He kept playing me week in week out, even though it was obvious my form was poor. It was like I had suddenly become a shadow of the player I was in my last season at Dundee and this Rangers team I had become part of were struggling in the league and the fans were really beginning to vent their frustration. It was noticeable that the team spirit wasn't great. Coming from a smaller club, I had envisaged great spirit and camaraderie among the elite of a big club. Some of the Jock Wallace treble-winning legends were getting on a bit. John Greig was having a hard time because these were guys he'd played alongside for years, winning trophy after trophy, and now he was trying to bring in younger players like me, effectively to replace them.

It was true, in that first year I did not really feel part of the dressing room at all. It is very hard for me to explain. It was just as though I was perceived as being different. In part it may have been because I was quiet and not prone to speaking up in the dressing room. I was very self-conscious about being deaf and would do anything rather than admit I couldn't hear. As a result, I would avoid situations that could expose my hearing problem. To survive in a football dressing room you need to have your wits about you, as some of the banter can be very cruel and merciless. It can and did get very personal sometimes. I suppose when a big club is struggling the situation puts players under enormous pressure to perform and get results. Players are human and I suppose everyone has to find a way to vent or hide their own fears and insecurities. When things are going against them some begin to take things out on others. It's easy to be a nice guy when things are going well and everything is running smoothly. The real test of character is when things aren't going well, because what matters is not just how you can pick yourself up, but also how you can help a struggling teammate. In fact, if some players focused or cared more about helping a struggling teammate, they would become less intense about their own scene. In an almost therapeutic way, you help yourself by trying to help others. By its nature, though, any professional sport can become very much dog eat dog!

In an incident in training one day I had a major bust-up with Rangers' most legendary hardman, Big Tam 'Jaws' Forsyth. Big Tam seemed to me at that time like a playground bully. He was a ferocious, hard-tackling centre-back who could be very intimidating to play against. I remember in a match once at Ibrox he pole-axed Paul Sturrock. 'Luggy' was left on the deck, blood pouring from his nose! This particular day we were playing five-a-sides on the ash park at our Albion training ground. I received the ball and I took it for a run, going straight past Jaws. He was getting on a bit and didn't appreciate anyone doing that to him – teammate or not! Next thing I knew was WHAM! I received a forearm smash right across the side of my face. Let's just say he was making his presence felt! Being a bit frustrated myself and not really enjoying the way my Rangers career had started off, I had just about had enough. The blow to my face was so severe and the intent so blatant that I just exploded in rage. Within seconds Big Tam and I were trading punches like two boxers coming to the bell at the end of round fifteen, but with neither really convinced they'd done enough to win the bout. My reaction I think had totally amazed everyone on the training ground, probably even me, but it demonstrated I was quite prepared to stand up for myself against anyone if the need arose.

As usual with these incidents, we were separated before any damage could be done. Big Tam, however, still wasn't happy and wanted 'afters' on the way back over from the training ground to the stadium. Still incensed and past caring, I was up for it too! Others intervened though and things began to calm down. This was a defining moment for me because in that instant I think maybe my teammates no longer saw me as a big, soft, silver-spooned country boy from the East. I'm sure Big Tam and I would laugh about it now.

I once described Rangers' late, great Davie Cooper as having as much skill as George Best. Coop, 'Elvis' or 'Moody Blue' as he was known, was indeed one very gifted individual. To witness what he could do with a football was amazing. There's no doubt Davie Cooper was truly world-class, as good as if not better than Ryan Giggs. Initially I found Davie to be a very strange guy. God knows what he must've made of me! His personality could change from one day to the next. Davie could be totally charming and be your best pal one minute then totally ignore or blank you the next. Some mornings if he was in a bad mood, he would just not speak to me, or anyone for that matter. Davie and I had a big fall out once and he didn't talk to me for ages after it. He was very used to getting his own way on the park, and during a league game against Partick Thistle at Firhill something happened that resulted in him ending up injured and on the treatment table. Basically we both ended up going for the same ball and instead of me kicking the ball, he got in the way and I kicked him instead. Davie being Davie was being a bit of a drama queen over it. I don't even really remember whose fault it was. It was just one of these things that happens on the pitch sometimes. We'd both expected each other to get out of the way and both got it very wrong!

When I came in for training on the Monday morning he was lying on the treatment table and none too happy with me. I went to apologise and say I was really sorry for what happened but he was in no mood for reconciliation and let me know what he thought of me. It was not complimentary! What didn't help was the fact that some players were delighting in winding him up about it before I arrived that day. It was fair to say we did not see eye to eye for a little while after that.

When I first knew Davie, he was notoriously suspicious of the media and rarely spoke to them at all. One of the nationals even sent in a particularly attractive female journalist over to Ibrox to try and entice him to speak to her, but Coop was having none of it. The interview I mean!

Apart from his enigmatic personality, Davie became a model professional. His attitude and work ethic improved greatly as he matured. On and off the park he was an individual and did things very much his own way. In my opinion, he was the most skilfully talented footballing entertainer of his era. His wonder goal against Celtic at Hampden in the Dryburgh Cup final was one of the greatest goals you will ever see.

I think Davie began to show more of his true self when he stopped playing and very ironically began a media career. One of the last times I spoke to him was when I was playing for St Johnstone and he was with Motherwell and in his mid to late thirties. As always when he had the ball at his feet, it was difficult to get anywhere near it. After the game we chatted and when he was in this mood he was good company to be in. It was so callously ironic that just at the very time in his life when his personality was really beginning to shine through as a media pundit, he suddenly died. Tragically his sudden death of a brain haemorrhage at the age of only thirty-nine robbed the footballing public of many years of what would've been a very good and capable media personality.

I remember going to his funeral. There was not a dry eye in or out of the church. There were thousands of fans out side in the street. Ex-teammates and good friends like Ally McCoist were weeping openly. It was overwhelming to see such an emotional outpouring from so many fans and people who knew him. He was sadly missed and I have no doubt he ranks as one of the most naturally talented left-footed players Scottish football has ever seen. Yes, I think he was better than Jim Baxter.

At games regularly some his family members would sit up in the stand and would be heard saying, 'Gie it tae Davie – just gie it tae Davie!' For most of my Rangers career that seemed like not a bad idea! Much of the time when I got on the ball it was Davie I would be looking to pass it to. I quickly learned that pass was to be not in front of him or never behind him, it had to be right at his feet, or you would just get the glare! I would then make a run into the box to look for the cross. Eventually and inevitably it would come, but not before he'd tormented and tortured the full-back a few times. Sometimes by the time he'd finished with the ball the opposition's defence had the time to be organised and picked up.

One night we played a friendly exhibition match against Feynoord. Playing for them was a very young Ruud Gullit and a very seasoned Johan Cruyff. I actually scored a really good goal in this match. I picked up the ball just outside the box and curled a beauty into their top right-hand corner. The weather was awful, it was driving sleet and rain. At the start of the second half I was standing opposite Johan and he just looked at me and smiled. Within the next ten minutes he'd had enough and was off! Don't think by that time in his career he had much to prove! Davie was superb that night though and later Ruud Gullit described him as a world-class talent. Who could argue?!

5

THE OLD FIRM AND
OTHER SCOTTISH FOOTBALL

Coming from the Perthshire countryside, religious bigotry was new to me. When I joined Rangers it took me a while before I even knew what some of the sectarian terminology meant. Words like Pape, Hun, Fenian, Tim, were just a foreign language to me. Any religious faith my Mum and Dad may have had ceased when my brother died. Although I am a Protestant and was christened in the church, I would not consider myself a religious person. In fact, I will go further and say I think religion generally is more to do with power and control than it is to do with the natural good-heartedness and well-being of the human spirit. I initially had no idea when I would hear some chants of 'We're up to our knees in Fenian blood, surrender or you'll die.' Pretty soon after I signed for Rangers it was clear my life was going to be very different! I have always been totally against all forms of sectarianism and racism and my views will never change.

One time I was invited to a party in Milngavie, just outside Glasgow. Standing quietly, minding my own business, I was approached by some guy who I'd never met or seen before. He immediately started trying to wind me up by saying I was rubbish, not worth the money and I played for a crap team. Again I knew he was baiting me, so I didn't rise to it but it didn't make

113

any difference. He was a bigot and I was his target of hatred. As I tried to ignore him and move away, he punched me hard in the face without any warning. It was quickly broken up and the guy was removed, but it left me with blood pouring from my lip. The next day at training, noticing my very swollen lip, I was asked by someone what had happened. When I told him the story, he asked me if I knew the guy's name and asked if I 'wanted it taken care of' and I am not talking about a written warning here. I made it very clear, though, I wanted no revenge on this guy and that I just wanted to forget about it.

The tension is inescapable when you play for either Rangers or Celtic and, like it or not, the truth is sectarianism is largely responsible for the unique atmosphere that surrounds the rivalry of the Old Firm. To me a bigot is just a bigot no matter what the colour of his scarf is, be it green or blue. It's naive to think it will all just go away because it won't. It never will. The wounds of history will ensure a portion of each new generation, no matter how small, will be indoctrinated in hatred.

I was also shocked one night at a local Rangers Supporters Player of the Year function. The players often went to these functions voluntarily to accept various Player of the Year awards and generally mingle with the fans. On the whole they were always fabulous PR exercises. On the odd occasion, however, you could get a troublemaker. On one particular night a fan came up to ask for my autograph and duly wanted me to sign FTP alongside it. I just couldn't believe it! What startled me was how normal this person seemed to think his request was. I told him he was welcome to my autograph but no way, under any circumstances, was I going to sign FTP! This person then took an aggressive tone with me and began to rant that I wasn't a true Rangers player, etc. He seemed genuinely upset that I'd refused his request. I must stress that in all my many experiences of going to official

114

Rangers supporters club functions, this was a very isolated incident. Generally speaking, the fans are wonderful and make you feel more than welcome and proud to be playing for the club. However, it underlined to me this mentality existed, albeit in a minority.

Possibly on a lighter note and more common was another incident, this time at a different function, when another person came up to me with his wife and asked me what I thought of her. I thought he was just trying to make conversation. Not wanting to offend the guy or his wife, I made sure I was complimentary and told them I thought she looked really nice. To which he then replied, 'Would you like to have her tonight?' She at this point was smiling invitingly at me but I was mortified and totally embarrassed. I tried to make light of it by mentioning that my girlfriend wouldn't be very happy about it!

However, getting back to the sectarianism issue. My own view is there is far more hypocrisy than hatred when it comes down to it. My own personal experiences of real bigotry or hatred were few and far between. Yes, there was plenty of bravado, a lot of huff and puff, but it was mainly all posturing. It's a great shame we can't just have the rivalry and passion but without that element of hatred. After many Old Firm matches there would plenty of genuine enough handshakes and pats on the back among the players. When it was over it was over . . . till the next time!

More recently, not long after his eighteenth birthday, I took my son Ian to a New Year's game against Celtic. It was the first game he'd ever been to at Ibrox and, when I thought about it, I realised it was also the first Old Firm game I had ever been to as a spectator, so it was also a unique experience for myself. The seats we had were opposite the main stand along towards the Broomloan end of the stadium, near to where all the Celtic fans were.

This particular game marked the fortieth anniversary of the Ibrox disaster in which sixty-six people, mainly Rangers supporters, died when a terracing barrier collapsed and there was a massive crush. It immediately became the biggest ever tragedy to occur in Scottish football. Before kick-off there was a commemorative ceremony followed by a one-minute silence. Former players from both teams strode out onto the pitch for the ceremony, including some of the ones who had played that day. Amazingly virtually all the fans from both sides began applauding. It was a tremendous show of unity and solidarity towards a tragic event. And when the referee blew his whistle for the start of the one-minute silence, I can honestly say that both sets of fans observed it completely. Ian and I had been in the stadium approximately an hour before the start of the game and he just couldn't believe the atmosphere as it built up towards kick-off. The fans were giving it to each other with all sorts of verbal onslaughts. There were the usual sectarian jibes and I even clocked a Celtic fan with a big imprinted IRA on his shirt, under his coat, which he opened to show off and wind up the Rangers fans. To me this proved a point. To most Old Firm fans, all the abuse and sectarian chants are just part of the tradition and a way for them to let off steam. But when it comes to a matter of life or death, you see that the vast majority are still respectful of the opposition. It would be naive of me to try to deny there are genuine bigots on both sides of the fence, but I still think they are in the vast minority, with the majority just using it as a conduit to vent frustrations in some cases that are maybe not even related to football.

How else can you explain all the Celtic scarfs laid down outside Ibrox when Davie Cooper died? Conversely, how else can you explain the respect Rangers FC and its fans gave to Celtic legend and all-round good guy Tommy Burns when he also

116

very sadly passed away. The red, white and blue of Rangers scarfs could clearly be seen lying outside Parkhead. I believe the human spirit, in the main, is naturally good and well meaning. In the end, it is not really what people say that truly matters because it's really what people do that counts.

Rangers' policy of not signing a Catholic came from the dark ages. There is no place for bigotry in a forward-thinking modern society. Graeme Souness made the best statement ever when he signed Mo Johnston. I think it was Graeme's way of letting people know that if he wanted a player he would sign him regardless of religion, colour or anything for that matter. The Rangers fans ultimately showed too that what means more to them than anything is what players do for them on the pitch. All else is just waffle and fresh air. We have to realise, though, that bigotry does exist, not just in football, in all walks of life. The only way to beat bigotry is to win the battle for hearts and minds.

On the lighter side, depending on your sense of humour, the funniest incident I can recall regarding the 'dark side' of sectarianism was when we played against Maltese side Valetta in the Cup Winners' Cup at Ibrox one night in season 1983/84. They really were just a pub team and in no time at all we had a barrowfull in the back of their net – including me scoring Rangers' 150th goal in European competition. (Coincidentally, I also scored Dundee United's 150th goal in European competition!) For them coming to play in a big stadium like Ibrox against the mighty Glasgow Rangers was a real thrill. As much as they didn't enjoy getting a thorough hiding, their coach wanted all his players to sample and savour the big-time atmosphere. With no more than roughly five minutes to go, he decided to give his last available substitute a run-out on the pitch. However, as he was preparing to go on the park, someone forgot to tell this poor chap that blessing yourself on the touchline in front of a partisan Rangers support is just not the done thing! The poor guy took such a verbal hammering from the crowd before he even came on! He had no idea why all the hissing and booing being aimed at him. Any time he came close to touching the ball he got completely barracked! You could see he was wondering what on earth he had done to incur such wrath from the crowd. I mean, it wasn't as if it was Celtic we were playing and they were 2–0 up and about to bring on Charlie Nicholas to rub our noses in it! This was just a part-timer that wouldn't have got a regular game for the Govan Girl Guides. Certainly it pays to be aware of religious protocol when playing football in Glasgow.

One of the most sickening experiences of sectarianism for me was when we played against Bohemians in Dublin in a European tie when Jock Wallace was manager. Quite simply, it was terrifying. Many loyalist Rangers fans had come across the border from Belfast for the game and it had all the ingredients of a recipe for disaster. For the record I think we lost the match 3–2, but that was irrelevant in terms of the scale of violence by two sets of fans hell-bent on war. How no one in our team was seriously injured was beyond me. In the first half at our end of the pitch we were being pelted by anything these maniacs could get their hands on, from half bricks to darts. In actual fact, I came very close to being hit by a dart. Standing in the penalty area defending a corner kick, this lethal thing was lobbed over the protective fence into the crowded penalty area and just stuck in the ground right beside me. Had it hit my face or head at that velocity it could've been very serious. Our goalkeeper Nicky Walker was very lucky not to get a serious injury from missiles been thrown into the goalmouth. The nutters throwing these objects could just as easily have hit one of their own Bohemian players.

Big Jock Wallace, ex-jungle fighter, was not a man given to fear anything or anyone and had gone out on to the pitch at half-time to try and calm things down. You could see that even he was shaken by it. The second half maybe wasn't as bad but, even so, that match should have been abandoned and the tie handed to Rangers. We left that stadium in our coach, heads down, lying on the floor, for fear of anything from a brick – literally – to a bullet coming through the bus window it was that bad. Luckily for us we won 2–0 at home thanks to two late goals, one from big Craig Paterson and the other from me right at the death, a diving header from another Davie Cooper cross which proved to be another late winner. It was becoming a habit!

'What's it like to play in an Old Firm game?' Believe me, I really would be a rich man today if I had a pound for every time someone has asked me that question. The one thing any Rangers or Celtic player will never forget is their Old Firm debut. Rangers v Celtic is quite simply one of the biggest club matches on the planet, and, who knows, even beyond it. Out-and-out tribal warfare, for the reasons previously stated. My very first Old Firm match came at Celtic Park in midweek, not long before the end of the season in 1980, and only a few weeks after I had signed for Rangers. It was the last Old Firm game of the season and although we were out of contention in the league there was more than just points to play for. After all, it was Rangers versus Celtic!

There is an added tension around that you can feel in the days leading up to an Old Firm game. You feel it mount as the clock ticks down to the big moment. There is an added edge in the dressing room and on the training ground. Late in the afternoon of the match the squad assembled at Ibrox, where we had our usual pre-match meal before departing for Celtic Park. Old Lizzie Love was buzzing around in the kitchen, preparing the food. Her daughter Tiny was also helping out. It seemed that Lizzie's whole family were an integral part of Rangers. The backroom staff at Ibrox was very much a closely knit family affair. There were those who gave their whole working lives to help with the running of Rangers Football Club. When we were playing Celtic everyone was just that bit more tense.

Our pre-match meals were always light. It was a choice of fish, grilled chicken, scrambled eggs, or some just had tea and toast with honey or jam. The players would arrive at the stadium late afternoon to relax a bit (or at least try), have the pre-match meal then get ready to depart for Parkhead, across the city to the east side of Glasgow. When it was finally time to leave and get on the bus, we'd make our way downstairs out the reception area and onto the team bus which was cordoned off, but only on Old Firm day, as there were usually droves of fans there cheering us on and looking for autographs. Right from the moment we left, heading east across the city, we had a police escort all the way. As we approached the stadium I could see thousands of fans walking along the streets already making their way to the game, the green scarfs giving us the finger or jeering and the blue scarfs giving us a wave or a cheer. I could quite literally feel the whole tempo rising as we got nearer and nearer Celtic Park. By the time our bus arrived at Parkhead, the whole place was jumping with the sheer atmosphere of a big occasion.

There was still over an hour and a half to go till kick-off! Police escort to and from the stadium is essential for a game of such magnitude, because without it there would be an increased risk of trouble or delay because of the huge increase of traffic volume. John Greig was noticeably more tense than normal. This was much more than just a league game for him. As a player he played in countless Old Firm games. As manager it was all outwith his control. Once the match started he could do nothing apart from watch and hope for the right result from his team. Managers of the Old Firm have previously risen or fallen by how their team performs in Old Firm encounters. Rangers v Celtic is not even so much about winning but rather more to do with not losing. John knew he didn't need to say anything to us, apart from where he wanted everyone at set pieces. Little to no talking is required in the build up to an Old Firm game.

All of us sitting in the Celtic away dressing room that night knew what was expected of us as a team and as individuals. Funnily enough, the only bit of real advice I got in the dressing room right before the match was from Alex MacDonald, Doddie. He advised the best way to get into the game was by getting in a tackle or two early on. He said, 'You'll quickly get our fans right behind you.'

Although I could sense the occasion and anticipation of a big game, nothing but nothing could've prepared me for the wall of noise that hit me as I walked out onto the pitch with my teammates. It was quite simply incredible. From the second the referee blew his whistle to start the match until he blew for full-time it was mayhem. Flat-out breakneck, 100 miles per hour mayhem! In the first ten minutes or so it's as if the crowd's noise is so loud it actually lifts the ball and keeps it off the ground. The tempo was so fast I could hardly get my breath. During that first ten to fifteen-minute period it was as though the game was going on round about me and I just didn't know how to get near the ball. Then I kicked Celtic legend and captain at the time Roy Aitken. No yellow card, our fans went mental and it was then I knew what Alex had referred to!

As the first half wore on I began to find my feet and felt at last I was a participant in the match as opposed to being a specta-tor! The second half was much the same as the first, with play raging from end to end and no one really dictating the match.

It was getting late on when Coop swivelled as only he could do and swung in a cross that I managed to get my head to and the ball was in the net! I couldn't believe it. With so little time left, I thought I'd just scored the winning goal in my very first Old Firm game! Typically of my luck at the time, though, the linesman flagged for offside and it was disallowed. It was marginal and often these decisions go in your favour, but not for me at this time.

Then, heartbreakingly but not surprisingly, with only minutes remaining Celtic went up the park and scored! Their recent big-money signing at the time, Frank McGarvey, got the goal that counted! I was totally deflated as the whistle then went for full time. As we trudged back into the dressing room, John Greig was totally gutted. He just wanted everyone out of Parkhead and onto the bus as quickly as possible.

It was always hard to be on the receiving end of an Old Firm defeat. Harder still for a guy like John, so used to success as a player and beginning to find it tough going as a manager. These moments, good or bad, meant so much to us as players during this era of football. If we weren't the ones running around daft on the park living out our dreams, we would otherwise have been standing on the terraces or sitting in the stands with our scarves on, being supporters! Many of the players of today get so much money but I wonder: do they have the same passion and affinity with the clubs the fans do? If you look at the top clubs in my day, there were very few foreigners. I'm not against foreign players at all, but merely stating a fact. There are much fewer successful clubs, if any in Scotland, that are built from a core of home-based players. During the Eighties you at least had Rangers, Celtic, Aberdeen and Dundee United. First and foremost we were supporters before we became players. We acted out our dreams as kids then lived them in reality as professional players. Because of this I think there was a greater bond between the fans and the players. They could relate to us more and we could also relate to them because we once were them.

The best Old Firm game I can ever remember playing in came very much in a backs-to-the-wall performance in a league game at Ibrox. It had come on the same week as a horrible 3–0 defeat by lowly Chesterfield in the Anglo-Scottish Cup. We'd gone down South in the wrong frame of mind and had taken our opposition too lightly and got severely punished. We couldn't afford this type of performance because it was too damaging to morale. Coming back up the road from England we'd taken such a slaughtering from everyone. The press, the fans, our manager, all that was missing was a good lambasting, or worse, from our wives and girlfriends! Just three days later we had to pick ourselves up and face our biggest rivals. In hindsight, it was exactly the match we needed. Had we been playing lesser opposition I don't think we would have felt so trapped and cornered. Therefore we would not have been so wound up for a life-or-death survival battle. Having just given our worst team performance since I arrived at Rangers, we now had nowhere to run or hide out on that pitch against Celtic.

I had never played in such a high-octane, up-tempo, good-all-round team performance in an Old Firm match as in that particular Old Firm encounter. We thumped them 3–0, and it easily could've been six, and I was voted Man of the Match. Journalist and ex-Rangers player Doug Baillie, writing for the *Sunday Post*, said of my performance: 'He's had his critics since signing from Dundee but they'll soon disappear if he can keep this up.'

I felt trapped and in a corner because of all the heat we were getting from the fans and the media. Instinctively, I think I just switched into survival mode. My game felt electric that day. Nothing was getting in the way. It's amazing how the brain can go from the anxiety of fearing consequence and outcome, straight into the present. This is when your mind is at its most powerful. When you are not thinking about what you are doing, you are just doing it!

At the end of that season, 1979/80, we finished poorly in the league but did get to the final of the Scottish Cup. Again our opponents were our arch-rivals from across the city – and not Partick Thistle. Of course, it was Celtic. Unfortunately, I was ineligible due to being Cup-tied, meaning I had already played for my previous club Dundee in the same competition. John Greig took me along for the ride though, to experience the build-up of a major Cup final. I sat alongside the subs on the bench and was close to the action. The occasion will only be remembered for one thing and that was the full-scale riot at the end, just after both sets of players had left the field. Rival fans from both ends of the stadium piled onto the park and met head-on in scenes that were more akin to some kind of open urban warfare. The police riot horses charged onto the park to disperse all the troublemakers who were running riot onto Hampden Park. These were among the worst scenes of football violence I had ever witnessed at close quarters. I am amazed that no one was killed. Well-known *Daily Record* sports photographer Eric Craig nearly was. He was hit on the head by a bottle thrown by some hoodlum and suffered a fractured skull.

On the football side there was very little to comment on. It was a very dull, unattractive match, but what stands out for me was the performance of our own Sandy Jardine. I had total admiration for the way he ran his heart out for Rangers that afternoon. I have never seen a full-back cover so much ground. Sandy was an athlete and pure class as a player. He was the best right-back

124

I ever played with. He was also a regular internationalist at a time when there were some top-quality Scottish players to chose from.

Celtic won the Cup that day through a goal in extra-time, scored by the skilful George McCluskey. I think even George himself, if pushed, would possibly admit his goal was a bit of a flukey in-off! His goal of course meant Rangers finished the season trophy-less. Even greats such as John Greig could not avoid the wrath of an impatient success-hungry Rangers support. John was now under severe pressure and I think it was around this time that he began to realise it.

During this era there were some well-known and colourful TV commentators. Arthur Montford of STV springs to mind. He was a gentleman and only ever commentated on the facts of the game. Some his sayings are unforgettable: 'and up go the heads' or 'there's a stramash in the goalmouth'. He loved wearing the Basil Fawlty-type sports jackets and looked like a bit of a stuffed shirt, but Arthur was pure class. The same could be said of Bob Crampsey, a man with an IQ that even Carol Vorderman would've been proud of. Bob was more of a radio pundit, though, and he had a great-sounding voice. If voices could be whisky, his was definitely a smooth malt.

I think Radio Clyde during my time were pioneers of after-match live football phone-ins. James Sanderson, or 'Solly' as he was nicknamed, was the man who really made it popular on Radio Clyde. He took a delight in winding up supporters who would call in, sometimes with a very animated point of view. There were times coming back on the team bus after an away game when we'd have the radio on and after a bad result be dreading someone calling in and having a go. Take it from me, it wasn't funny if you happened to be the one that was getting it on national radio in front of all your teammates on the way back home from a defeat at Aberdeen or Dundee. Solly, though, was as sharp as a tack and always quick on the draw when dealing with the fans: 'Were you actually at the game today, sir?' he would invariably enquire. For the fan's sake, he really needed to say yes or his credibility was blown sky high and he was toast verbally.

On one hilarious occasion a very animated fan came on right after an away match at Dundee:

JS: Where are you calling from, sir?
Rangers fan: Am at hame.
JS: And where is home sir?
Rangers fan: Dintoaker.
JS: Ah, you mean Duntocher.
Rangers fan: Aye, Dintoaker.
JS: And were you actually at the game today, sir?
Rangers fan: Aye a wuz.
JS: Well can you please tell me how much it cost to hire the helicopter that got you home in time to make this call?
< Brrrrrrrrrrrrrrrrrrrrr! >
JS: Oh, we seem to have lost that caller!

It was guys like Jimmy Sanderson, Arthur Montford, Bob Crampsie and BBC's Dougie Donnelly that really kept the pot boiling in Scottish football in terms of media interest. To me, their enthusiasm and passion for football were obvious. There were others that followed, but these were the ones I remember with fondness and respect. I always thought Archie Macpherson was a bit of an egotist and hadn't the sense of humour that some of his peers had.

The next season, 1980/81, was a memorable one for me in more ways than one. Pre-season was full of promise. Jim Bett was signed from Lokeren of Belgium along with big burly rough-round-the-edges striker Colin McAdam, from Partick Thistle. Jim, or 'Jazzer' as he was known, was a very good player. He'd been playing in Belgium and making a name for himself when John Greig brought him to Ibrox as a midfield playmaker. In a pre-season match against Tottenham Hotspur Jim and I combined really well against a Spurs midfield that included the brilliant Glen Hoddle and World Cup-winning Argentinian superstar Ossie Ardiles. Ibrox was packed that night as we outplayed Spurs. Admittedly they were a bit behind us in terms of their pre-season. It had been between Jim and me for Rangers' Man of the Match that night. It was especially good for me to put in a really good performance against top opposition in front of our home fans. I could really feel some form beginning to come back, and my confidence levels, along with fitness levels, were much higher going into the new season.

There was another big development for me at this time and it was one that did not go down well with my parents, particularly my dad! He'd been sceptical all along about my relationship with Jeanette. I think he saw it as a distraction and potentially damaging to me, rather than seeing that it may actually have been good for me at the time. Dad was in the kitchen early one morning as I was having some breakfast before leaving to go to Glasgow for training. I think he'd begun to get wind of something and said to me, 'I hope you are not thinking about going to live in Glasgow with that girl.'

To which I replied, 'Well, that's funny because, now you mention it, that's just what I have decided to do.'

Well he hit the roof and began ranting about what an idiot I was, among other things. It got really heated as usual. Having quickly decided I'd had enough of his 'opinion', I downed a bit of toast before jumping into my car and heading off to Glasgow.

He'd been so concerned about my relationship with Jeanette he was threatening to leave me out of his will. In retrospect, I wish he had. At least from that day I would've known exactly where I stood.

Jeanette was six years older than me and I was still only nineteen when we began our relationship. We'd first met in Dundee not long before I signed for Rangers. Possibly she was attracted to me initially because I was becoming well known, a local celebrity if you like, but she was good for me and provided some much-needed stability in my life. After signing for Rangers it would've been impossible for me to continue living at home for various reasons. To me it all made sense – well, at my age I suppose it would do! I did get a bit concerned however when, not long after we moved in, her mother cornered me and asked when I was going to make an honest woman of her. YIKES! I was not ready to get married – far from it – and neither was she. I think I can reconcile it all by saying we just met and hit it off at a time when it was good for both of us. I think we both knew it wouldn't last forever but we simply enjoyed what we had at the time. She never struck me as being the marrying type and I certainly had no plans to do so. My life had changed so much at nineteen years of age: I had gone from living at home, playing for Dundee to within months moving in with my first ever girlfriend and playing for Glasgow Rangers! It was surreal!

Frustratingly, despite all the early promise of the new signings and new season, it was not too long before the team were struggling again and falling away out of the championship race. We somehow lacked the consistency and defensive discipline. We also didn't score enough goals against the top teams. We seemed to be more of a Cup team than a team that ground it out over the season to win a league.

128

Once again by early New Year the Scottish Cup was all there was to play for in terms of winning majors. In the first round we disposed of Airdrie 5–0 away, in which I scored a memorable goal. In the second round we were drawn away against the team I'd first supported as a boy, St Johnstone. At the time they were battling for promotion to the Premier League from the top of the First Division. Their ground, Muirton Park, however was full of good memories for me. Right from when I was a schoolboy I always seemed to play well there and always seemed to score. These feelings became so strong I used to sense it before I even took the field. For me playing against Saints that day was like going home. Many of my family and relatives still live in the Perthshire area. That day was massive for me, even if maybe it wasn't quite so emotional for the rest of the squad. St Johnstone obviously were not fancied at all, but they did however have a talented young teenager in their ranks by the name of Ally McCoist! It felt as though the whole of Perth would be there and I knew many would love to see me get my nose rubbed in it in front of my family and friends. I was really excited about the match and just maybe a part of me was feeling confident enough to want to show what I knew I was capable of.

The game kicked off on a Saturday afternoon in March 1981. The atmosphere was electric inside Muirton Park that day. I recognised so many faces when out warming up pre-match. The game began really well for us, as we scored two goals early on in the first half. The first came after Ally Dawson combined well with Willie Johnston down our left-hand side towards the town end before Ally crossed and the ball was headed in by our big burly striker, Colin McAdam. Our second was a rare right-footed finish from me inside the box after Saints failed to clear a deep searching free kick from Sandy Jardine. My feelings, or intuition if you like, had not let me down, I just felt I would score in every game I played in that stadium and think I just about did! It really looked like we were cruising all the way to the quarter-finals but maybe, just maybe, we had begun to switch off, thinking the game was already in the bag. St Johnstone had other ideas and pulled one back when we failed to clear the ball defensively. It was played wide then cut back square across goal, past our already committed keeper, Peter McCloy, before being stabbed into virtually an empty net by an ecstatic Jim Docherty. That made it 2–1 at half-time and reminded us this game was still not over. In the second half it really didn't help matters when our normally very reliable gigantic goalie Peter McCloy, the 'Girvan Lighthouse' as he was known, let a rather tepid John Brogan effort from no more than ten yards slide under his body and into the net. It was now 2–2 and the alarm bells were ringing!

Legendary Saints striker John Brogan still wasn't finished. A free kick lobbed harmlessly enough into the box wasn't dealt defensively. The ball broke to a Saints player, who fired a very weak effort at Big Peter, who allowed the ball to break from him pretty much like a bar of soap would get away from you in the shower! As the big Lighthouse again attempted to get his hands on it, the toe of John Brogan got to it first and poked the ball under him into our net once again. Our normally rock-solid big goalie just had a particularly bad day at the office and our defence was awful in dealing with two situations. That was all it took to put us into the nightmare scenario we now found ourselves in. St Johnstone now led 3–2, with not much time left to play.

With the clock ticking down we were in big trouble. John Greig was getting desperate, and brought on utility club stalwart Alex Miller. 'Squeaky' was one of those players that was 100 per cent loyal to the club. He was Rangers through and through. Never quite fully establishing a position for himself in his own right, he was a player who could be relied upon to do a job. His finest moment I can remember was when he scored one from long range at Parkhead in an Old Firm match, which we won. It was as rare a goal from him, as it was a beauty!

'Squeaky' was running around like a maniac shouting, 'COME ON, COME ON! REMEMBER BERWICK, REMEMBER BERWICK!' Berwick incidentally was where Rangers suffered their most humiliating defeat ever, losing to Berwick Rangers 1–0 in the Scottish Cup. In hindsight, it was hilarious, he was running around, screaming something that many of the younger squad had little or no recollection of. In fact, at that precise time nothing could be further from the minds of the players who were trying to find a way out of the enormous hole we had dug ourselves into! Yes, the club stood on the brink of another major disaster. One from which I don't think John Greig would've survived.

I have never felt so physically sick on a football field. Our fans were going mental at us as the pressure mounted. 'Bottles' were seriously on the brink of crashing and the home fans were loving it. To our credit we seemed to wake up from our self-induced coma right at the cliff's edge, to discover this was not the dream we were living, more like the nightmare of staring down into the abyss. At that point we began fighting not just for Rangers but for our own credibility as footballers.

It was not until deep into injury time that my timely intervention came. During that last period of the match as we were heading for defeat, there was only one thought in my mind and that was to score a goal. Never in my career had I felt such a desire and need to get a goal. My mind was completely and utterly present with no thoughts at all about any consequences. No mulling over the humiliation and despair in the dressing room of the aftermath of such a result.

There was no awareness of anyone watching me, no thoughts

of friends or family and no consideration of the little matter of the wrath of more than just a few thousand Rangers supporters who'd paid good money to come to Perth that day who without doubt would be baying for our blood. All I could see was the field. In my mind there was just no way I was coming off that pitch without scoring another goal. I wasn't even interested in getting on the ball at that point. I left that to Russell, Cooper and Bett. I decided to keep making runs into the box to try and get on the end of a cross. All I needed was one whiff of a chance and I knew I would take it.

Just as it really was looking like game over, Davie Cooper picked up a throw-in from Alex Miller down their right-hand side. His touch and familiar mesmerising swivel all in one move-ment created all the space he needed to whip in an inswinging cross with that priceless left foot of his. As I saw Davie controlling the ball, I was already anticipating what was coming next and was making my way into the box. I somehow just knew this was the one I'd waited for. Saints goalie George Tulloch, who wasn't the tallest goalkeeper around, committed himself to coming off his line to punch it clear. It wouldn't have mattered either way because in my mind I was scoring regardless! Our big robust striker Colin McAdam went for it too but he was slightly behind me as I got there first. As I climbed to meet the ball I seemed to hang in the air to get slightly above the ball. Tulloch's fist was a just a fraction slow as my head made downwards contact on the ball – just like the hundreds of times it did when Dad used to throw a ball for me to jump and head it against the garage door. As if in slow motion the ball took ages as it veered downwards, almost hitting the goal line before bouncing upwards into St Johnstone's net. Well before it did though my brain was already celebrating, as I knew I had scored. GOAL! 3–3. It was game over and the replay booked back at Ibrox!

As long as I live I will never forget the feeling of relief and joy that surged through my veins as the ball crossed the line. It was indescribable! One of those very special moments in your life that only lasts a few seconds.

Thinking of it, Davie Cooper supplied so many of the crosses that I scored from with my head for Rangers. When he was on the ball I seemed to instinctively know where and when it was coming into the box. He knew all he had to do was put the ball into the right spot and I'd somehow get there. It was a good understanding. He also had an almost telepathic understanding with midfield genius Bobby Russell, another gifted footballer of his generation. I can still see Bobby today making those devastating blind-side runs and Davie slide-ruling the defence-splitting pass to perfection. It was great to watch.

Archie McPherson, commentating on that fateful day at Muirton Park for BBC *Sportscene* ranted, 'I DON'T BELIEVE IT! REDFORD HAS JUST SAVED RANGERS!' Quite literally we had saved ourselves from one of the most humiliating defeats in the club's history.

Back in the tunnel after the game it was mayhem. John Greig was going bonkers. Someone, whoever was responsible, had not come to open the away dressing room and we were all stuck outside in the corridor waiting for access. In sheer frustration and anger, John stormed up the corridor past everyone, got to the door and straight-legged it off the hinges, I guess in pretty much the same fashion he had straight-legged a few opponents in his day as a player! I would not like to have been on the receiving end of his left boot that day. It wasn't often I saw that side of John but he was one scary guy to be anywhere near at that moment. In the dressing room that day John was ranting like a mad man, he had finally blown his top and it had been a long time coming! When he finally calmed down he thanked me in front of the whole team for scoring that vital last-minute goal. Eventually when we were all sat in the bath mightily relieved to still be in the Cup, Willie Johnston's comments were very prophetic. He simply said, 'That's it, lads, after what we went through today our name is on the trophy.'

The goals we lost against St Johnstone that day though were an absolute joke. It was this type of performance that was putting everyone under more and more pressure. It was costing the club league titles. Not to mention John's reputation as manager of Rangers Football Club. Despite the odd outburst, in my opinion, John Greig could never have been as ruthless a manager as Sir Alex Ferguson or Jim McLean. I just don't think deep down he had the same desire for management that he had as a player – the big difference being that John had already proved himself as a very successful player, whereas Sir Alex and Jim hadn't to nearly the same degree. As such I think they went into management with a feeling they still had it all to prove.

I saw the same thing more recently in Davie Moyes of Manchester United. When I first knew Davie he was a player with Celtic and seemed to be the fans' scapegoat whenever things weren't going well. In the year I went to obtain my advanced FA coaching licence at Lilleshall, Davie was in my group. It was so obvious, you could see the desire he had. I mean no disrespect to John Greig at all. In fact, this should be taken as a compliment to him as a person. I believe because of his complete fulfilment as a player, subconsciously he just didn't feel that much of a need to pull up trees or stamp on throats to be a successful manager.

Look at the way Sir Alex got rid of players or dropped them no matter who they were or how big their reputations were. I never saw that mentality in John. He was just an all-round good guy and I think, to a certain extent, still wanted to be seen as one of the lads in the dressing room. His task of going from player straight to manager was an enormous one.

It's incredible to this day how many people from Perth still remind me of the goal that cost St Johnstone the best result in the club's history at the time and in doing so saved Rangers from the worst result in theirs. Although the team itself was not playing particularly well, I was slowly but surely beginning to establish myself as a Rangers player at last. I still somehow wasn't quite able to express the individuality and spark I had shown at Dens Park as a Dundee player, but I was consistently playing a decent standard of football. I think the majority of Rangers fans at last began to at least appreciate my attitude and effort. I even had my own supporters club from Kilsyth called the Ian Redford Loyal Rangers Supporters Club. It seemed as though I had traded most of my devil-may-care attitude at Dundee, where the fans had christened me the 'Sundance Kid', in return for being a more rounded, mature and reliable performer at Rangers. I don't think it was really me, though, and I felt like something got lost along the way between my injury at Dundee, coming back and then joining Rangers.

The next round of the Scottish Cup was the quarter-finals in which we comfortably disposed of Hibs 3–1. Typically semi-finals are very tense nervy affairs. In this one we were drawn against Morton at the neutral venue of Parkhead. It was a tough, bruising encounter which we won 2–1. For a change our defensive discipline was good and we scored twice to kill them off. Mind you, they did not a bad job of that themselves with getting two players sent off. Big mercurial genius Andy Ritchie got a penalty back for them late on but it was never going to be enough for them. We were just relieved to be in another major Cup final. Our opponents in what was to be my first Scottish Cup final was Jim McLean's revolutionary Dundee United, who'd taken care of Celtic in the other semi-final and who were on course for a League Cup/Scottish Cup double and, come to think of it, Old Firm double.

As was customary for Rangers, the squad was taken away to the Troon Marine Hotel for a few days to prepare for the match. Personally I think there was a case for not making an issue of the fact this was an incredibly crucial game for the club. Brian Clough was a master at this. On the eve of his first European Cup final as manager of Nottingham Forrest he took his team for a stroll and ended up buying them all a drink in a bar! What better way to remind them this was a moment to savour and enjoy rather than fear. He knew a couple of beers would have a relaxing, beneficial effect on his players, and he was right. That's the sort of simple thing a great manager would do on the psychological side.

I felt in our build-up to that game there was far too much tension in our camp. I have sympathy for John Greig though because he was very much feeling it. He was carrying the weight of expectation of a great club on his shoulders. With the league now gone, the Scottish Cup was the only major issue of the season still to be resolved. All the media attention and focus switched on to the match, as there was not really much else to talk or write about. The pressure was gradually building as the week went on. This was no picnic outing to look forward to for Rangers because it was our last chance to win a major and it would be the only major trophy the club had won in two seasons. That was unacceptable to the fans. The pressure on John Greig and all of us was enormous. In this scenario there was no buzz of excited anticipation. There was only realisation that winning the Scottish Cup had become an absolute must. Having already bagged the League Cup by trouncing my old club Dundee 3–0, the pressure to win was not as great for Dundee United as it was for us. On paper and based on form they were maybe even the better team (they certainly were defensively) and probably favourites. Yet all the pressure was on us to win in the national stadium, Hampden Park, that week.

On the morning of the match I remember waking up in my hotel bed really early and feeling very tense and nervous about the occasion. I lay awake for a while until I knew breakfast was being served. I quietly dressed and tip-toed out of the room so as not to wake Jim Bett, my roommate. It was around 7am. It was very therapeutic for me to just be able to sit on my own, eat breakfast and contemplate the day ahead.

Sometimes at the table if I switched off for a second, someone would quickly shout my name to distract me. Of course being totally deaf in one ear I had no idea which direction the sound was coming from and it would make me look really foolish. As long as I could see who was speaking it was no problem but sometimes I got mentally exhausted just trying to keep up. It was an added tension that made things more difficult for me than they already were. If I became over-tense before a match my legs would feel very heavy and I would feel very tired and lacklustre. Normal nerves are good and are nature's way of preparing you for an event. Fight or flight, if you like, but if you are struggling to cope with a situation mentally then they can get the better of you and block you from performing. You will always perform better when the 'big picture' or your subconscious is settled and working in tandem with your conscious thought. I think this was a major problem of mine throughout my career.

Good sports psychologists are not magicians; they are just people who know how to help you put anxiety levels into perspective and deal with them through a good cognitive thought process. Better still is to develop a good core mental philosophy. If you have this you can take on and deal with anything. I didn't really have either when at Rangers and we were all very much on your own in that department, as there was no one on the coaching staff who knew how to convey a good psychological mindset. It was simply sink or swim! John was becoming a bag of nerves and I'm sure sometimes without even realising we were picking up the signals.

After a relaxing breakfast I headed back upstairs and went straight back to bed and slept for another two or three hours. By lunchtime we had our official pre-match meal and this was really more or less the only time we were in a group that morning before we left. As usual, just after the pre-match meal John gathered the squad for one final team meeting. After that it was onto the bus and up the road to Glasgow. I remember it was a nice day and there was a real feeling of spring in the air.

The journey from Troon to Hampden Park was under an hour. As we got to the outskirts of Glasgow we were beginning to see more and more red, blue and white scarves and flags. By the time we got close to the stadium all that could be seen was an ocean of red, blue and white. It was impossible not to be amazed by it. Looking out the window and seeing the expressions on the faces of our supporters, there was no doubting this was a huge occasion.

Coming into the stadium in the bus that afternoon was similar to arriving at Parkhead for an Old Firm encounter. Maybe there was a bit more of a party atmosphere from the fans than the sheer intensity of the build-up to an Old Firm clash. I was so taken aback by the emotion. I could feel everything welling up inside me and a tear came to my eye. I wiped it quickly away so that no one would notice! It was overwhelming and I'm sure any other Rangers player lucky enough to have experienced this will know exactly what I mean.

This occasion is what I had dreamed about as a wee boy kicking

THE OLD FIRM AND OTHER SCOTTISH FOOTBALL

a ball around in the garden, up against the garage door, against the wall, in the field at Errol Station with the Clark brothers playing keep-ball-from-Skipper, my mental Springer Spaniel, who if I allowed to get possession would sink his teeth in and burst the ball! (Eventually he didn't get to burst so many!) This was when I dreamed of one day scoring the winning goal in a major Cup final. I don't think you really appreciate it so much at the time, especially with a big club when winning Cup finals are the norm and anything less is just seen as failure. These moments, though, are as rare as they are priceless when it comes down to how you assess your own life. They stay with you forever when many other memories fade and die over the years.

As always, Mum and Dad were there along with all their regular friends who travelled with them to the games. This was a huge day out for them. I don't know if they ever thought when watching me as a young boy kicking a ball around the garden or when playing for Errol Rovers that they would be coming to the national stadium to watch me play for Rangers in the Scottish Cup final. The sadness in their lives was such a contrast to what they must've felt that day. I really hope it lifted them and gave them some pleasure.

The tension involved in the build-up to any major Cup final when playing for Rangers is just immense. Much as the Rangers fans get behind their team on such an occasion, achievement or success is measured by only one thing: winning! With most clubs just getting there is viewed as a nice bonus with something to look forward to. With Rangers it's all about the expectation of winning. The fact the club had been trophy-less for two years was now weighing immensely on our shoulders.

On match day, 9 May 1981, the build-up to that final was fantastic. The atmosphere on the pitch before the game, the pipe bands marching up and down, created a carnival flavour, the colour of all the scarves, and flags of both sets of fans – it was something to behold. As individuals and as a group we'd spent the whole week being told how crucial and how critical it now was to win a trophy. Dundee United, on the other hand, I don't think enjoyed the idea that they were being viewed as slight favourites to beat Rangers in a major Cup final. With success comes expectation and with expectation comes pressure. They had earned this right but I'm not so sure they were comfortable with it.

John Greig played me up front as a striker but, more surprisingly, left Davie Cooper, along with goal poacher John MacDonald, on the bench. Davie had been having a hard time of it, and his head had been down a bit. It was rumoured that earlier in the season he had gone to the manager and asked to be left out of the team. In a team of good individual players not many were playing to their full potential. John MacDonald was another major talent not producing what he was capable of. In their places on the day John Greig preferred the experience of Tommy McLean and Willie Johnston, both creative wide players. To a certain extent I was in danger of becoming a victim of my own all-round ability because I was potentially as good a striker as I was a midfield player. John seemed to have more options in midfield than he did up front and so I was sacrificed as a midfield player to play as a main striker. John also gave me a spell at left-back and it worked, too, because at one point I was being tipped for an international call-up in that position.

Typically with all the excitement and fervour related to the big occasion, the game itself was such a let-down. I honestly can hardly remember even touching the ball. It was all just so nervy and tense from start to finish. My legs felt so heavy and lethargic, like I was trying to run through quicksand. Agonisingly, it went all the way to the last minute with barely an incident of note until Bobby Russell was fouled inside the box – PENALTY!

The referee duly pointed to the spot, however, I noticed that all my teammates were now looking the other way. No one appeared to want to pick up the ball and take the responsibility. Surprisingly, I was the nearest thing Rangers had to a regular penalty-kick-taker at the time. Having scored one in particular against Dundee United at Ibrox a few weeks previously, I was the last Rangers player to have scored from the spot. However I was not mentally prepared at all for this eventuality because nothing prior had been spoken of or agreed. At Dundee I knew if we got a penalty it was my job to take it, which I was happy to do. At Rangers it was as if I had just acquired this role without portfolio. Finally in the absence of any other volunteers, I picked up the ball and decided to take it on. As I put the ball down on the spot, Frank Kopel of Dundee United came over to me and said, 'Watch and not kick the ground, son.'

As I tried to put the ball on the penalty spot I struggled to find any decent bit of turf. The surface was so poor. No matter how I tried, the ball just kept wanting to sit down into the ground. It was a bit like a golfer trying to hit his driver off a bare lie! Eventually I got it settled on a manageable bit of bare surface within the allotted white-dotted spot. I then looked up and saw 40,000 Rangers fans directly in front of me behind the goals. I went at the knees and my heart began pounding uncontrollably. It was frightening because I thought it was going to burst straight out of my chest. My breathing had suddenly become very shallow and constricted. My throat tightened as if I had tied a tie far too tight. I knew somehow I had to try and get a grip of myself. I tried my best to get my mind back into the present but I couldn't. For some reason I fidgeted with my socks as if pulling them up, but they were already up! My conscious mind was already writing the scripts of the only two possible outcomes. Hero or villain!

I kept trying to say to myself, 'Just hit the target. Just hit the target. If you hit the target the chances are you will score, just make sure you hit the TARGET!' As I steadied myself, United goalkeeper Hamish McAlpine appeared to grow larger in stature right in front of my eyes. Particularly his hands and gloves seemed to be getting bigger and bigger. The height and width of the goals suddenly seemed to look narrow and shallow. 'Buggering Hell!' I was thinking. 'This is not good, Reddy. This is not good at all.' My anxiety levels were such that my brain had gone into overload and were now stir-frying in a wok! I had lost control of my emotions and thought process as my pulse and heart would've confirmed by off-the-scale readings!

Under the circumstances I tried as best I could to continue to focus. I knew the odds would still be in my favour if I could, so I took a few paces and paused, tried in vain to take a deep breath. The referee blew his whistle, giving me the go-ahead. It was as if the whole world stood still and even I could've heard a pin drop inside Hampden. I decided to get my body over the ball and kick it downwards with the top of my left foot to keep it low and on target. I see so many players miss penalties because they lean back and hit it with the instep, thus opening up their body, and the ball just goes miles up in the air or past the post. Believe me, your odds increase dramatically if you hit the target!

I didn't make great contact but at least it was on target! Hamish had made an early decision and dived away from the ball, but as the ball was not really directed to a specific corner of the net, it hit him on the legs and was deflected away from goals. The referee then blew his whistle almost immediately to end the match. It was literally the last kick of the game. Now we were into extra-time. I was shattered. There is a picture of me sitting on the ground at the side of the pitch at the end of normal time in utter exhaustion, despair and disbelief. And now we still had another thirty minutes to go. Amazingly, though, I will never forget the way the whole Rangers support immediately forgave me and tried to lift me by chanting my name. It was an incredible show of support from a set of fans that had not been enjoying the best of times watching their team. It's another moment that stands out for me and is something I have never forgotten. It showed to me that day why Glasgow Rangers can be such an incredible club to play for.

In extra-time both teams could hardly raise a gallop. The game crawled predictably across the finish line at 0–0. Much as I was heartbroken to have missed the penalty and effectively the chance to win the final for Rangers, I think it would've been an injustice had any team won that day. Two good attacking teams on paper had just literally bottled it on the big occasion and cancelled each other out! As a Scottish FA Cup final it was a total and utter non-event. What didn't help, in my opinion, was the poor state of the playing surface. Hampden always seemed to be like this in May at the end of the season. Here we had two teams full of very skilful players but it was hard to be confident in your control of the ball on a hard, dry, rutted surface.

In the dressing room after the match I sat there, gutted at the thought of having to go through all this again. Eventually by time I came out, the press were all waiting for me in their droves. Big Derek 'Bah' Johnstone kept them away from me as we made our way out of the stadium onto the bus. It was a nice gesture from the big man. Although he was very much the joker of the dressing room, Derek was a decent, well-meaning guy.

The celebration buffet back at Ibrox was muted to say the least. Adding insult to injury for me was club chairman, surgeon Rae Simpson. In his after-match speech he mentioned how sorry he was for 'Jim Redford', who had missed the penalty kick. Old Rae was famous for his gaffes – as if I wasn't feeling bad enough! It was a tumbleweed moment as no one knew what to do or say to me, but to be fair most of my teammates understood how I was suffering. Having missed that vital chance to win the Cup for Rangers, I was feeling numb and distraught. I was so exhausted by it all emotionally. At that time I just wanted to go away and forget about football. It had been a really long, difficult season and I really felt completely drained.

It's amazing how quickly time heals and soon I began to stop feeling sorry for myself. There were two things that helped more than anything and that gave me the mental strength and belief to lift myself again going into the replay: John Greig came out and immediately said I would be the first name on the team sheet for the replay, and because the Rangers supporters had been so vocal in getting behind me, I knew I just had to repay that faith. It gave me the belief and the determination to lift myself and do it all again just three days later, on 12 May 1981!

The replay will be remembered (apart from us winning 4–1) by those who were there, for the individual performance of Davie Cooper. Left out of the team on the Saturday, Davie was back for the replay along with John MacDonald and me moving back into my more familiar Rangers role of left midfield. There was only one thing more dangerous than an on-form Davie Cooper and that was an on-form Davie Cooper with a chip on his shoulder!

The atmosphere at Hampden was again superb. It had been raining and the surface was slick and greasy, suiting the many and varied ball players in both teams, none more so than our Davie. The tempo of the match was breathtaking from start to finish. We got our noses in front early when the normally solid United defence failed to clear the ball and it broke kindly to Coop, who nudged it goalwards with his knee, committing United keeper Hamish McAlpine before calmly slotting it past him neatly into the corner of the net. His goal was our catalyst! It seemed to electrify the whole team, not to mention our incredible support, who were going crazy.

Goal number two came quickly when Davie then whipped in a superb cross that beat everyone except Bobby Russell, who had ghosted in at the back post and struck it first time into the net. Bobby was magnificent throughout, as was John 'Solo' MacDonald, who on the night was at his very best. I was getting on the ball more in the wide-left areas and that was also causing problems. Jim Bett was a powerhouse in central midfield. It was as though all our creative players caught fire and a whole range of differing skills were on display. It was still not over, though, and United had their moments. Bannon, Milne and Sturrock – all superb individual players – were also showing great touches and fighting hard. They pulled one back when Sturrock slipped a cute pass into the path of Davie Dodds, who finished it well. We were still on the rampage, though, and Davie again did the damage when I knocked a pass to him, before he split the United defence with a slide-rule special, to put John MacDonald in and his finish was clinical, 3–1. It was a long way back for United now.

In the second half it was still end to end. To their credit, United kept battling away. The final nail in United's coffin came when I picked up the ball wide-left, just inside United's half. John MacDonald was in good position so I picked him out with a long curling pass that put him right in on goals. Again the finish was clinical and it was effectively game over.

Without doubt Davie was the maestro that night and I can only ever remember one other all-round team performance of that calibre in my days with John Greig as manager. This was his Rangers team at their very best. On that form no team would've lived with us, because we had just hammered the best team in

Scotland at that particular time. It was such a shame we were seldom able to replicate that performance. If we had, then winning the league would not have been an issue.

With the creative talents and goal-scoring ability of players such as Cooper, Russell, Bett, MacDonald, Derek Johnstone and myself, it was hard to see why we became known only as an occasion team but remained an enigma when it came to the league. Was it because we didn't have enough grinders? Was it perhaps because the defensive side of the team was too old? Was it because we were not organised enough as a team unit and just played as if we became too dependent on the individual brilliance of certain players? Whatever the reasons, John Greig wasn't able to find a formula consistent enough to win a league title. We certainly had all the necessary ingredients but just couldn't get the recipe right. Personally, I am leaning towards the fact that I think we were not disciplined enough as a team. Too many times we just didn't have eleven individuals all fighting for each other and playing within a system or formula. Over the long, hard slog of a whole season, that is what wins league titles.

As we emerged with the Cup outside Hampden Park, there was Dad, along with my sister Jill, who I don't think had ever been to see me play before, and Graeme, my brother-in-law. They were all standing there in the rain among hoards of others who'd waited to see the team emerge with the trophy. I could see the emotion on Dad's face. There were tears in his eyes. My relationship with Dad seemed to be measured by how well things were going for me in my career. If things were good and I was playing, well then, he was fine. But if things were not going well, he struggled to hide his disappointment. This I found difficult to handle. He did have his moments, though, and that night at Hampden was one of them.

As a farmer Dad couldn't get his head round the concept of professional sport. He saw what I did every day as no more than just a couple of hours' work, followed by time wasting – not realising that some days coming off the training ground I just felt totally exhausted and needed to rest up and recharge the batteries. Yes, it can seem wasteful and unproductive, but that is the nature of the beast. Any proper athlete will tell you that rest is just as important as what you eat and drink and how you exercise. Bearing in mind right at the start of my Rangers career I was also driving back and forth between Glasgow every day, it was certainly not as easy as it perhaps looked to him.

I did a lot of things to try and keep in his good books. Finally to try and appease the old man I had the idea that maybe I could start a business to run in my 'spare' time! Jeanette being a hairdresser, we had the idea that we could buy a salon and she would run it. Having found an ideal premises in the West End of Glasgow, I put the idea to Dad and he agreed to act as guarantor for the sum of £25k. This was what I needed to acquire the lease-hold and business as a going concern. Well, going concern was pushing it. Let's just say it was already a salon! It was situated in Hyndland, the posh bit of Glasgow's West End. Jeanette and I were both sold on the location and were sure it would prove to be a good business venture. Subsequently, with Dad acting as guarantor for the money, I bought the salon with my girlfriend Jeanette as my partner.

Having really begun to establish myself in the previous season, somehow in 1981/82 I struggled to recapture the form I had shown the previous year. Again we were inconsistent in the league, and within a couple of months I found myself dropped and out of the team.

Amazingly, at the start of the season I had scored four goals in a League Cup game at Ibrox against Raith Rovers but still came off the park feeling low and down because I had missed so many other chances and was getting lots of stick from the fans. Had I scored the chances I missed that day I would be holding the record for the most goals scored in a game by any player! I began to get really down about spending more time on the bench than I was in the starting eleven. My frustrations led to me feeling depressed. I had always enjoyed a few beers at the weekend after games, but now I had started drinking more often, during the week and even more heavily at weekends.

When I was drinking it was just blotting everything out temporarily but it solved nothing. When it wore off, all my negative feelings and problems were still there but were made even worse by the depressant effect of the alcohol. I had a hard time feeling accepted in the dressing room at the best of times. I could handle and reconcile things when I was in the team because playing gave me a sense of worth and purpose. However, when I wasn't in the team sometimes I would wonder what on earth I was doing in Glasgow. I was unhappy, feeling sorry for myself and was drowning my sorrows and because I was drowning my sorrows my fitness went, which ensured that my form stayed poor. It was a vicious downward spiral.

The salon was also struggling to get off the ground. The working overdraft was right up to its limit. Not only were things not going well on the pitch, I was also now feeling under financial pressure too. It got to the stage where I needed to ask Dad if he would be prepared to extend his financial guarantee to enable the business a bit more leeway in terms of cash flow. I decided I needed to speak to him about it.

Early one Sunday morning, I got in my car with a massive hangover and drove from Strathblane up to Perthshire, unannounced. When I arrived at Errol Station I could see Dad's van parked outside the chicken houses just beside the level crossing

148

at Errol Station. I thought rather than going to the house first to see Mum I would pop in and surprise him. I parked beside his van and went in to the shed to find him.

Between the intense smell of ammonia and noise of the chickens inside the shed, it was taking me all my time not to throw up. My head was spinning and my stomach churning both at the same time. Dad had no idea why I had come up the road to see him that morning but it was clear from the onset he was in no mood for me. I didn't therefore waste much time before cutting straight to the chase. I explained the situation: that cash flow was really tight and the business needed a bit more time to get on its feet. I went on that we'd been taking very little to nothing out of it and that we were genuinely struggling to make things work. His reaction was not encouraging: 'Well, if you have come to ask me to guarantee you more money, you can fucking well forget it!'

With my head also buzzing now from his verbal onslaught, I took no more. Without saying anything in reply, I turned and walked away from him. Outside I quickly threw up a couple times before getting back into the car and heading off home. I felt so bad I didn't even want to go and say hello to Mum. We didn't speak again for quite some time. Apparently he had gone over to the house later, expecting me to be there and was even more annoyed that I had just jumped in the car and driven straight back through to the West. Maybe Dad in his own way taught me my first lesson about the realities of business! Thankfully the salon began to turn the corner and the overdraft slowly began to come down without any more outside intervention.

During this period I was not really enjoying anything about my football career. The constant pressures, the expectations, the jibes, the bitching and backbiting that seemed to get worse and worse, the more the team struggled. In truth, my lifestyle was a big part of the problem. Too many distractions, too many boozy nights after games. I began to put on weight, my fitness was poor and because I was not playing regularly again my match sharpness was sadly lacking. Overall, it was not a happy time to be playing for Rangers. There was a heavy cloud hanging over the place. There was generally a lot of discontentment within the dressing room. The fans were on our backs, and rightly so, because we were not delivering the goods. That said, I was letting myself and the club down with my self-destructive attitude.

As a typical example of how I was living at the time, Big Derek Johnstone (DJ) called me up on a Saturday lunchtime, just after our game had been called off due to frost. He was in a hotel in Drymen (not an appropriate name for us at the time!), which was very near to where I lived in the village of Strathblane. Jill and Graeme had come to stay for the weekend. DJ told me he was with his friend Billy Connolly and asked if I wanted to join them for a few drinks. At the time Billy Connolly was really beginning to make his name nationally as a comedian and entertainer. Big Derek was good company, and me also being curious to meet Billy Connolly, I agreed to join them along with my brother-in-law. It was not long after we arrived at the hotel that I began to realise that the other 'Big Yin' really enjoyed a bevvy session too. Consequently, that Saturday ended up a massive all-day bender.

I found Billy to be very much as he portrayed himself, a typical Glaswegian comedian with sledgehammer wit. He was incredibly funny to be around, but as the day wore on and the more drunk we all became, I could tell he was also a man with his own set of demons. Goodness knows how much we all ended up drinking that day! What brought it home to me though was the way Billy kept asking Derek and me, 'What's it like to run out in front of 50,000 fans? What's it like to score a goal in front

of all these people? What's it like to play in an Old Firm game?'
Billy was very much still a football punter.

To try and restore a bit of much-needed team spirit and harmony to the dressing room, John took the squad off to Portugal
for a few days' 'bonding' and also to play a friendly match. It
didn't do me much good, as I ended up getting myself sent off
in the first half and locked in the dressing room for the second
half, for the benefit of my own safety. It was just a friendly but
I reacted severely to an opponent who had, it seemed to me,
literally tried to put me in hospital in what was a very late and
nasty tackle. Luckily I saw it coming and just managed to take
evasive action. It was the intent of it that made me so instantly
angry. Down came the red mist and he knew it because as I went
after him he started running away from me.

It must've looked hilarious to the neutral eye. He was zigzag-
ging all over the pitch as if trying to avoid a pursuant crocodile,
but I caught him a beauty with my left boot and inserted it right
up into a place where the sun never shines! Without even looking at the referee, I knew I'd done more than enough to get an
instant and automatic red card. My opponent's challenge trig-
gered off a reaction that had been building up in me for some
time. As I made my way up the tunnel, I had to run the gauntlet
of some very irate Portuguese fans. The whole of the Rangers
bench I think just sat in total disbelief at what they'd just witnessed from me. I'm sure John Greig, not to mention the rest of
the squad, must've thought I had finally flipped!

In 1981, the same year we beat Dundee United in that classic
Scottish Cup replay, we met them in another major Cup final,
this time in the League Cup final in the season of 1981/82. The
way things had been going for me, unsurprisingly I found myself
on the bench for the match. Even though I knew I had not been
playing well, I saw myself as a good bet for a goal or an assist in

any big game. Especially if it came right down to the wire. My attitude and spirit during this phase of my career was very poor, though, and without doubt I was losing my way. Not only was I was not working hard enough, I wasn't working at all at my game. I couldn't really explain a lot about how I was feeling at the time but, looking back, I can see that I was very depressed.

First-team coach Joe Mason was the only one who seemed to even attempt to get to the bottom of what was going on with me. Joe was manic and could be very funny; he often came away with some classics in the dressing room. I remember one night when he was taking the reserves in a league match against part-timers Hamilton Academicals, Joe went ballistic. Coming in at half-time we were 1–0 down. Joe cried, 'I am not going to be beaten by a bunch of butchers, bakers, candlestick makers. There's no way I'll accept being beaten by Hamilton Addacemi-cals, err Hamilton Ammademic, emm Hamilton Accadama ... FUCK IT! – HAMILTON ACCIES!' I liked Joe Mason – he could be volatile but he had a heart and he was one who did reach out to me in those difficult early days.

Going into this final, for the first time against any of the Old Firm, Dundee United were actually clear favourites to win. It was a sign of the rising force Dundee United were becoming in the Scottish game. It was a dark dreich Sunday afternoon in November at Hampden Park, but as usual, there was a great atmosphere. They were playing us off the park in the first half and should've had the game won by half-time. We were just rubbish. In the second half favourites United took the lead. United's Paul Sturrock, probably the best player in the league at the time, collected the ball just inside our half and, with back to goal, turned Alex Miller inside out before releasing Ralph Milne with a defence-splitting pass. Ralph Milne, who was the quickest thing on two legs in Scottish football, sprinted onto it before cutting inside slightly and releasing a left-foot drive into our net for 1–0. It was a great goal and well deserved, as they were without doubt the superior team.

As the second half began to wear on I had begun to give up thinking I would have any role or part to play in the match. It was sheer torture for me having to sit and watch. The way the team were playing, I couldn't see any way back for us. My pride was really hurting. My friend and fellow teammate Billy 'Bleeper' MacKay had also just about given up the idea of getting on the pitch, and so we began to tuck into a box of chocolates that had been lying unopened in the back of the dugout. We were both depressed and had decided to indulge in some comfort eating! Our manager didn't seem to have any inclination to change things and time was running out even if he wanted to.

Suddenly, with no warning at all, John Greig shouted, 'Bleeper! Get warmed up.'

Billy, like a madman, was immediately out of the dugout, thinking he was going on, and began running furiously up and down the track to get himself ready.

Meanwhile, I was still stuck in the dugout, feeling even more depressed thinking my chances of getting on had gone completely! Then, with no more than around five minutes of the match remaining, John suddenly shouted at me, 'Reddy, get your tracksuit off. You're going on – NOW!'

I nearly choked on the last remaining chocolates as I suddenly quit the comfort eating and stumbled out of the dugout with tracksuit trousers already at half-mast and furiously trying to get my tracksuit top off. It never ceased to amaze me how long it could take to get a top and pair of trousers off. As I moved towards the touchline, I was still fumbling and undressing.

I had been on the pitch no more than seconds when Davie Cooper picked up the ball on the halfway line on the right-hand side of the pitch and, as usual, cut in on his left before picking out John MacDonald with a typically superb pass. As John ran onto it he was fouled right on the edge of the penalty area. It was a direct free kick. In this situation there was only one man who was going to take it and that would be Davie.

The strike was deadly and explosive. It was up and over the wall yet still well under the bar, and with total power and precision. United goalie Hamish McAlpine got a hand to it but no way would any keeper have saved it. 1–1.

In the space of two minutes I had gone from depressingly munching chocolates on the bench, thinking it was game over, we're going to lose, to being on the pitch, match all square and GAME ON! It was Davie this time who pulled us back from the brink and kept our hopes alive once again.

At this point you could see how deflated United looked. They must have been wondering what they had to do to win a final against Rangers! With so little time left to go in the match, again I had only one thing in my mind . . . scoring the winner! Instantly my mindset became a carbon copy of what it had been in the latter stages of the 3–3 match at Muirton Park.

All I felt was an incredible desire to get one moment or chance to win the game. No coincidence again either that Davie Cooper played a part in what was the definitive moment of the game. From the right-hand side well into United's half he took a free kick. I think I held back from attacking it because the box was already full of players and decided to anticipate the ball breaking back out of the box. As Davie's cross came in, United defender Paul Hegarty got his head to it first but didn't get the power on it required to head it well clear of danger. For some spooky reason my decision to stay out of the box proved to be the right one, as Hegarty's floaty-headed clearance landed right at my feet. Or rather my left foot!

154

It all happened within a split second. Outwardly there was no time to think, yet inwardly I felt like I had all the time in the world. It was another of these rare moments where I felt complete and utter clarity of mind. As I controlled the ball, I was aware of a gap or space just inside the top left side of the United goal. I knew if I could float it accurately into that space, I had a great chance to score. My first touch had been good but my second touch was even better as I chipped the ball with my left foot precisely at my prior calculated target. As the ball left my foot, I knew immediately it was good. However as it hit the left-hand side net of the United goal that lucid moment was again gone forever and immediately replaced by utter mayhem. GOAL! And my lifelong dream came true. I had just scored the winner in the last seconds of a major Cup final! In front of me, behind the goals, were all those same thirty to forty thousand Rangers fans that had witnessed me unable to control my emotion and miss that last-minute penalty earlier in the year. Like a maniac I was off and running uncontrollably. Had the stadium doors been open I would've needed a fiver to get back in!

The release I felt at that moment after weeks and weeks of depression and anxiety at not playing was just unbelievable. Up to that point in my career nothing had equalled or bettered that moment at Hampden. Eventually I was caught by some of my teammates, who had been so deflated when I had missed *that* penalty. This time I had spared them another bout of extra-time!

Then instinctively I broke away from them and turned to face the Rangers support behind the goals, who were all going crazy. I saluted them in a manner that showed my respect to the ones who stayed loyal and supported the team through and through. But I guess there was also part of me that wanted to gloat to the ones who had been giving me and other players a hard time.

There were too few of these rare gems in my time at Ibrox and

I suppose in my career in general but even to have experienced one moment such as this made everything worth it. Let's put it this way: if someone asked me how many days of my life I would be willing to trade to relive such a moment, my answer would be quite a few!

These incredible experiences I have had still fascinate me from the psychological perspective. Interestingly, the contrast between missing the penalty in the last minute of the Scottish Cup final and scoring the winner in the last minute of the League Cup final demonstrate the huge differences between having time to think and contemplate the outcome of an action, as opposed to having no time to contemplate an action. With that winning chip I had no time to think about the outcome, and the result was a goal. This showed me I had the instinct and ability to react well under pressure. On the negative side, when I had to take the penalty and was given too much time to contemplate the outcome, my skillset didn't fire up and I allowed my thoughts to get in the way. I think it also proved when, given time to think, my self-belief levels were not what they should've been.

I think I had also allowed my feelings to become a bit soured. I was in a major rut and felt I was going nowhere. I was not really earning much money apart from just being able to pay my mortgage, run a decent car and eat well. This was fine if it was a job guaranteed for life, but I knew my career was not going to last forever and it was most certainly not going the way I had anticipated at Rangers. Overall, to me, my game felt inhibited; it was clumsy and awkward much of the time. There were of course also many consistent performances, but the bottom line was I knew I was underachieving massively in terms of what I was capable of.

With the benefit of hindsight I can see I had allowed my mind to become distorted. My teammates were just my teammates.

156

Why should I have expected any more or any less from them? Instead of allowing the sarcastic comments to prey on my mind, I should've knuckled down and tried even harder to overcome my situation. It was a time in my career when instead of feeling sorry for myself I should've shown more determination and resilience. Scoring wining goals in major Cup finals was without doubt fantastic, but that should have just been the icing on the cake instead of the whole cake itself.

Being a top performer is about grinding, week in and week out. I have to be honest and say at this point I was just not doing that at Rangers. It is always easy to blame circumstances and others when things are not going well, but if you have the talent the ability and the mental toughness as I had, there should never have been any excuses for drinking and abusing myself and not being a dedicated professional. When times are tough you simply have to dig in, keep trying and as long as you are still breathing, never give up! Success comes when effort and preparation meet opportunity.

I suppose it said much about the way I was feeling when I decided I didn't really want to celebrate the win with my team-mates at the official after-match celebration. Instead I went back to Blanefield to celebrate with Jeanette and her friend Jennifer. Jennifer, a very attractive girl with a bubbly personality, had temporarily moved in because we'd headhunted her from one of the top hair salons in Dundee to come and work with us at Brims. It did raise a few eyebrows! My reputation was maybe not growing on the park at this time but it was now certainly growing off it!

The three of us ended up at one of the nearby local pubs and met up with a few friends who we'd got to know. I got very drunk and now the demons had taken over. In my infinite drunken wisdom I decided I wanted to go and show face at the

157

official Rangers party, which was being held in a hotel in Glasgow. I think scoring that winning goal had unleashed a posse of demons inside me and I think, in my own way, I was intent on a bit of gloating and ramming it down a few throats. A lot of my problems, though, were born of the subconscious and had little to do with my situation at the club. I was unhappy with being out of the team but was blaming everyone else or external factors and was not realising the problems I had were internal not external.

Although I am honest enough to admit many of my problems were internal. There were things about the club that at the time that seemed regimented and institutional, or old-fashioned if you like. Many of the younger new players like me who were brought in found a lot of it to be pointless and unnecessary. For example, even on the training ground you were not allowed to wear your socks at your ankles or have your jersey outside your shorts. These were very old-fashioned traditions started way back in Victorian times. Jim Bett always liked to wear his jersey outside his shorts and I was one who liked my socks at my ankles in training. It gave me a less restricted feeling. Playing for Dundee sometimes I would have my socks at my ankles. The new young players,such as Jim Bett and I, rebelled against this and were constantly being chastised about it. You were also not allowed to turn up for training unshaven. This was just plain nuts to me and some of the younger ones in the squad!

I have a feeling some of John Greig's problems came from a combination of trying to move the club forward in his own image, yet trying to appease the 'Politburo' sitting above him in the boardroom. They were all for change regarding the brand new all-seated stadium, yet for a huge club like Glasgow Rangers for most of the year we trained on a mud heap and an ash car park called the Albion. This was not befitting a huge club like Glasgow Rangers. The 'Politburo' wanted to move the club into the 'big league' and would pay big transfer fees for players of potential, such as myself, yet wouldn't pay the players top wages. Our bonuses at that time were very poor and just didn't reflect modern thinking at all. What the club should've done was also buy fully established players and pay accordingly. Forget the new stadium, at least until the team is bringing home real success.

Up-and-coming clubs with modern ideas like Alex Ferguson's Aberdeen and Jim McLean's Dundee United were paying far more in incentives than Rangers were. It was no coincidence they were getting real success. It was almost a 'fur coat, no knickers' mentality. In my opinion, if a club has money and they want success then there's only one thing that will bring it: a good team on the pitch. To get that requires investment in the best players and the best training facilities. In my era Rangers had neither. We were a top-four Scottish club side, who, on our day, were as good as anything in Scotland, but that was it. It was plain crazy too because the club had, and still has, one of the biggest and most loyal sets of supporters in the world. Would they have traded a nice new stadium for a team wining trebles and getting success in Europe? You bet they would!

In my opinion, with a brand such as Rangers FC you get it right on the park first then everything will 'follow follow' from that. Tradition is fine but the club was too ensconced in 'you play for the jersey'. That's fine up to a point, but not if you want to be the best. Like it or not, expecting professional players to have that attitude was unrealistic and only going to take you so far.

With the League Cup final won, the partying was well and truly over; my form continued to be inconsistent and lacklustre. I was very much in and out of the team. To make matters worse, my relationship with Jeanette was on the rocks and complicated by the fact that we were running a business together. On the positive side, in December 1981, by an eerie coincidence on virtually the anniversary of my brother's death, I met the girl I fell in love with and eventually married. It was the day of the players' annual Christmas party, or rather 'piss up'. It usually started at lunchtime in a Glasgow city centre bar and continued all through the afternoon and into the early evening! As always Billy and I had broken away from the pack and found a pub somewhere that could accommodate our needs. It was a long, long afternoon and by early evening Bleeper decided he wanted to go and visit his old girlfriend, Margaret, who happened to be a student at Glasgow University. She was living in a flat nearby Sauchiehall Street, where we were drinking.

I decided to tag along and cadge a cup of much needed black coffee. We both arrived at the door of her flat in a very badly boozed-up state. When the door opened, however, it wasn't Maggs but rather a very beautiful brunette by the name of Janine, who just happened to be Margaret's flatmate. I think I fell in love straight away. We were both welcomed in and the girls began making us lots of cups of coffee to begin to try and sober up the pair of us. Eventually they gave up and actually decided it would be more fun to join in. By this time Billy and I had got our second wind so we all ended up heading out into town for a night out.

Our night with the girls ended up with me solely kipped up on the sofa and Billy and Maggs having a reunion in the bedroom. The state Billy was in that night didn't get much past Maggs tucking him in and turning him on his side so that he wouldn't choke on his own vomit! Breakfast came much too quickly for our liking as we were still well under the influence, but we now both had to get up and go to training. We knew

160

we were going to suffer because knowing that we'd all been on the piss, we were going to have to pay the price in sweat and pain on the track, and we did just that! The biggest bonus of the whole affair for me, however, was that Janine agreed to see me again. As always, with me nothing was straightforward, as she herself had just been in a serious relationship and the last thing we both needed was to be diving headlong into another one. It was the start though!

Billy MacKay was the closest I had to a real friend at Ibrox. We seemed to have much in common – not least he was also from the East of Scotland. On nights out, however, Billy and I were like matter and antimatter. When you put us together with alcohol the results were inevitably explosive. Billy I think was much like me in that he was also a bit lost and out of things. He'd been given his Rangers debut very young, at sixteen years of age, but had not really been able to fulfil his potential and spent most of the time in the reserves or on the fringes of the first team. Billy was also an academic and didn't really fit the profile of a typical footballer. Like me I think he was shy and self-conscious, and also like me, I think he drank to alleviate the pressure and his inhibitions. Billy was very shortsighted, wore contact lenses and got slaughtered in the dressing room for it. We were sometimes known as 'Hear No Evil – See No Evil!' Unfortunately when we got drunk together the release valve would just blow its top and all the pent-up, suppressed aggression was released into the wild! There were no sports psychologists around at that time in football. You would've been laughed out the dressing room door for going to a psychologist, but in fact probably 90 per cent of that dressing room needed a psychiatrist, never mind a sports psychologist!

Gregor Stevens was a player that John Greig brought to the club from Leicester City. He joined not long before me. Gregor had built up a good reputation as a classy defender but he seemed to struggle mentally with the never-ending intensity that goes with playing for a big club and made worse by the fact this big club was a struggling one. I think Gregor really began to feel it, as did some of the rest of us. Without doubt he had the ability and the talent but he could be extremely volatile and reactionary on the park.

During a particularly bad run of form, John had arranged a 'friendly' match down at Kilmarnock, as there had been a lack of games due to bad weather. Gregor was having a very hard time of it, as were all of us that day. At half-time John came in and went ballistic in the dressing room. It was clear that he too was a man under real pressure.

Gregor was obviously at breaking point because within a minute or so of the start of the second half, he launched himself into a tackle that resulted in one of the young Kilmarnock players having his leg very badly broken. It seemed as if the pressure had just become too much and he momentarily lost the plot. Playing for a massive club like Rangers during these lean and difficult times was not easy for anyone at the club.

Nobody on that pitch was interested in playing football any more that day. Without a doubt it was not easy to ignore the constant pressures that were building up within the four walls of Ibrox due to our lack of success on the field. Gregor off the pitch was an absolute gentleman, a quiet introvert. Eventually something has to give. His quiet, gentle nature, perhaps pushed beyond the boundary of his mental coping mechanisms. We are all human, and under constant pressure we all have our thresholds.

Another time, not long before Gregor left Rangers, he was put out on loan to Hearts. One day when we played them at Tynecastle, Gregor was actually in opposition to us. I spent most of the second half trying to make sure I was well out of range from one his tackles. He had lost it again and was so wound up he was running around bawling, 'Get into them ...' The thing was, Gregor was only out on loan so he also still happened to be one of us, to which he was referring. After the match though, in the players' lounge, normal service had resumed. Over a cup of tea and slice of fruit cake Gregor made friendly and polite conversation: 'Hi, Reddy. How are you doing? How are things with you?' It was as if nothing had been going on at all out on the pitch.

In season 1981/82, about the only major bright spot for me was scoring that winner in the League Cup final. We were nowhere in the league but it seemed, as always, we were again in the Scottish Cup final against Aberdeen. No joy in this one either for me, as I was suspended for it, but I know the way things were the chances are I wouldn't have started. More likely I would've been on the bench. For the record, it was another very poor final but we were deservedly beaten by a better team. Alex Ferguson's name and reputation as a young manager was growing and, from this point, it was not too long before he was off to Manchester United.

Despite my heroics in the League Cup final, I was *really* glad to see the back of that season. In the space of those twelve months it seemed like I had managed to fall out with everyone meaningful in my life. My parents, my manager, my girlfriend! Jeanette and I finally split up. It wouldn't have been me, though, without added complications. We still had a business to run and, having no car, Jeanette needed mine to get herself back and forward to Glasgow to the salon. In the end, because I had to keep the business going and as it was starting to seriously bring down the overdraft, I ended up giving her my car, which was a lovely little black Ford Fiesta Super Sport with wide tyres! 'Fortunately' for me, I already had a club-sponsored car – well, if you could call it a car! Unfortunately for me, it was a 1980s Austin Princess and they were hideous! Mine was a horrible dirty brown colour and looked more like a lump of triangular-sliced cheddar cheese. The suspension when driving felt like a waterbed. Believe me, I knew what a waterbed felt like, as I had one in my apartment at Blanefield! Having moved out of my own flat and given my car away, I had offloaded all the 'baggage' it was now just me and my new apartment.

Thankfully I had a good friend, Alistair, who lived in the Darnley area. He offered me a room in the large apartment he shared with his mum, Anne. Anne became my temporary landlady and surrogate mother! Thank God all this was going on in the close season. I was not on good terms at all with Holmlea. I don't think I had much contact at all with anyone during that close season. Janine and I had seen each other briefly but decided we had things in our lives to sort out before we could start anything, so we went our separate ways. As much as I appreciated staying with Alistair and Anne, I knew I needed to find a place of my own. Luckily I found a place relatively quickly. It was a two-bed, ground-floor flat in a converted Edwardian sandstone villa beside Maxwell Park, in the residential area of Pollockshields. Being part of an original old building, the rooms were large, all with high ceilings. It was an area of Glasgow I liked very much and it was close to Ibrox stadium. I paid £29,000, for it! For me it was perfect and I couldn't wait to move in and effectively start all over again. Having persuaded Jeanette that the flat in Blanefield had to be sold, she too was making plans to leave. Thankfully, Jennifer had really begun to enjoy life through in the West and so when Jeanette finally left, she took over and became my manageress. This was a lifesaver for me at the time because, without Jennifer, I would've struggled to keep the salon going in the right direction. However, I knew a longer-term solution would need to be found.

There comes a time when you hit the low point and begin to bounce back. I had badly needed to get some peace and solitude in my life and when I moved into my flat in Pollockshields, it became my sanctuary. I hadn't a problem living on my own – quite the opposite, in fact. I quickly discovered I was beginning to enjoy my new-found freedom and my life again. Spending this time in the close season had given me the time to reflect. I was on holiday and for that spell there was no pressure. It was just me and my thoughts. I was enjoying my surroundings and the fact I had no one to answer to. I took pleasure from getting up in the morning, putting on my kit and going for a jog in nearby Bellahouston Park. I enjoyed cooking for myself and at night I felt really relaxed with the feet up, watching TV, enjoying a cup of coffee. Just doing some really simple things in the peace and tranquillity of my own surroundings was making me feel better. This was a complete contrast to my life, which, up to this point, had seemed like a never-ending stock car race! There's much to be said for allowing your thoughts and wishes to come to you rather than actively pursuing what you think it is you want. If you leave your mind alone in peace and quiet, things will come to you and you'll gravitate in the direction you want to go. Life can be so hectic and pressurised that often we never get this chance to find ourselves.

After a few weeks of this unwitting self-imposed solitude, I was beginning to come to some important conclusions about myself and the direction I wanted to go in. I began to realise what I still badly wanted most of all was to be a successful footballer, playing in a successful Rangers team. Yes there were things about the job that were very stressful and could get me down, but I knew I had the will and the strength to overcome the negative forces that were holding me back. I realised the solutions lay totally within me. I realised I needed to get back to working hard to turn my situation round. First things first, I knew relations between John Greig and I had soured considerably. I therefore wanted to demonstrate to him that playing for Rangers was what I really wanted. I decided to call him up and ask if I could come to see him before the squad came back en masse for pre-season. There had even been speculation about me leaving Rangers and that John Greig had decided to get rid of me. When I met him it was very much cap in hand from me. Basically, I told him I was sorry for having had such a bad attitude last season when I was dropped. I told him I really wanted to turn things round again and re-establish myself in the team. I told him I wanted to turn over a new leaf and get my career back on track. I also told him I would be happy to play in any position.

I really missed feeling fit and playing well. John, I think, was initially taken aback by what I had said. I'm sure he thought I had wanted to come in and ask for a transfer. He agreed he too would wipe the slate clean and judge me by what he saw in pre-season training and matches. I was actually a very fit footballer but sometimes mentally I had a tendency to lose focus and determination when things were going against me. I wasn't a Ralph Milne, the quickest thing on two legs, but I had enormous amounts of stamina. Looking back, I sorely regret every single day that I lost the plot and didn't look after myself as well as I should have. I know at times that must have cost me in terms of consistency of performance. To play any kind of top-level professional sport, you must be dedicated all the time, not just some of the time.

Going into the next pre-season, which was 1982/83, I had probably never been as fit since my early days at Dundee FC, under the cone-meister George Blues. I think John immediately could see that I had made the effort to prove I meant what I said. At certain cardiovascular endurance exercises I was right up there with the very fittest of players at Rangers, or any other club for that matter. At the start of the season, John began to play me at left-back. Initially I was not happy, but I did not show it and accepted it without question; however, it seemed with every season of my career at the top I was making my way further and further back on the team sheet. From left-winger to striker, striker to midfield and now midfield back to left-back. I wasn't complaining, though!

The team generally also got off to a great start. We were play-ing a fast, high-tempo, attacking-style football. We looked like we could become serious contenders in a league that also com-prised of a very strong Aberdeen, Dundee United and Celtic. One other crucial event that pre-season was the signing of Swedish internationalist Robert Prytz from Malmö. He was like a bumblebee and buzzed about the midfield, getting on the ball and making things happen. Typically as a Scandinavian, he had great technical ability. Prytzy and I really hit it off in the early days. He was, like me, young, free, single and enjoyed a beer or two at the weekend.

Within a few games, John soon had me back in a really strong four-man midfield, comprising of Bobby Russell, Jim Bett, Prytzy and myself. Like Russell, Bett and myself, Prytzy was very com-fortable on the ball. It did take him time to adjust to the culture shock and rigorous tempo of the Scottish league though, but his English was getting better: 'Reddy, what fucks you do, widda ball up in da air all de time? Ya canna do dat.' That said, there was not a better-equipped midfield four in the Scottish Premier League at that time, as far as I was concerned.

John Greig too deserved much credit for the way we played

at the start of that season. I'm sure at last he thought he had a Rangers team playing consistently in the way he wanted: playing skilful attacking football and scoring plenty of goals. I was really enjoying my football again, though, and was doing things with the ball I would never have had the audacity to do in the previous seasons. My mind was much more relaxed and confident. John, I'm sure, saw that I had made a real effort to change my ways. My attitude had improved enormously. I was still prone to drinking too much on a Saturday night after games, but when you are young and super fit, you think you can do anything and get away with it. Without a doubt, though, binge drinking catches up with you, and there are no exceptions!

Since the start of that season we had gone on a very impressive unbeaten run and were at last looking like a championship-contending team. Our 4-4-2 formation, with a very strong midfield, was working well. Davie Cooper was relishing things again and playing well in a more or less free role. Our weaknesses were potentially still there though. We lacked defensive discipline and a thirty-goals-a-season striker. John 'Solo' MacDonald fitted the bill and was capable, but he struggled with lack of fitness due to various injuries and a bad back. John was about the same age as me and had made his breakthrough early on in his career. In the dressing room he could be a monumental pain in the butt and sometimes I could tolerate him more than others!

We still also lacked a really top-class central defender and goalkeeper. Craig Patterson was signed from Hibs and although he had it all as a player, unfortunately he was another who was dogged by injury. To Craig's credit, amazingly he still managed to keep playing to a decent level, but he was not a Willie Miller or a Dave Narey. Big Craig also got a hard time from a section of the fans, but they didn't know or understand how much pain he was constantly battling just to stay on the field. Legendary goalkeeper Peter McCloy was getting past his reliable best and Scotland internationalist Jim Stewart was as potentially as good a keeper as there was in Scotland, but he too seemed to lack a bit of consistency or confidence, perhaps. Also, how was it possible to replace a player of the calibre of Sandy Jardine, one of the best attacking full-backs Scottish football has ever seen, in my opinion? Dave McKinnon was signed from Partick Thistle for the right-back slot and although he was a trier and would tackle a rabid Pitbull, he was not remotely in the same class as Jardine. I think if you look at great league-winning teams over the years without a doubt the one thing they all have in common is a strong core. Goalkeeper and central defence is where it starts. In McCloy, Jackson and Forsyth, Rangers had that. Unfortunately by the time John Greig took over, they had all become that bit older and past their best.

Our impressive early season form took us past Borussia Dortmund in the first round of the UEFA Cup, beating them 2–0 at home after a good solid 0–0 away result. This underlined the way we were playing and augured well for the rest of the season. In the second round we were drawn against FC Cologne, who were even tougher German opposition. As always, John Greig liked to prepare meticulously for these big European games. You could tell he too savoured these occasions. Sometimes, however, he could get flustered with excitement and said some unwittingly hilarious things. In our hotel during a team meeting, as part of our pre-match build-up, he delivered a gem! John liked to go into detail about the strengths and weaknesses of each player in the opposition. Sometimes in his eagerness he struggled to find a suitable description or analogy. The main danger man for that FC Cologne team was without doubt the world-class right-winger Pierre Littbarski. He was one of the stars of the German World Cup team in 1982. When speaking of Littbarski, John reckoned he wasn't the bravest player in the world but then he seemed to struggle to come up with an appropriate simile and he seemed to have temporary brain freeze. Eventually he blurted out: 'Ehhh, that Littbarski, he's got the heart of . . . ehhh . . . emm . . . A NEWLY BORN PARROT!' How we all managed to keep our faces straight I'll never know but it was a very funny moment.

My mission that night was stop Littbarski and get forward myself. As always on European nights, there was a huge crowd and the atmosphere was electric. How I loved this type of occasion! I was so up for it the hairs were up on the back of my neck in the tunnel. I just couldn't wait to get on the park. There was no anxiety at all, only nervous excitement and anticipation. There was just nothing like Ibrox Park on a night like this. I was feeling so fit and full of running at the time, and my mind was clear, for a change! My confidence was growing along with the teams. John Greig was happy for me to patrol the whole left side of the park, defence, midfield and attack. I knew Littbarski would be a very difficult opponent, as he really was world class. I also knew I had to try and unsettle him early on if possible or he would give me a very tough night. It worked well for me and fortunately I managed to keep him pretty much under control, so much so that I still managed to get forward and create some things down the left-hand side. It was one of my best ever performances in a Rangers strip.

On the night we ran out winners 2–1 with goals from Derek Johnstone in the first half and a late winner from another John Greig signing, Irishman John McClelland. As an indication of how I had turned things around for myself that season, Peter McCloy paid me a rare compliment after the match by telling me he thought I had been 'immense'. The return leg, however, was a different affair altogether and was probably one of the main reasons why our early season form came to an end. We knew our lead from the first leg was slender but we were playing well and were looking very good going forward. This time tactically I was in a more central orthodox midfield role, with Ally Dawson at left-back.

The stadium of Cologne was magnificent and the atmosphere from the 61,000 spectators was just fantastic. The hairs were again up on the back of my neck as we lined up for the national anthems. Again I was feeling great mentally and physically and really looking forward to the game, as I always seemed to do on big European nights. Having started the match really well, Pierre Littbarski then really showed everyone why he was such a star for Germany in the World Cup. He picked up a ball outside our box, played a pass in, got the return and weaved past a couple of defenders before hitting a solid drive past our goalie, Jim Stewart. It was a bad blow to us so early in the game and it seemed to really inspire them. Before long they got another, then our roof just caved in. Before the end of the game they had stuck five goals past us in a devastating display of attacking football. This was the Germans at their very best. It illustrated once again that under the toughest of examinations defensively, as a team we came up well short. Again, though, I was happy with the way I competed and played against a top-class German team. I realised I had nothing to fear from anyone on a football field when my mind and fitness were in harmony. However, from the team's point of view, this was a psychological hammer blow we did not need and it knocked the stuffing out of our fragile recovery that season. We came back from Germany deflated and with confidence shattered. A season that had started so well, with so much promise, was teetering on the brink once again.

Sure enough, within another few league matches again the big black cloud had descended over the club. It was around this time I can first recall the whispering campaign beginning to allure that the smart money was already on the impending departure of John Greig.

I have my own view about what contributed most to the dramatic slump that ensued after the Cologne hammering. For a club playing well and with a bit of belief, one bad result should never determine the rest of the seasons. Right at this junction was the very time we needed John to keep us on track but critically I think he chose the wrong method to put things right. It still rankles me that if John had just taken the Cologne result as a one-off and stuck to the plot, we could well have won the league that year. But after a punishing early-season schedule, instead of easing off and giving our tired and weary legs a bit of a break on the training ground, he increased our workload. We just seemed to do nothing every day but run our legs off for hours and hours on a muddy, heavy training pitch that was the Albion. Come the Saturday, players were complaining about feeling tired and lethargic. In hindsight maybe John, under pressure, panicked much too early in the season. In terms of fitness from a personal point of view, mine had rarely, if ever, been better. From where I was I could only go backwards fitness-wise. You reap what you sow, though, and it was no surprise that out of the next ten league games we won only twice. Consequently, we fell rapidly off the pace in the league, and although we weren't out of it, most of the real damage to our league campaign had been done.

With confidence levels and moral now fragile, by early December we were back at Hampden to defend our title and face Celtic in the final of the League Cup. This was another truly massive game for us psychologically, and we didn't go into this game in the best frame of mind. Celtic, on the other hand, were much more up for it than we were. They were strong at this time with some very good individual players, and none better on his day than Davie Provan.

Normally tactically astute, I think John got our tactics wrong on this occasion. He wanted me out of midfield and back into the left-back area and to stop Davie Provan. Possibly he was thinking that as I had handled Littbarski well at Ibrox I could do the same with Provan. In principle, I had no problem with this at all. Davie Provan was great player but he was no better than Littbarski. What was really concerning me, though, was the way in which he wanted me to stop Provan. John was worried not only about Provan running with the ball at our defence, he was also very concerned about stopping the supply to the feet of their exciting new young wizard Charlie Nicholas. Charlie had not long broken through into the first team and was in sensational form at the time for Celtic. John instructed me not to get too close to Provan because if I did then the channel ball in behind me would be much easier for Celtic to find the feet of Nicholas, and he could turn defenders on a sixpence. Call me old fashioned if you like, but I always thought one job on a football park was hard enough to deal with. Especially when you are playing against the calibre of player of Nicholas and Provan! So when I was asked not only to stop Provan on the ball but also to deter the channel ball in behind to the feet of Nicholas, I think I could possibly be excused for politely asking, 'What on earth is this all about?'

Hampden Park was absolutely buzzing that day; the atmosphere, as always, for a major final involving the Old Firm was incredible. It was a dark Saturday afternoon, the floodlights were on, the stadium was packed; you could smell the big occasion. It was also, if I recall, a bit drizzly, which made the suspect surface at Hampden perfect. The conditions really suited both teams in an attacking sense, as both had outstanding, individual, skilful players. It was my first major Old Firm final and again I was feeling very fit and confident in my own capability, even though my brain was still a little confused tactically going into the match.

It wasn't too long after the start, however, that it was obvious I didn't know if it was New York or New Year. Davie Provan had a field day down the right-hand side as I lay off him enough to allow him to get the ball, turn and run at me. Davie was one of the best dribblers of a ball in the game, and as a defender trying to stop him, the only chance you had was to cut him off at the source. That meant closing him down before he got on the ball. After he got on the ball it was too late. You were already dead!

The channel ball into Charlie Nicholas should never have been a concern to me as long as I was able to do my job stopping Provan. Standing off him was like giving a bank robber a set of keys to the safe! When you play against a good team with good individuals, you each have to stand up and defend your own bit of turf. That is when good teamwork and tactics play a crucial role. Get that side of it wrong and you are asking for problems. Our central defenders of John McClelland and Craig Patterson were well capable of handling Celtic's front players of Nicholas and McGarvey. Even though they were both top-class players and a handful for anyone, we also had individual players that could hurt any opposition – so why spend too much time worrying what they might do to us? In my view, John got himself too concerned about Celtic's strengths when he should've focused more on what we were capable of doing to them in an attacking sense. To me that was the main reason we lost the match 2–1. My performance at left-back was slaughtered by the press, but to be honest, I couldn't really have expected anything else. In my defence, though, I felt like a boxer going into the ring to fight Mike Tyson with both hands tied behind my back – never mind one! Celtic pounded us and the goals came from – you've guessed it – Charlie Nicholas and the killer goal from Celtic midfield dynamo Murdo MacLeod. We did get one back, through a delicately struck Jim Bett direct free kick. Overall we had been well beaten when, with a more positive approach, we were just as capable a team as they were.

I was not just disappointed but also very frustrated at what had been expected of me tactically in the match. Despite all of this, I was still happy with my own form. Tactically I had been ripped to shreds by Davie that day, but when I did get on the ball, I more than held my own. My physical and mental attitude was strong and I had no doubt I was capable of continuing to play well. I began to feel as though I had established myself that season as one of the more consistent performers in the team.

Off the pitch things were going much better too. Janine and I had finally got back together, got engaged and got married, all within a year! Most thought it was a shotgun job, as we certainly didn't hang about. Surprisingly for many, no kids came along within the first few years! There was also a bit of controversy in the papers because a Rangers player was marrying a Catholic. However it blew over and was treated as very insignificant.

With the team now out of Europe, losing to Celtic in that League Cup final and losing ground in the league, Ibrox was again not exactly a bed of roses. By Christmas time 1982 it was pretty obvious all we really had left to play for again was the Scottish Cup, and once again we got there to meet Aberdeen in the final. Remarkably, I once again had to sit it out because of an accrued suspension. For the record, we were thrashed 4–1.

Sadly, what had started as a very promising season finished again trophy-less and with more major disappointment.

Our finishing position in the league that year was just above mid-table mediocrity. Unacceptable! It was becoming clear the fans would not tolerate this continued lack of success. John Greig summed up his feelings after one particular Old Firm match late on in the season when they defeated us at Ibrox 1–0, thanks to a Charlie Nicholas wonder goal. In the dressing room after the game, emotions were running high and the heads were very down. No one spoke. No one knew what to say. What could we say? There was just silence, apart from a few boots being clattered off the floor. Otherwise you could hear a pin drop. Finally, John broke the silence and bawled: 'GO AND GET YOUR BATHS, THE LOT OF YOU, AND I HOPE YOU ALL FUCKING DROWN IN IT!' I think that really said all about the way he was feeling.

The fact was in Scottish Football at that time, there were four or five strong teams in Scotland all capable of winning the league and competing in Europe, all with the nucleus or core of home-based Scottish players. It was a much harder a task for John Greig to produce a title-winning Rangers team than for probably any other Rangers manager in the history of the club, with the possible exception of the Jock Stein in the Lisbon Lions era. As an example, when Graeme Souness came to the club he had such a tremendous advantage over everyone else. His budget stretched to going out to buy virtu-ally any top player in the UK. He was able to go and sign top English internationalists such as Chris Woods and Terry Butcher. Walter Smith did an undisputedly fabulous job since coming back to Rangers but, in all honesty, where was the challenge coming from? If his teams were beating Celtic they were winning the league, end of! The John Greig era is much maligned due to the fact we didn't win the league, but the teams I played in were on a level playing field with some other very good teams in Scotland.

Dundee United under Jim McLean were a top side who feared no one in Europe. They had got to the semi-final of the European Cup. Aberdeen under Alex Ferguson had beaten Real Madrid in the final of the European Cup Winners' Cup. Celtic were a classy team of top individual players, guys like Tommy Burns, Davie Provan, Charlie Nicholas, Paul McStay and, of course, the titanic Roy Aitken. Even Hearts were strong and could compete with the best. So you have to put things into perspective: just because we weren't winning leagues it didn't mean we were a crap team. It did mean there were others consistently better than us, however. John, unlike Graeme and Walter, was competing on different and much harder terms.

It wasn't just a case of John getting the chequebook out, because in doing so he had no real advantage. Yes, he could spend more than Dundee United or Aberdeen for a player, but he was still struggling to beat any of these teams when it came to the overall package including the players' personal terms. The bottom line was the club had a policy of not giving players decent money. John was also now competing with all these clubs for the young talent that was coming through on what seemed like an endless conveyor belt at the time. It seems barely conceivable but I was making more money when I moved to Dundee United than I was when I played for Rangers.

Not too long ago I took a trip down memory lane where I actually sat down and wrote a list, without even hardly giving it any thought, of talented Scottish players from my era, the only criteria being that they be good enough to be playing for Scotland today. I also tried not to include other older definites like Sandy Jardine, Willie Johnston and Derek Johnstone. Here goes. Aberdeen: Strachan, Miller, McLeish, Weir, McGhee, Black, Simpson, Cooper, McMaster, Hewitt. Dundee United: Narey, Hegarty, Sturrock, Bannon, Milne, Dodds, Malpas, Thomson. Celtic: Nicholas, McGarvey, Burns, McStay, Provan, MacLeod, Aitken. Rangers: Cooper, Bett, Russell, MacDonald, Dawson, Redford (not counting those like Jardine, Forsyth, etc., who were earlier Scotland regulars but were at the tail end of their careers during my time.). Then you had the likes of Mo Johnston and Frank McAvennie, who started with lesser clubs, and of course all the top Scottish stars that were playing for the biggest and most successful clubs in England: Dalglish, Hansen, Wark, Brazil, Nicoll, Gillespie. As I said, that was just in my era of the late Seventies early Eighties. There would be even more no doubt, if I gave it some extra effort. But these names just rolled off my tongue without even a moment of thought. Any one of these players mentioned above would've been capped regularly today.

The point I'm making is that we had tons of players of that calibre in my era. I have listed forty players! That is incredible when you think about it. I didn't include Ally McCoist either, simply for the reason I was trying to stick to players slightly more of my Rangers era. That above list is equivalent to more than three teams! I was never selected for the full national team whilst playing for Rangers, despite there being a couple of spells when I think I was playing well enough to at least be included in some squads.

There were some real personalities in the Scottish game at that time and I can remember playing in the national Under-21 squad with talented guys like Peter Weir and Frank McAvennie, who were playing for St Mirren. In fact, as another indication of the talent our game had at the time, I played in the only Scottish national team ever to beat an Italian national team on their own soil. As I was only nineteen when I joined Rangers, I was still eligible for the Under-21s for a couple of seasons. We had drawn Italy in the quarter-finals of the European Championship and played them in Catanzaro in the first leg. Frank was starring for St Mirren and proved his class at international level in that match by scoring the winner. Frank was as daft as a brush! But what an engine he had and he was a cocky git!

I remember hearing a story being told about Frank when he was a young player at St Mirren. Apparently one day he'd opened his pay packet in the dressing room and had a look of consternation on his face. When some of the other players noticed he seemed to be a bit concerned, they asked him what was wrong. Frank apparently was not happy at all: 'I cannot FUCKIN' believe this FUCKIN' National Insurance crap, I already paid that last month.' Don't know if it happened, but it's a great story!

Actually, in that Italian team we defeated were players like Giuseppe Bergomi, who became a stalwart for Inter Milan and Italy in World cups. I remember taking a forearmed smash from him that even my 'teammate' Tam Forsyth would've been proud of, in the first half. Also playing for Italy that day was none other than Franco Baresi of AC Milan, who became captain of Italy and became one of the best defenders the game has ever seen.

Playing for Scotland at any level was always a huge honour for me, but there were always some things about being in Scotland squads that were so amateurish and laughable. Scotland Under-21 coach at the time, Andy Roxburgh, was an impeccable organiser when it came to everything to do with team and match preparation. What Andy had no control over, however, was budget constraints!

The match against Italy in which we got ourselves into the record books was played in Catanzaro in front of a huge partisan Italian crowd. The atmosphere was absolutely fantastic and again I felt really up for it. I think there were around 35,000 crammed into a tightly-knit stadium. When I think about the quality of some our players that day – Ray Stewart, Stevie Nicoll, Frank McAvennie, Charlie Nicholas, Jim Bett – the list goes on and on! It was a very tough-fought and close game but McAvennie's goal was enough to give us a lead going into the second leg back home at Pittodrie home of Aberdeen FC.

After the match it was straight onto the bus and off the airport for the flight home. As it was in the middle of winter, the weather was bitter cold. When we got to the airport we trooped off our coach and into the departure lounge as soon as possible. Here we were the Scottish national Under-21 football team huddled together, dressed in a bunch of shell tracksuits that looked so threadbare you could've shot peas through them from a hollow wet Woodbine! Meanwhile, the Italian bus pulled up only minutes behind us, and as we all sat in a huddle like a bunch of scavenging vagrants, Baresi and Co. swept through the departure lounge in full-length Armani cashmere winter coats. They looked like a bunch of movie stars on the way to an awards ceremony. We looked like a bunch of beggars playing 'peevers' on a street corner! It was embarrassing but I suppose, in view of our result, it did go to show that appearances can be deceptive.

The 1982/83 season may have ended on a low, but on the positive side, I had a wedding to look forward to. Janine and I were married in Pollockshields Church on 14 June 1983. The wedding was very much a case of East meets West, Janine's family being from Ayrshire and my family coming from Perthshire! Not long after we were married, Janine also played a pivotal role in

My parents on a very happy occasion

Strawberry fields forever! Dad's berry farm at Middlebank, Rait, Perthshire

Douglas, my brother

Check out those early Rangers strips! Dad, my big sister Jill, cousin Gavin, Douglas and me

Out of acorns . . . The first Errol Rovers team, including me, Gavin and Raymond Stewart

After scoring my own and Dundee's fourth goal v St Mirren in August 1979

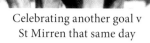

Celebrating another goal v St Mirren that same day

Celebrating that League Cup final win v Dundee United in 1981, in which I scored the winner

If the cup fits, wear it!

When tackling was allowed. I was the most fouled player in Scotland 1980/81

Smokin'! In the league 1983/84 v Hibs at Ibrox

Mud bath v Falkirk in the Scottish Cup

Celebrating with Iain
Ferguson v St Mirren
1984/85

A peek over my right
shoulder reveals a very
famous face: one of my
all-time heroes, Johan
Cruyff. Rangers v
Feynoord at Ibrox in 1984

Boiling-hot action:
another Old Firm
encounter at Ibrox in
1983/84

That memorable night in Germany in 1987 v Borussia Mönchengladbach. I came very close to scoring

Scottish Cup final 1987, Dundee United v St Mirren, trying to put in a cross

That magic night v Barcelona at Tannadice in 1987

Head down, eye on the ball for Dundee United in 1987

Early Eighties. Scotland v Italy, Under-21 quarter-finals of the European Championship. I am being closed down by *the* Franco Baresi, who was later voted AC Milan Player of the Century in 2004

Under-21 squad, taken before the game at Hampden v England, in the semi-finals of European Championships in 1982

With the full Scotland squad, pre-European Championship qualifier v Belgium in 1987

Tractor Boy! Playing for Ipswich Town, season 1988/89

Taking a full six-pack! St Johnstone v Falkirk in the early Nineties

Adventures in Cairo, mixing business with pleasure in 2009

The great Sergei Baltacha: my
Ukrainian friend and partner
in crime. Ha ha!

My Natalie with Sergei Baltacha junior and his now very
famous sister, Elena

An angelic-looking Ian Redford junior.
Don't be fooled!

My gorgeous wife Janine and our two
beautiful children, Ian and Natalie, taken at
Natalie's graduation in 2012

helping me manage the business. She ran the reception, doing the bookings and cashing up. This was a huge weight off my shoulders, till we found the long-term solution I had been looking for with the salon.

There was a general feeling 1982/83 would be make or break for John Greig and there was also a feeling that some players would be moving on out of Ibrox. John, during his reign, apart from me, had also bought: Gregor Stevens, Colin McAdam, Jim Bett, Craig Patterson, Robert Prytz, John McClelland and Dave McKinnon, but his last big signing eventually proved to be one of the best in the history of the club, a certain Ally McCoist from Sunderland.

My first encounter with McCoist came in a reserve match at Dens Park when I was still a teenager with Dundee. I had just been attempting to come back from injury. McCoist was a young sixteen-year-old playing for St Johnstone. He bundled me off the ball at one point and when I glared at him he just laughed at me! He was cheeky and cocksure of himself, but there was just something about him that I knew was different.

Ally also played for St Johnstone in that famous game at Muirton when they came so close to knocking us out of the Cup, save for my late equaliser. Soon after that match he signed for Sunderland for a fee of around £300,000. It was a huge fee for someone so young and inexperienced. Ally didn't really hit it off down South, as was not uncommon for some young Scottish players. John Greig brought him to Ibrox to solve our continuing goal-scoring problem. We already had big 'wheechar', the wholehearted Colin McAdam, but he was more of an old-fashioned 'rumble 'em up' type of player, and not a natural goal scorer. John, in an emergency, had also brought back Gordon Smith from Brighton in the hope he could rekindle the flame that had once burned brightly at Ibrox.

Derek Johnstone had left to join Chelsea and, as previously mentioned, John MacDonald's injury problems just seemed to get worse. Despite an impressive enough goals ratio as a front player, John Greig had other ideas for me. In truth, I knew I was not the answer, as I never saw myself as a natural goal-poaching striker. Young Aussie Dave Mitchell was given some chances late on in John's era. Dave had come on trial and had impressed enough to get a contract.

At the start of the new season 1983/84 I found myself getting more and more frustrated. With another great pre-season under my belt, I just never really seemed to be getting played in any one position. I felt as if I was being continually moved around to accommodate others in the team. I wasn't happy about this and the way things were panning out for me during our pre-season matches. I remember things came to a head with John after a pre-season match against Antwerp, in Belgium. I had played outstandingly well and, in fact, I heard that one or two of the directors of Antwerp had made an enquiry about me after the game. John was not giving me much encouragement and seemed to prefer the likes of Robert Prytz or anyone in my best position. Thoroughly cheesed off again with the whole picture, I had gone out of the hotel at night for a drink. There was some kind of festival on and the whole place was alive and it seemed like a good idea at the time. I didn't over indulge at all and though I was late back in my hotel room, I broke the curfew by no more than ten minutes. John was waiting for me and was not amused, but he was a man under pressure and had much more to worry about than just me. We ended up having a real bawling match at each at other and I said a few things that I shouldn't have, and so did he. It was not a nice situation at all and I felt bad about it afterwards. John thankfully wasn't the type of person to hold a grudge but I did feel from this moment on it was never really the same for me with him as manager.

With McCoist being the main new signing for the 1983/84 season, as had also been the case with me when I came to the club, much was immediately expected of him. The fans were now becoming very impatient with the team and that was making things worse. I believe that had Ally hit it off at Sunderland we would never have seen him playing back in Scotland. He would have ended up playing his best days out at the top levels of English football. Where the similarities ended between Ally and me was that he went on to become one of the truly great Rangers players, whilst I eventually moved on, never really fulfilling my potential at the club. It still quite hurts me to say that, because I would dearly have loved to have done that.

The McCoist transfer, I think, went some way to explaining what John Greig's real problem was as manager of Rangers. The big successful players wanted to play in England and it was only really young players of unfulfilled potential or those on the rebound that John seemed to be able to attract to the club. This was not John's fault; this was ultimately down to the club's policy regarding pay structure.

Season 1983/84 began as 1982/83 had ended, with the team struggling and most players trying to find some form. The rumour mills were beginning to spread the word that John would be leaving before Christmas, as there was no noticeable improvement from the previous season.

The fans now really had begun to turn against John. It was almost at the point of no return. Just about the worst moment in my entire career was after we'd lost yet another league game at home. We were all sitting in the dressing room, heads down in silence. Outside in the street from within the dressing room the chant could be heard over and over: 'GREIG MUST GO, GREIG

MUST GO!' John was hurting really bad, that was obvious. Actually, latterly you could see how stressed he was becoming, because his jaw would sometimes be trembling when he was talking. It was a shame that things went this way for such a great loyal servant to the club. 'Just listen to that outside. See what we've all brought upon us,' he said, or words to that effect.

Much worse was to follow that day because as we began to leave the stadium after the game, we were being abused by those fans who stayed to protest their dissatisfaction. It was horrible. We had to have a police escort to our cars to save us from some of our own fans. Their anger was very understandable but some of the things that were shouted to us that day by some individuals were an utter disgrace. If had not been for the police there would've been some violence, I have no doubt about it. Poor Ally McCoist. He'd not long joined the club. He must've wondered what on earth he'd let himself in for.

Very soon after this, and without giving much warning, John finally succumbed to the constant pressures. One day after training he called everyone into the dressing room. He very quietly and with great dignity informed us all that he had just resigned as manager. He went round the dressing room and made a point of shaking everyone's hand and wishing everyone all the best. Although it had been expected, when it came it was still a shock. I honestly had mixed emotions because I genuinely felt very sorry for John and knew how stressed and upset he'd become. On the other hand, I had really begun to feel that my Rangers career was over under him.

As always in football, some players are glad when a manager leaves because it can often trigger a change of direction for those who've been either on the fringe of the team or out of things altogether. In the interim, the experienced Tommy McLean, John's assistant, took over. He took me aside one day and told me that he thought I really had something to offer the club. He told me to knuckle down again and that I would get my chance. He was true to his word and played me in my best position in midfield. Not long after John had departed, after a very good performance against Celtic at Ibrox in the league, Tommy told me to keep it up and that my performance had demonstrated I had a good future at Rangers.

Just before John left he had me on the bench against the Portuguese giants FC Porto in the first leg of the European Cup Winners' Cup. The team won 2–1. But by the time we got to Porto for the second leg, John was gone and Tommy was in charge. I liked wee Tam, but as a player he could be a bit lippy on the park, especially to the younger players. Tommy latterly, though, became more mature when he stopped playing and was on the coaching staff. Much like his brother Jim, he was very astute tactically. I knew he had faith in me, as he brought me back for the return leg in Porto. Despite the fact we played well and worked incredibly hard, we lost 1–0 and went out due to the away goals rule.

Incidentally, the noise when Porto scored that night was like nothing I had ever heard before, outside of an Old Firm match. I thought the roof of the stadium was going to come off, as seventy thousand Porto fans went totally berserk. There were strong rumours that the Porto players were on a bit more than just baked beans for their pre-match meal. No one outside the Porto camp would've ever known for sure. The difference in technical ability throughout the team compared to Rangers was there for all to see.

I have no doubt at all John Greig was a forward thinker. I believe he wanted to change Rangers from being known as a big, physical, strong running team, to a skilful, technically efficient team that could play and compete on level terms in Europe. I also believe despite all the difficult factors of his era. He came much closer to achieving this, than many fans realise. However with the John Greig era now over, I don't think anyone at Ibrox could've been prepared for what happened next ... the return of Big Jock Wallace.

6

THE RETURN OF JOCK WALLACE

They say it's never a good thing to retrace your footsteps or to try and rekindle the past. So in November 1983, when Jock Wallace returned to his beloved Glasgow Rangers FC to try and resurrect the glory days he first created as assistant to Willie Waddell, there were those who doubted he was the man to reverse the club's fortunes and bring that much elusive league title back to the club. The Rangers supporters craved the Wallace glory days of a treble-winning Rangers team. Ibrox, without doubt, was his spiritual home and big Jock was first and foremost a Rangers fan. Ironically, he'd also been the mastermind behind the most humiliating defeat in the club's history. As player-manager of Berwick Rangers, they unceremoniously dumped the club out of the Scottish Cup in 1967.

The Wallace/Waddell partnership brought immediate success to the club because in 1972 Rangers won the European Cup Winners' Cup, after which Jock was installed as manager, with Waddell moving upstairs to the boardroom. But in 1978, Jock, having delivered two league titles in 1975/76 and 1977/78, surprisingly resigned as manager. It had been a real shock to the fans because no one seemed to know why. Jock was never one for spilling the beans and apparently never spoke of his reasons. There were some who reckoned Jock had asked for more money; and who could blame him for that? His loyalty to Rangers was not in question but there came a point when you would need to question how loyal the club were being, in return, to their most successful and loyal servants. It surely has to cut both ways? After a managerial spell down south at Leicester City, he returned north to take charge at Motherwell in 1982 before finally returning to his beloved Rangers the following year, in 1983.

My first encounter with our new manager came in a hotel room at Aberdeen. We'd travelled up on the Friday night in preparation for a league game at Pittodrie the following day. This was Jock's first match back in charge. I was rooming with Billy MacKay, who'd known Jock well, as he'd given Billy his Rangers first-team debut as a raw sixteen-year-old. Billy told me what to expect and it was noticeable; even the older, more experienced guys who'd previously worked under him during his first spell at the club were all very much on their toes.

After dinner we'd all gone to our rooms early. Jock was going round chapping on all the doors with interim assistant Tommy McLean. Tam obviously knew Jock very well from his days of playing under him in the famous treble-winning team. There was a knock at the door. As I opened it, there stood the big man, poker-faced, eyes peering over his bifocals. He didn't initially say anything. It was wee Tam who broke the ice! As they came in, Jock simply brushed past me and initially spoke only to Billy. He just asked him something like how he'd been.

He then turned to face me and I was immediately aware of those laser eyes focusing in on their target! 'I hear you're a bit of a troublemaker in the dressing room, son.'

I was very much taken aback by both this and his intimidating glare. 'I'm not sure what you mean,' I said, throat tightening.

'I mean, I hear you like to talk back and voice your opinion, son,' he growled.

I was now thinking, 'This is just great. Someone has been winding up the new boss, telling him I'm a rebel without a cause. Just brilliant!' But I managed to reply, 'I am, err, not sure what you mean, boss.'

'Okay, enough chat,' he quickly growled. 'I just want you to know that you'll do things my way and I don't tolerate trouble-makers, understood?'

'Okay, boss,' I choked.

Jock had made his point and was not interested in anything further I had to say. He then turned and walked out of the room. Wee Tam just smiled as he passed me on the way out behind Jock. I had just experienced at first hand an example of Big Jock's sledgehammer management and was thinking to myself, 'That's it, my Rangers career is over.' That could not have been further from the truth. I didn't need Pickfords on speed dial . . . yet! The next day I was in the starting eleven of his first team selection since his return. We lost at Pittodrie 3–0. We were well and truly humped, but at least we'd shown a bit of spirit and bottle.

Very soon it became apparent there were huge differences between the managerial styles of John Greig and Big Jock. John had wanted his teams to play a more entertaining, skilful football more suited to the football purist. Big Jock, however, wanted power football. He wanted his teams to get the ball forward as soon as possible, by whatever means, and play in the opposition's half. In terms of footballing ideals, it was the Rolls-Royce versus the Steam Roller. The single-shot technical accuracy of the rifle versus the scatter-spread approach of the sawn-off shotgun! Sometimes it wasn't pretty but certainly it was effective.

I initially responded very well to Jock's type of management. He loved a trier and I was all that. Jock was more of a motivator than John. He was more about getting players charged up and willing to do battle. When he first arrived, the training sessions were like boot camp. He even had some of the older players like club giant Peter McCloy jumping to attention like he was a little school kid. He was such an intimidating man with a huge physical presence. He didn't speak; he growled. Jock was such a great motivator and I responded to him without being able to understand half of what he bellowed!

As a natural matter of course, a football club gets a lift when a new manager is appointed, for no other reason; it just gives everyone a break because the fans automatically wipe the slate clean and get behind the new regime. Even if that can sometimes be temporary, it's still a welcome relief for the squad. As I said, the atmosphere during the last few weeks of John Greig's tenure had been horrible for everyone at the club. It's a bit like when it's been raining and miserable for a long time and suddenly the sun comes out it gives everyone a bit of hope and a bit of the feel-good factor. The fans needed something new to cling to but it got to the stage where the players did too. When a downward spiral at any football club gets to the point where the large majority of fans want change, then the inevitable is never very far away. There were few better candidates at that time to give the whole of Ibrox a lift than Jock Wallace, and to be fair, he had the whole place buzzing to start with. Our form and results immediately began to pick up and there was once again real hope and optimism around the place.

Back at Ibrox the following week for his second game in charge we had Dundee United. This was Jock's first home game since his returning to Ibrox. I remember the atmosphere vividly. It was electric inside the stadium. Dundee United were a top-class team but we outplayed them with our own brand of high-tempo, fast-action football. The game, however, finished 0–0. More importantly, for us it ended a dreadful sequence of four league defeats in a row, including a 2–1 defeat by Celtic at Ibrox. After that Celtic match Wee Tam came to me and told me I had played really well and that I had a good future at the club. I think he knew then change was coming. As previously mentioned, it was really Wee Tam that brought me back into the team almost as soon as John resigned.

From day one Big Jock's training sessions were timed to military precision. Even to this day I can tell you what we did on a Tuesday, which normally was the hardest day of the week. Often we'd get a Monday off if the performance was good on the Saturday. First thing, we'd all troop through to the away dressing room where we would do rigorous sets of various exercises – circuit training if you like – to strengthen legs, arms and core. Typically it was lots of press-ups, various leg pushes and abdominal stuff. Jock would be in the middle of the room, barking out instructions and getting into anyone that remotely threatened to slack off. There was a real edge to it. Everyone was on their toes; it was up-tempo stuff and this was just the warm-up. We'd then take the short brisk walk over to the Albion. As said, there were two pitches, one grass and the other was ash. We would begin with the whole group jogging round the park together. Jock loved to stop the group then select someone to come out and give a demonstration of an exercise. There was one in particular that he knew I struggled to do. It involved legs and arms moving at the same time but in different directions. For some reason, I always seemed to clam up and not be able to do it, much to the amusement of the rest of the squad and Big Jock. I just felt like a total chump!

We'd then go into ball practice. We did a lot of full-sided games at the start, as Jock wanted to really get to grips with all his players and see them playing in their proper positions. It was all quick-fire stuff. Jock wanted everything done at pace, his sessions were awesome in that first spell of his return. Finally we'd head back to the stadium for some track work. Typically we would do something like half a dozen 150-yard sprints. You'd start behind the goal and run on the cinder track, along the back behind the goals then round the corner and up to the halfway line. Then walk across the pitch and back round to the start with so many seconds' rest period before you went again. Always by that last run you could feel the legs going into meltdown and vomit was just around the next bend!

In all, we'd maybe trained for two and a half to three hours at the most. But once you had finished you were good for nothing for the rest of the day. The up-tempo training was initially taken onto the park because our performances were noticeably better. Personally, I was playing very well and can remember a couple of players saying to me they thought I should be in contention for the national squad. I'm not so sure but for fellow pros to be even talking about me in those terms was an indication of how good my form was at that time.

There was one very scary moment for me, though, when I thought more than just my Ibrox career was over. As usual the first-team squad were running round the training pitch doing the Big Jock warm-up routine, with him barking out the instructions. He then started speaking to me but I could neither hear nor make out what he was saying. I know that some who had perfect hearing struggled to understand his gruff voice at times. Not knowing he was treading on eggshells with regard to my deafness, he started calling me a useless deaf so and so in front of all the rest of the players.

To me this was abuse, I suppose much in the same way a black footballer would feel when he is racially abused. Now I could handle most things, but when it came to my hearing I was very sensitive about it. Only because, to me, it was a genuine disability or impairment. It was a problem that I had to deal with

192

on a daily basis. I did not like it being exposed, especially in front of all my teammates. Jock obviously had no idea that my hearing was a serious problem, as I had never made it out be. In fact, I would do anything other than admit I was deaf. But Jock didn't know or understand and was just taking the mickey and went on. 'HOLD IT, HOLD IT. REDDY, YOU STUPID DEAF BASTARD. GET OUT HERE AND SHOW US ALL HOW IT'S DONE.'

I was now extremely embarrassed and annoyed at him so I snapped back, 'WHY DON'T YOU JUST FUCK OFF!'

At this point the whole place came to a standstill and no one said a word as the ex-Korean jungle fighter Jock Wallace walked over to me. I thought, 'This is it. I am dead.' To his credit, he immediately realised he'd touched a nerve and let it go by saying, 'Come and see me after training.'

Later when we spoke he didn't outright apologise but went on to say that he thought I was doing a fantastic job for him and that, if I could keep it up, I'd be playing for Scotland. This was a measure of the man. Jock realised I had a genuine problem with my hearing and accepted that.

I came away from training that day thinking even more of him. And I thought a lot of him before that. Jock was a very tough man who had been through hell in the jungle as a soldier. He'd obviously fought and seen colleagues die in the war. Much was made of his fearsome reputation but I liked him a lot. It was very simple: if you ran your guts out, you had nothing ever to fear from him as your boss, and I can honestly say I ran my guts out for him.

Having represented my country at all international levels, youth, Under-21s and being one of the youngest ever players to play for the Scottish league, my full international debut still eluded me. My form initially under Jock was so good there was even talk among the media of me being included in a full squad but for some reason once again it didn't come. To be fair, it was an era of very stiff competition and it was not easy to get a full cap for Scotland during this period.

The following week it was back home to Perthshire for me with an away league match against newly promoted St Johnstone. This was my first game back at Muirton since I scored that very late equaliser to deny Saints their finest ever hour. They had been making rapid progress since our Cup encounter, and with the money they got from the sale of Ally McCoist, they very prudently had climbed up the leagues and were back in top-flight football once again.

It was a dirty Saturday afternoon in November. Once again I had been looking forward to going back to Perth. My confidence was up and my form was good. I was really enjoying working under Jock. The atmosphere around the dressing room also seemed less odious – if even superficially, there seemed to be more togetherness about the place. My instincts and intuition were again telling me to expect good things. I'm not sure what the odds were on me to score that day, but in my mind I was a certainty! My goal came in the second half and was a very rare, right-footed power drive into the Saints' net for the only goal of the match. St Johnstone again had given us a real scare, but this was our first league win under Jock and our first league win in seven games. At last we had begun to stop the rot, because we did not lose another match in the league that season until we were beaten 3–0 away against Celtic. That game had ended a run of sixteen matches undefeated and included ten wins and five draws.

The Scottish League Cup seemed to be my favourite tournament and in the quarter-finals second leg Dundee United came to Ibrox knowing they had to win as they could only draw with us 1–1 at Tannadice in the first leg. In front of a packed-out Ibrox stadium we won 2–0 in a match which was to be the third and final instalment of the Redford/McAlpine trilogy. United legend Hamish had thwarted me in the Scottish Cup final by saving my penalty. But I had taken revenge on him in the same year by chipping him to steal the winner in the late show of the 1981/82 League Cup final. So it was all square! We led 1–0 from the first half through a super effort from Sandy Clark, one of John Greig's later signings from West Ham. But it was back to Redford versus McAlpine in the second half. I was revelling in the atmosphere that night and was in the form of my Ibrox career. Seldom did I play better over ninety minutes for Rangers than I did that evening.

The icing on the cake came around midway through the second half when the ball was played forward to Big Sandy around the halfway line. For some reason the United defenders all seemed to get caught very square and very drawn towards the ball. Meanwhile, I had read the situation and broke quickly from deep into the huge space ahead of me. Sandy, obviously noticing I was already on my bike, knocked a pass through the advancing United defenders who'd all been caught moving forward at the same time as I broke past them, but moving in the opposite direction towards Hamish. Suddenly I had no one in front of me but the moustachioed United legendary goalie! Hamish showed his hand by coming off his line a bit too early, his goal now left unguarded and completely empty. The ball then took a lovely bounce up off the ground in my favour as I moved onto it. So with the combination of Hamish coming off his line and the kind bounce of the ball, the decision was made for me. I knew if I could just add a decent touch to the ball, momentum would carry it over Hamish's head and into the net. With very little time to contemplate my actions, I put a nice

195

touch on it with my left foot and lobbed the ball over his head and into the empty net – right in front of a total mass of Rangers Bears, who were going mental before the ball had even crossed the line. Hamish had been caught in no man's land, but to me all that mattered was the ball being in the back of the net, and Rangers were in yet another major Cup final, which was later to be remembered as the McCoist final.

What an incredible feeling it was for me at that moment, knowing I had scored before the ball had even crossed the line. It's like everything was in slow motion. As soon as I put my touch on the ball and saw the trajectory of it, I had earned the luxury of watching the ball on its way to the empty net. In reality, maybe no more than a second or two had passed between me lobbing the ball and it actually crossing the line. In these moments, though, just before the mayhem of the ensuing eruption, I could see and feel everything so clearly. I had total clarity of mind. The stadium was wired to the moon that night and when I scored that crucial second goal the whole place just went wild.

Jock Wallace had arrived on 10 November 1983 and, discounting the defeat in his first match at Aberdeen, by end of February 1984 we still remained unbeaten in all competitions. Totalling seventeen games, winning twelve and drawing five. Not exactly statistics of a struggling club! For the first couple of months, Jock, without doubt, lifted the whole place. Clearly there was a tempo and spark in the team that hadn't been there for a long time. However, there was no getting away from it. We still trailed in the league and by the end of that season we finished fourth – in other words, nowhere – with only fifteen wins, which was less than 50 per cent of our entire league fixture, the only positive slant being practically all the bad results had come before Jock had arrived. For one man in particular there were was a massive

silver lining behind a very black cloud. Ally McCoist was enduring torture week in, week out from the fans. Under John Greig
they had given him no time at all to settle in. It wasn't his fault
that the club were struggling when he first came. Ally found
himself in and out of the team and some of the fans seemed to
be on a mission to destroy him. Things really came to a head on
17 March 1984, when we played Dundee at Ibrox in a replay of
the quarter-finals of the Scottish Cup. It was a massive game for
us because although out of contention for the league, we could
still have done the Cup double, as we were already in the final of
the League Cup, which was to be played the following Sunday.

Dundee could smell blood as they sensed how much pressure
we were under. In their ranks they had two players capable of
causing problems for anyone: Cammy Fraser and Iain Ferguson.
Iain in particular was well known to me, as we had been teammates at Dundee. I knew how dangerous he could be if given
half a chance in front of goals. There was a huge crowd at Ibrox,
and with Dundee coming so close to putting us out at Dens,
there was real anticipation that an upset could be on the cards.
We got off to a really good start in the match but Dundee pegged
us back to 2–2. The crowd were getting really impatient and I
remember feeling the enormous pressure of expectation on our
shoulders as Rangers players. Ally was also having a very tough
time in the match, and it got so bad for him that at one point
the whole of the Rangers support began chanting, 'ALLY, ALLY,
GET TAE FUCK.' I don't care who you are, when approximately
30,000 to 40,000 people are chanting their displeasure at you, it
has to hurt.

In the middle of the second half Robert Prytz got himself sent
off but worse was to follow. I stupidly overreacted in the heat of
the moment and needlessly got myself sent off for an altercation
with Dundee's Albert Kidd. I had allowed the whole pressure of

the situation to get the better of me, and as I trudged off towards the dressing room, there already sitting in the bath was Prytzy!

'Don't suppose you could pass me the shampoo?' I said.

'Reddy, wot fucks you do?' He said in his best Swedish-Scottish accent!

Prytzy and I were both sitting in the bath absolutely gutted. Heads down, not saying a word when we heard another goal had been scored and it was not in our favour. We knew the lads out there had gone down and when the remaining nine players trooped into the dressing room, the whole place was like a morgue! Jock came through from the dressing room and gave me a real roasting for my stupidity. As the rest of the team came slowly trudging through, McCoist looked particularly distraught with it all. We all just sat in the huge communal bath together, no one speaking a word. Suddenly Ally just broke down into tears. I think the weeks and months of constant pressure and constant abuse had driven him right to the very limits of his tolerance levels. I'm sure no one but no one would've thought it possible for him to come back from such depths of seemingly utter despair. Football, however, is a game of fate and a roller coaster of fortune.

The following week we had Celtic to play in the League Cup final. It was our last chance of a trophy that season. My goal at Ibrox had ensured us safe passage into the final, but my sending-off against Dundee ensured that I would miss the match against Celtic. My sending-off along with Robert Prytz's however also probably ensured that Ally would play against Celtic. Had Prytzy and I both been available then I honestly don't think Jock would've selected Ally for that final. The crowd were just so much against him it was getting to the stage it was affecting not just Ally but the rest of team. Jock, however, had little choice but to play Ally at Hampden. The rest, as they say, is history! Unbelievably! And in the most incredible circumstances Ally scored all three of our goals in a very famous 3–2 victory. The winner came in extra-time from a penalty he took that was actually initially saved but rebounded back to him. Some things are just meant to be!

I was really pleased for the lads and Ally in particular for pulling himself out of the football equivalent of the abyss. It was incredible to think that things got so bad for him that Big Jock even apparently tried to offload him to Carlisle United. But much to his credit and determination, Ally had refused to go, insisting he wanted to remain and fight for his place in the team. As for me, I was truly despondent that I had missed yet another chance to play in a major Cup final.

The rest of that season, as I recall, petered out in very unspec-tacular fashion. We seemed to draw more games than we won and ended up again a poor fourth place in the table. There was one more very memorable moment, though, from Big Jock the day before we were due to play Celtic in a league game.

Typically on a Friday after training he would assemble the squad in the boot room for his pre-match team talk. Usually he would indicate his line-up then and so you knew whether or not you were going to start the following day. I liked this, as it gave you a good chance to go and mentally prepare for the match the following day. Jock though on this occasion got a little bit more than carried away. As I've said earlier, he was not a great one for tactics; he was much more of a motivator but really, in all honesty, the last thing any Rangers team needs is to be wound up the day before they are due to play Celtic. Anyone who has ever needed to be motivated for this game just does not deserve to be playing in it.

The boot room was small, with little room to manoeuvre, but the big man was standing in the middle of us all as we were cir-cled around him. He began his speech and, to try and illustrate

199

clearly what was going on, you have to try and visualise a mad man! 'Right, lads, it's Celtic tomorrow so it's time to fix bayonets, and when you get the first goal you stick that bayonet into your opponent! When you get the second goal you twist the bayonet inside him and when you get the third goal you stick that bayonet into him again and again and again again!' By which time we were all looking at each other then looking at Jock, but his eyes had glazed over, as if he was back in the middle of the jungle in Korea taking on all comers. It was actually very scary to see him in this mode and I have to say this was the most graphic team talks I ever witnessed in my entire career.

From memory and for the record, the match was on 21 April 1984 at Ibrox and we beat them 1–0. No matter what, it's always good to get the last laugh of the season in an Old Firm encounter. There were no such things as meaningless Old Firm matches!

With the 1984/85 pre-season already looming Jock's second honeymoon was over and the pressure was on right from the start. Before our scheduled pre-season trip to Switzerland, Jock pushed the squad very hard physically. Included was our traditional foray to the sand dunes of Gullane. Much has been made of Jock Wallace's love of sand dunes. The truth is he saw running in sand, particularly uphill, as a very good means of stamina-building. Gullane was actually no more than one day's hard labour and I can't remember hurting any more at Gullane than any other hard day at pre-season. Running till you drop is running till you drop – whether it be on sand, grass, ash or any other surface. The net effect is just the same.

A week or so into pre-season I had aggravated my knee in training. It was tendonitis due to stress on the joint. Over in Switzerland Jock wanted me to take a cortisone injection to play in our first pre-season match. I refused because I was very anti-painkilling injections. I'd heard so many horror stories about older players and the disastrous long-term effects. Jock was none too pleased at my refusal and went in the huff a wee bit. I think we actually lost a bit of ground in our relationship after this. He could be stubborn; he couldn't accept my view that I may have been risking some longer-term damage. It was only pre-season and there were still weeks to go before the real stuff started.

There were spells at Ibrox when some of us used to enjoy an odd game of golf on a day off. I didn't play much golf at that time but really enjoyed it when I got the chance. A regular four-ball was developed between McCoist, Craig Patterson, Bleeper and myself. Usually Ally and I teamed up against Craig and Billy. They were better than us off-scratch and, more often than not, they would take the money. I decided enough was enough and that our turn had come to win. Sure enough, on this day on the seventeenth green Ally and I took the money. As we stood on the eighteenth tee getting ready to play the last hole, I went into my golf bag and pulled out a bottle of champagne and two large cigars. I handed a glass and cigar to Ally then popped the champers! We lit up the cigars and duly celebrated our win, much to the consternation of Craig and Bleeper, who were none too amused at having their noses rubbed in it!

The following week a story appeared in the Rangers News about Ally's and my famous victory celebration on the eighteenth tee. McCoist had relayed the story to them, only happening to mention that it had been he who had the idea to bring along the champagne and cigars! When I collared him about it in the dressing room, as usual all I got from him was his stock trade wide-eyed grin and maniacal laugh of his. This was typical of McCoist! As a young player Ally was a tonic for any dressing room. He was someone you wanted around when things weren't going well because he dug in like no other player I have ever known. It was not really surprising for me to see what he achieved as a player during his Rangers career.

With pre-season preparation over the coming season was going to be vital for Jock, as this was his first full season in charge. No one could really have blamed him for us finishing so poorly in the previous season, as he only came to the club in November. His record for the remainder of that 1983/84 season was actually pretty good but it had to be maintained and now the heat was on. He'd spent approximately half a million bringing in a catalogue of new players. Also added and brought to Ibrox by Jock that season was the incredible 'Tin Man', Ted McMinn, signed from Queen of the South. He'd impressed greatly in a match against us in the previous season and had been attracting a lot of interest.

Hope and optimism are the lifeblood of a football fan. Without it they would not keep coming back for more punishment. Through the early Eighties the Rangers support could be forgiven for not exactly exuding much of either. Typically they came in their masses at the start of our league campaign. Pre-season preparation had gone well for me, and despite the tendonitis in my knee, I was in good shape going into the start of it. Disappointingly, on our opening game in front of a massive crowd we drew 0–0 with St Mirren. Expectation had taken a jolt already and the fans' impatience was already beginning to seep into the fragile confidence levels of the players. A win at Dumbarton the following week with goals from myself and McCoist restored a bit of much needed faith. A week later, in the season's first Old Firm encounter we again drew 0–0, not exactly awe-inspiring stuff.

The following week we were up at Dens Park in a match that we really needed to win to get us back on the rails. It was in this match I reckon I scored the best goal I ever scored in my entire career. The fact I scored it in the stadium where I reckon I expressed more individuality in my career than anywhere else I don't think was a coincidence. Picking up the ball around the halfway line, I went on a run, or 'mazy'. I wasn't thinking about anything, at this point scoring was not on my mind, but it was like I had that feeling of being in slow motion again, where everything suddenly became crystal clear with no conscious thought involved in what I was doing. As the challenges were coming in I was just moving the ball and my body away from them.

In what was probably a matter of no more than a few seconds, I found myself at the edge of their penalty box but had been forced away from the goals by their opposing defenders. Instinctively I pivoted round to get the ball back onto my left foot, facing the target area. It seemed like I now had the whole Dundee defence round me. There was nowhere to go, all roads were blocked. My mind was so clear, there was no panic or thought about being dispossessed. In what seemed like all the time in the world, I just knew what to do next was aware that their goalkeeper was slightly off his line and had left a small but vacant area in his top right-hand corner.

Without any doubts or hesitation I simply chipped the ball, pretty much like a golfer would do with his sixty-degree lob wedge, up and over the Dundee defence and over the out-stretched hands of their goalkeeper. Maybe you can get lucky once, but when you do something time after time it is more than luck, it is a developed skill or technique. A skill practised so much, repeated so many times, until it becomes the your first reactionary thought when under pressure. As the ball glided gently on the correct trajectory path to the target, I can even remember seeing a piece of mud on the ball as it homed in on its target. As soon as I made contact and saw the path of the ball,

I knew it was a goal. For that second or two, it was like sitting watching a lottery draw, already knowing you have the winning numbers! That incredible feeling of almost being outside myself, watching the execution of my actions and the amazing feeling of complete awareness of everything around me. Yet what was I consciously thinking of? Nothing. For sure if I could've harnessed or bottled these occasional feelings or experiences then I would be making a fortune selling them today. Unfortunately I wasn't able to harness this mental aspect often enough to enable me to do this more consistently.

In all, I played approximately 250 games for Rangers. Out of all these games I reckon I was totally at one with myself mentally and physically in no more of them than you could count fingers on one hand. That's not to say I played badly in all the rest of them, because I didn't. It does mean, however, that in the rest of them I just didn't play to anything like full extent of my creative capability. I'm of the idea to get out of the way of yourself and function in 'the now', you need to be able to not allow your scene to become cluttered with historical events and future images. The big driver of the mind is the subconscious, or your big picture. If you have something deep down that is not resolved within yourself, then I believe it manifests itself by your negative conscious thoughts and actions when something majorly traumatic happens to you in your life, no matter what that might be. I am suggesting that a seismic shift occurs in the way the subconscious part of your brain feels things and therefore processes things.

It is reckoned that if you have a desire or ambition from a very early age that lies deep within you, almost from day one your subconscious mind begins to go to work on how to get you there. As an example, it can explain the reason why so many top stars talk about total dedication, practice and never giving up.

If real desire exists within your subconscious mind, it becomes part of your thought process and the driver responsible for your conscious actions, or the part of you putting in that extra bit of effort and determination. Conversely, if you are subconsciously ashamed or guilty about something major, then I believe that unless you seriously begin to accept something and forgive yourself, it can be as though you are on a mission to punish or destroy yourself without consciously realising it. The mind is a totally miraculous and unbelievable piece of biotechnology, more sophisticated than any man-made computer (so far, that is!). I also believe we are still thousands of years away from the mind being developed to even half of its capability. We tend to get little glimpses of what can be possible now and again.

The complexity of all our thought processes are all so uniquely different and individual. The subconscious is fed a constant stream of data from the day you are born, but I believe it is the ultimate decision-maker concerning who you are and what you want to achieve. How many times have you been driving along the road listening to the radio when suddenly a song you maybe haven't heard for a long time comes on? Immediately your brain tags that song with an emotion or a feeling in your memory. That memory can lie archived almost forever but as soon as some-thing connected triggers it, immediately it is thrust into your conscious thought. To me that is nothing short of miraculous!

I believe the subconscious mind is your driving force, your willpower, your determination or conversely, unless you rec-ognise it and take steps, it can become your own weapon of self-mass destruction. When Tiger Woods was a baby his father played golf with him every day in the garage or in the garden and, when he was old enough to walk, on the golf course. His brain was being fed golf from day one. Granted he was also lucky enough to have the physical attributes required of a top athlete and for the true greats a combination of the right mental keys, talent and athleticism is needed for greatness. That is why such high levels of achievement are so rare and so revered when we witness them.

That afternoon at Dens I believed I achieved in my own self my own little bit of greatness in terms of what I could get out of myself. Not for one minute am I trying to compare my own moments with anyone else's, but I am suggesting every single person has the ability to surprise or amaze themselves with what they can get out of themselves.

Not very long after that memorable moment at Dens, it was clear in terms of the league campaign, again we were stuttering and stammering. Too many 0–0 draws were just not convincing enough for our fans. In a welcome break from our league campaign we were also in the UEFA Cup that year. In the first round we disposed of Bohemians of Ireland, but not before we had to endure the gauntlet of a hate-filled mob in Dublin. In the second round we got a very glamorous draw, being paired with the Italian giants Inter Milan. This was an absolutely stunning fixture for the club and I was so looking forward to playing in Milan in the first leg. It was the first time I had ever been to Milan and the atmosphere around the whole city was fabulous. We were staying in a hotel right in the centre of Milan and managed to get out and have a wander round, looking at all the beautiful shops, cafés and restaurants. Although we had such little time to enjoy the surroundings, this to me was always a very enjoyable part of the build-up to a big European night. The last thing I was thinking was we are going to get 'humped'!

Inter Milan are a huge club with world-class stars but I always loved to play against this type of opposition, just to see how well I could do against the very best. I'll never forget arriving at the San Siro stadium about two hours before kick-off and walking out of the tunnel at the side of the pitch. The fans, even this early, were hysterical and were trying to pelt us with anything they could get their hands on. Thankfully no darts, beer bottles or half-bricks this time. The cartons of milk, yoghurt and fresh fruit, such as apples, oranges and bananas, were thrown from a much more health-conscious Milan support! I'm not sure what we got was special attention because we were no doubt viewed as an anti-Catholic club, or whether the fans just reserved this type of welcome for all their opposition.

Underneath the main stands, near the dressing room area, they had a special gymnasium where all the players of both teams would go to warm up properly before taking to the pitch. Playing for Inter Milan at the time were world stars such as Giuseppe Bergomi, (who'd almost rearranged my jaw back in that famous Under-21 victory); Alessandro Altobelli, world famous for scoring in the World Cup final in which Italy beat Germany in 1982; Liam Brady, the Irishman from Dublin, ex-Arsenal and one of the best left-footed players in the world, similar in some ways to our Davie Cooper but Brady was more of a midfield creator whilst Davie being more of a winger or wide player. The big star of that Inter team, though, was with-out doubt Karl-Heinz Rummenigge, German internationalist and one of the deadliest strikers and best players in the world at the time. I recall when I went through to the gym to do my warm-up routine there he was already in the middle doing his. He looked more like a ballet dancer than a footballer. I had never seen such a physique on a footballer. His legs were like tree trunks and his upper body was just rippling with muscle. He was not nearly as tall a player as I had thought but was just incredibly athletic and powerful-looking. Unfortunately for Rangers, we were to see how graceful he really was out on the pitch.

In the dressing room, as we readied for the match, we could sense the fantastic atmosphere that was building outside in the arena. It was awesome! When we eventually trooped out onto the pitch, the atmosphere was among the best I'd ever experienced, apart from maybe Cologne and Porto away. Big Jock's game plan was pretty basic and straightforward: keep it tight at the back, keep our discipline and not lose an early goal. Easy! Unsurprisingly, we didn't get into the game and they took complete control as they attacked us in wave after wave. I think possibly as a team we were overawed by their reputation and the occasion. Meanwhile, Brady's left foot was spraying passes all over the place, probing and opening up our defence at will.

Rummenigge was giving everyone in the stadium a bird's-eye view of how balanced, graceful and skilful a footballer he was. In an utterly magical moment in the second half, in our penalty box with his back to goal, he jumped off the ground, scissor-kicking the ball into our net from a height which, it seemed, most centre-halfs would've struggled to header! It was about the most incredible bit of athleticism I had ever seen. Had it not been disallowed for dangerous play, as he caught one of our players in the head with his right boot, it would've surely been without doubt one of best goals I've ever seen. Rummenigge protested furiously, went on his knees and thumped the ground in frustration as his bit of genius was tagged 'the wonder goal that nearly was'!

We did have the odd moment in that first half, though, as I had my slice of a wonder goal that nearly was! Lurking outside the box from around thirty yards, I picked up a loose clearance from their defence. The ball sat up beautifully for me as I controlled it with my left thigh. I then thumped it on the volley with my left foot just as it got to a perfect height for me to generate enough power and accuracy. I made perfect contact as the ball flew goalwards, dipping slightly as it narrowed in on its target. I knew it was good and thought I had scored one of the best goals of my career. Just as I thought it was sure to hit the back of their net for a spectacular opener for us, it smacked full pelt off the crossbar and shot straight up in the air. Their goalkeeper, also thinking it was on target, made a valiant effort to stop it but got nowhere near it, and with him now on the ground and out of the picture, the ball was dropping down, quite literally in front of an open goal. Ally McCoist had been lurking around instinctively, as most good goal scorers would do. His reactions were initially the quickest of all in the situation. However, as Ally immediately got underneath the ball, I think he got impatient waiting for it to come down again and possibly thinking a defender was sure to be making a challenge to clear it. Whatever was going on in his mind at that moment, he'd jumped much too early and had already landed back on the ground again before the ball came down. Just as McCoist landed and was rooted to the spot, the ball hilariously hit him on the top of his head and went out of play for a goal kick! The ball actually could just as easily have still ended up in the net but luck was not on our side. I'm sure Ally, looking back, can see the funny side of it now, as I do, but he certainly didn't at the time and neither did I!

Another who wasn't amused was BBC commentator Archie Macpherson, watching as was usual from the commentary box: 'McCoist must score ... DEAR, OH DEAR, OH DEAR. WHAT ON EARTH WAS RANGERS STRIKER ALLY McCOIST TRYING TO DO THERE?'

That Ally McCoist chance was more or less the only time we threatened in the entire match. Eventually we succumbed to the constant barrage of pressure and went down 3–0 as Milan all but extinguished any hopes of overcoming the deficit in the away leg. Playing in the San Siro was still a great experience and another one I've never forgotten.

Before the return leg at Ibrox, we had the little matter of another major Cup final, history once again repeating itself by pitching us once again with Dundee United but gave me and United goalie Hamish McAlpine the chance to continue our long-running duel! It was a typical Cup final, with tension playing a big part and both teams cancelling each other out. That day I had my own personal man marker in United's stalwart utility man Billy Kirkwood. I swear had I gone to the toilet during that match Billy would've been standing there handing me the soap afterwards.

The game itself wasn't quite as bad as the Cup final when I missed the penalty but it wasn't far off it. When it came to big games and Cup finals, I always seemed to be more than just a bit-part player. No surprise either that Davie Cooper was largely instrumental in creating the only goal of the game. In one of the few genuine creative moments of the entire ninety minutes, it was the combination of Davie and me that set up my team-mate and pal Iain Ferguson for the winner. There were very few players I would rather have with a goal-scoring opportunity in a major match than Iain Ferguson. He was, apart from my striking partner at Dundee Billy Pirie, the best finisher I ever played with. In my opinion, Ferg was a better finisher than Ally McCoist, but Ally had other attributes – not necessarily all down to technique – that made him the better all-rounder and, of course, in the end the statistics were indisputable.

Davie Cooper picked up the ball over on the right-hand side

THE RETURN OF JOCK WALLACE

of the park and I saw him looking up to make a pass. I knew he would release me if I could just get away from my man magnet. I broke diagonally into the penalty box, just managing to sneak a yard on Kirkwood. Coop played me in with a reverse pass. It was the type of play he did with Bobby Russell all the time. As usual, his pass was perfection. As I moved onto it, I was still running diagonally away from the United penalty box. I controlled the ball with my back to their goal, instinctively spun round and immediately noticed Ferg lurking in a great position. I slid the ball square into the box, threaded through a couple of defenders and right into his path. All that was required now was the finish. Typically he nearly burst the net! Goal! 1–0! That one piece of clever play was enough to land Rangers another major trophy and me my third winner's medal as a Rangers player. From then on all we wanted to hear was the final whistle. It was not a particularly enjoyable game for us because the pressure of expectation to win another trophy for the club and for Jock was enormous.

Not much time for celebration this time, though, because we had the second leg v Inter Milan to play at Ibrox. In that return leg against Milan we gave a tremendous performance and at one point gave our fans some hope as we took it to 3–1. Unfortunately they scored quite early on in the first half, giving us a mountain to climb. Our scorers were Iain Ferguson with two and Aussie 'Dingo Dug' striker Dave Mitchell, who was beginning to slowly assert himself at the club. It was a very gallant performance, though, and one from which we all could take real heart. After the match I swapped shirts with Italian World Cup final-winning goal scorer, Milan legend Alessandro Altobelli. His jersey, without doubt, is one of the most memorable items of all the football memorabilia I have collected over the years.

211

Sadly to say, our league form remained unspectacular and by the time Milan had put us out of the UEFA Cup, which was in early November, it was again already looking obvious we were not going to be seriously challenging for the league. Different clowns maybe, but same old circus – perhaps this was along the lines of what our fans were already beginning to think. As we approached the end of 1984, we had two big matches to play over the festive period against Celtic. Although the league campaign was again in the crapper, much credibility could be restored by taking maximum points from our biggest rivals. The first was a 1–1 draw, with Davie Cooper getting our goal, but I will always remember this game for reasons other than football.

After Janine and I got married, tensions began to ease a bit with Dad. The Friday night/Saturday morning phone calls still came but I had begun to chill slightly and maybe was able to be a bit more mature about things. Under normal circumstances, Dad would never have missed an Old Firm match, so when he didn't call on either the Friday night or the Saturday morning, I sensed something was wrong. As I went off to the game, I just had a bad feeling about things.

On the way over to Ibrox in the car I was beginning to curse myself for not phoning him but I had to try and get my mind on the game. It was not as though I was massively worried but this was just more of an instinctive, intuitive feeling. It was so unlike him not to call, even from the point of view of telling me how many tickets he needed for his pals. Usually I played well in Old Firm matches, but in this one I had a shocker. What summed it up for me was when I tried to shoot for goal with a first-time effort and almost hit the corner flag! I was just awful. Jock didn't say much to me though after the game and I thought I had got away with it!

After matches in Glasgow, normally I would make my way over to the salon to see Janine and see how her day had gone in the salon. I always looked forward to that, as the salon gave me something else to think about. Saturday was always our busiest day of the week, and with it being just before Christmas, that day was our busiest day of the year. As I walked by the shop front and looked in the window, I saw Janine's face. I could immediately tell something was wrong. She told me that one of the neighbours from Errol Station had called to say Dad had been rushed to hospital with a suspected heart attack and was in intensive care in Perth Royal Infirmary and the next twenty-four hours were crucial.

Dad, as usual, was being his awkward self earlier that day and was refusing to go to hospital until the doctor told him he was having suspected coronary failure and if he didn't agree to be hospitalised he would likely be dead within twenty-four hours. That did the trick! The ambulance soon arrived to take him to hospital but as he was being stretchered downstairs he insisted that his Saturday betting slips be put on for the day! Not only that, he also insisted that I was not to be told until after the match. Apparently he'd also had the audacity to try and arrange a wireless for his room so that he could listen to the match on the radio! Nothing like getting your priorities in order. Just what you need to keep your heart stable, listening to an Old Firm match live on the radio!

It was very awkward for me sitting with him in the hospital because he had never really made it easy for me to be tactile towards him. I awkwardly put my hand on his and told him he would be fine. He just looked back at me with a helpless resigned look in his eye and didn't say anything. Very heavily sedated, he knew his life was in danger and I'm sure at this point he was feeling very afraid.

Monday morning back at Ibrox was a very strained affair for me. Big Jock was not happy at all with me. I didn't tell him of the subsequent events of the weekend and that my mind had been distracted, that all was not well back home. He laid into me and told me that my performance against Celtic had been unacceptable. It was very difficult for me to disagree, and so I just had to bite the bullet and take the flak because I deserved it. I should've called home to see what was wrong then I would've made Big Jock aware of the situation. I was just doing what I always did and that was trying to just get on with things regardless of how I was feeling.

My situation with Jock got worse when he did actually find out what was going on. What upset him more than anything was the fact that I had not trusted him enough to go and tell him. No doubt he would've told me to go and take some time off and come back when things had stabilised. That's the type of guy he was. From that time I think it was as though he felt I had let him down. It was fair to say that my career at Ibrox from then on really began to deteriorate. There was also genuine competition for my midfield place with the young talent that was coming through. Promising younger players such as Derek Ferguson and Iain Durrant were beginning to stake their claims.

The league campaign was again over by early New Year, eventually ending with us finishing a very poor fourth and incredibly twenty-one points behind winners Aberdeen. This was not exactly inspiring stuff and way not good enough for a huge club like Rangers! What's more, it was obvious to the fans the club had not moved forward at all from when John Greig had been replaced. By the end of season 1984/85, and it couldn't come quickly enough for me playing in the reserves, it was becoming increasingly clear that my future was looking elsewhere. Jock just seemed to have made up his mind I was not going to be playing a major part in his plans anymore.

With there being no Cup final either at the end of the season, I was in holiday mode as the close season had just begun for me. The final that year was contested between Celtic and Dundee United. United's reputation for blowing it in Cup finals at Hampden was growing about as much as Rangers' reputation for blowing league title campaigns was growing!

On the day of that final Janine and I were at home in the flat getting ready to go and spend a few days down in Saltcoats with her parents. The phone rang and it was Dad, right out of the blue. We were chatting about things. He too was very disappointed that my career at Rangers appeared to be over, this time, though, I got the impression he seemed more understanding and on my side. We also spoke about the Cup final and how we thought it would go. I told him I respected the way Dundee United played football and maybe it would be a good idea to play for them. I knew there was something else, though, and I asked him if everything was all right. I could tell he was hesitant but he then started to tell me he had developed a severe pain in his left ankle. I told him not to worry but to make an appointment and go see the doctor just to make sure everything was okay. I didn't say anything to him but I was concerned, given his condition and what he was describing.

After the call I couldn't help noticing how at ease I had felt talking to him and was a bit puzzled by it. I knew things had slowly begun to get better between us but this feeling I had was more than that. He had never made me feel at ease for a very long time but weirdly that is how I felt after I came off the phone with him that day.

Janine and I took off to Saltcoats, arriving there mid to late afternoon. Later on, around teatime, we were in the breakfast room of her parents' house just relaxing, chilling out and enjoying being on holiday, when the phone rang.

Luigi went through to take the call but when he came back in to the room I could see something was terribly wrong. He told me to sit down and that he had something to tell me. He had just taken a call from Errol. It was Kate Fillingham, our next-door neighbour and a friend of the family, to say Dad had died suddenly, collapsing at the wheel of his van, whilst driving on his way back from the doctors in the village. I was in total and utter shock.

In no time at all, Janine and I were back in the car heading back to the North-East to be with Mum. It was such a tremendous shock to everyone. I was thinking more and more about our last conversation. Did he have a feeling and know he was going to die and had that been him just trying to reassure me? How sad that we spent most of our time together being awkward in each other's company. So many things could've been put right had he lived longer, when we would've been older and wiser. I sensed he was beginning to mellow towards me, but now he was gone and I just felt completely empty.

I was a mixture of emotions. With the grief and sense of loss also came feelings of almost a sense of relief that I no longer had the burden of his expectations on my shoulders. Once again I was left feeling very mixed-up and confused about the whole range of emotions I was going through. It was never straightforward for me. Dad always used to say, 'If you ever get tired of playing football just jack it in and come and work in the business.' But again I knew this had never been an option to me as I knew it would never have worked, but with Dad gone what role was I supposed to play now? Was I supposed to just turn up and expect to be given the reins of his business? The truth was I had spent all my working life playing football. I didn't know how to run a farm, especially one the size of what he raised and built from out of the dirt.

When I think about it, I never tried to do much else other than try to live up to his expectations. I also think, in hindsight, this was where my mind had got things confused. Looking back, I think I had to have been a very resilient character but there was something in my mind that wasn't right about the way I perceived things. Subconsciously had I been trying too hard over the years to please him? I know he was on my side and I have been told by others how proud he was of me playing for Rangers, but I only ever seemed to feel this when things were going well.

Unfortunately in my time at Rangers there were spells when things weren't going well. I remember the time we beat Kilmarnock in the league 8–1 at Rugby Park and I scored two goals. It was the first league goals I had scored for the club. One was direct from a free kick and one was a penalty. I had cadged a lift off of him and his pals on the way back from Kilmarnock to Glasgow after the game but he was in the huff with me because he thought I should've scored a lot more goals and played much better on the day! When we got to Glasgow I remember I just got out of the car, shut the door and walked away without even saying cheerio. If it had been Jim McLean, Jock Wallace or John Greig, I would've handled it no problem. They were my gaffers and stick was just part of the deal.

With everything that had gone on over that close season, for the first time ever in my career I was not looking forward to or feeling optimistic about pre-season. I already knew Big Jock was not going to see me as a first pick and, to be honest, I was actually really beginning to feel for the first time I wanted to leave Rangers. In virtually two seasons since Jock had taken

217

over, nothing had changed for the better in terms of results in the league. The team was still far too easily beaten. Despite all the new signings nothing had improved.

There were still big issues within the dressing room. Many players were unsettled, including our recently appointed club captain, Northern Irish internationalist John McClelland. Mostly the players' issues at Rangers were about money, or rather lack of it. John refused to re-sign and extend his contract because the club had offered him nothing by way of incentive. Other clubs were beginning to move on in this respect, but Rangers weren't. I had been at Rangers for nearly six seasons yet both my career and the club were no further forward than they had been on the day I first joined.

As I expected, Jock froze me out of the first-team squad when we reported back from the summer break. Suddenly I found myself under the watchful eye of reserve coach John Haggart. Thankfully John was a very reasonable guy and did not make life difficult for me playing with the 'stiffs' through pre-season. I knew there was no way back for me and it was time to move on. Quite frankly, at this stage I felt so depressed I didn't even know if I wanted to continue playing football any more. The word was out that I was surplus to requirements and I was quickly getting some discreet approaches from nearly every other club in the league apart from Celtic! Honestly, though, at this stage, mentally I wasn't giving a shit about football! I knew Mum was really going to struggle on her own and my instincts were telling me that I needed to move back East to be nearer her and the family business. Maybe I was just looking for excuses because my playing career had hit the skids. I'm sure many must've thought with Dad dying and me being the only son I now had it made financially, but again this just wasn't true. The way Dad left the will meant any assets left to me were mainly in the form of land and tied jointly with my sister. She, along with her husband Graeme, ran the farm. Practically the only liquid assets I received from Dad's estate were in the form of shares that were eventually made over to me and, true to form, within only a matter of weeks before the great stock market crash of 1987. Get your lucky white heather!

The decision, I suppose, was finally made for me literally a couple of days later. It was on the Monday morning. We'd all been given the day off but I got a call from Ibrox to say Mr Wallace wanted to see me. I'll always remember driving the short distance from my flat over to Ibrox that day. It was absolutely lashing down with rain and the sky was totally black. I had a strong sense that something was about to give. I parked my car just outside the main door and walked into the stadium for the last time as a Rangers player.

Jock was quite animated when I went in to see him. He hadn't been this way with me for some time. We shared pleasantries; to be fair he did also ask me how I was coping with things on the home front, as he knew about Dad dying. When we got down to business he told me there was more than just one offer on the table. There was genuine interest from Hibs, Hearts, Aberdeen, Dundee and Dundee United. I had been giving things some thought and had only been able to come up with one conclusion. There was only one other club in Scotland I was interested in playing for and that was Dundee United. I made it very clear to Big Jock they would be the only club I would leave Rangers to play for in Scotland. Jock knew his hands were tied, even if another of the interested clubs were prepared to pay a bigger fee than United. He knew I meant what I said, but he understood the big picture and didn't stand in my way. In the end we agreed the deal and it now only remained for me to go and agree personal terms with my new employers.

With all that had gone on that summer I hadn't felt as low or depressed for some time in years. I was leaving Rangers for sure and that was bad enough, but what I wasn't sure of at this time was whether I ever wanted to play football again. This was not the frame of mind to be in when going to work for the infamous Jim McLean, manager of Dundee United.

7

DUNDEE UNITED

Before I finally met Dundee United manager Jim McLean, I had only ever previously spoken to him on the phone. Anyone who knows anything about the history of Scottish football will know what a fearsome reputation he had as manager of Dundee United FC. His dressing room outbursts are still legendary. All I can say on this is that if Alex Ferguson was known as the 'hair-dryer' in the dressing room then Jim McLean was without doubt the 'blowtorch'!

For some reason all through my playing career I loved playing at Tannadice. Even as a Dundee FC youth, I would sometimes go and watch United's reserves playing in midweek. There was something about the playing surface and the floodlights that just made me want to be out on that pitch. Dundee United played great football throughout the Eighties and, along with Celtic, were probably overall one of the most entertaining teams to watch. For a provincial Scottish club such as United to win the Premier League as they did in 1982/83 then get to the semi-finals of the European Cup the following year, only to lose narrowly in the end to Italian intimidators FC Roma, was an incredible achievement.

When I knew I was leaving Ibrox, the main reason I wanted to play for Dundee United above any other Scottish club was because of the way they played the game. Their style of play was European, they had a continental/cosmopolitan feel about them, even though the team comprised mainly home-based Scottish players, including a few who were actually born and bred Dundonians. Jim McLean or 'Wee Jim', as he was known (I'm not really sure why, as he wasn't as small as his younger brother Tommy, who I'd worked with at Rangers), had this thing about insisting his players live within a five-mile radius of the stadium. Any signings he did make from the West of Scotland would therefore have to be prepared to relocate and live in Dundee or the surrounding area.

United were the only type of club I could honestly see myself fitting in at, on the football side at least. With Dad's death very raw and my mind in turmoil about what to do, it was not the best time for me to be making big decisions about my future. Maybe I should've been more like McCoist and kept on fighting for my career at Rangers. Indeed had I known what was imminent at Ibrox, with the pending David Murray/Graeme Souness era, I surely would've knuckled down, worked harder and again fought for my place in the team. Much as I came to appreciate and respect Rangers, though, as one of the big clubs to play for, I have to admit I was never a 'dyed-in-the-wool' type of Ranger like some players of my era were. I became more of a Rangers convert, someone who came to love and appreciate the sheer magnitude of the club, despite what I saw as mainly hypocrisy regarding all the sectarian issues.

United's manager Jim McLean knew me well. He'd first tried to sign me when I was a schoolboy playing for Errol Rovers, but Dad would not let me go to Dundee United. He knew of McLean's reputation for the apparently harsh way he treated players. Jim McLean had a reputation for either making or breaking you. In any case, I don't think it would've worked. I have no doubts that when I was in my early teens I was not the type who would've been able to handle any abuse. I would've either ended up walking out or punching him in the face. In fact, probably both!

Wee Jim knew about my personal situation, he knew about Dad dying and he also knew I wanted to return back East. I think what concerned him most about me was he probably thought I was in the position where I didn't need football financially. Like many others in this respect, he was very wrong. There's no doubt I would've enjoyed being in that luxurious position but unfortunately for me it just wasn't the case. In the end I convinced Jim that my ambitions were still intact; in truth, however, I had no idea where to turn.

I was totally confused about what to do with Dad gone, and very down about leaving Rangers at such a low point. It's possible I initially saw United as a kind of halfway house or stepping stone to give me some breathing space to see how things were going to pan out back home with the family business. Maybe I was kind of hedging my bets, so to speak. I certainly knew one thing for sure: they played the type of football I thought would suit me.

Having convinced Jim that I still had the desire to win things and be successful, he put a six-year contract in front of me, three years with an option of another three years. The option being the club could keep me if they so desired. But of course meaning that if I want to dump you I can and I will. The basic wage was again low, even lower than I had been earning at Rangers, but to be fair to Jim, he accepted that and made an exception for me in as much that he guaranteed to pay me the first-team basic wage regardless of whether I played or not. There were few other players at the club who had this in their contract. One of the reasons why Jim McLean was able to dictate so much at

United was that if he dropped you from the first team and put you in the reserves he had the power to lower your basic wage with it. Believe me, if this happened it was breadline stuff! I would never have signed for United unless they had agreed to guarantee me a half decent basic wage.

The big gain financially in playing for United was the way they incentivised you for winning matches. Jim McLean, as well as being insanely ambitious, was also a realist. He knew he would never be able to keep a lid on his best players unless he at least offered them good bonuses for success. At the time, because United were winning regularly, the win bonuses were superb for a small provincial club. The only caveat being you had to earn them!

Being in no real frame of mind for serious negotiations, I agreed to the terms he offered. To be fair to Jim McLean, he gave me a decent signing-on fee and also offered me an extra bonus incentive for scoring so many goals. He didn't need to do this but it was his way of convincing me the rewards could be there if you worked for them. In reality, at the time I couldn't see my career lasting much longer and thought my time at United would be no more than a stepping stone towards me quitting the game.

Having committed myself for six years, I consoled myself with the idea that there was no other team in Scotland that suited my game like Dundee United. And it was as good a deal financially as I would've got from any other Scottish club. My judgement was maybe very clouded but my assumptions, particularly relating to the playing side of things, proved to be absolutely correct!

So in August 1985 I finally put pen to paper and became a Dundee United player. Having just done so, little did I know at that time I would go on to play a big part in one of the most exciting and successful European runs ever seen by a Scottish club! That same week, on 17 August 1985, I made my debut for United against Aberdeen, in a match we drew 1–1. It was an unspectacular start, I mean I did okay but I knew I had let my fitness deteriorate badly in the off-season. It was not so much the match itself I remember, though, it was the after-match team talk of my new manager Jim McLean that is still vivid in my mind! Standing outside the home dressing room that day was my father-in-law, Luigi. I remember him saying the noise coming from behind the door of the home dressing room was like nothing he'd ever heard before! The screaming, the bawling, the ranting! It was incredible to think it was all coming from the one source, Jim McLean! Sitting there in the dressing room utterly dumbfounded by what I was hearing, for the first time in my whole career I was beginning to think being deaf was going to be a huge advantage playing for this manager! Of course, over the years you had no choice but to harden to it or you would simply not be able to cope playing for the club. It also didn't seem to matter whether it was win, lose or draw. He still went totally mental after almost every game!

Typically if he singled you out, which was not unusual for me and certain others, Wee Jim would come right up to you and put his finger so close to your face you could smell what soap he'd been using. His face would be completely contorted in rage – and on occasion there may even have been some white foamy stuff gathering at the side of his mouth too! His eyes looked like they were about to start bleeding and pop out of his head. His breath, or the blowtorch (as I have since christened it!), was all over you like a rash. Wee Jim was quite something to behold, and no one but no one escaped his venomous outbursts. There were no real favourites, only varying degrees of victim! In his mind, if you deserved it you got it, and more often than not, in his mind you totally deserved it. It was that simple!

Some players sitting in the dressing room after matches, before the real fun and games began, reminded me of the way the old man's gun dogs looked, just when they knew they were about to get a tanking for disobedience! Then it would begin: 'SEE THAT BASTARD OVER THERE? YES, THAT FUCKING BASTARD SITTING THERE IN THE CORNER. WELL, HIS PERFORMANCE TODAY JUST COST YOU ALL YOUR FUCKING BONUS MONEY.' Then he would really begin to take off. In some ways it could be quite funny too and I used to find myself dying to laugh at the way he sometimes ran out of breath before he ran out of words. Occasionally the last part of his tirade would come out of his mouth in silence, as if he had suddenly started miming!

Sometimes when he was ranting I would try and conjure up an image of something my mind could compare to what I was witnessing. One day I thought of Wee Jim playing the role of Linda Blair in the original *The Exorcist* movie – particularly the bit where she is possessed and spouting all this evil bile whilst rotating her head 360 degrees! That, for me, was what 'Wee Jim' was like. We never quite got the 360-degree head rotation but in the state he got himself into it would not have surprised me!

Without a doubt, I thought Jim was a strange guy but he wasn't all bad. Far from it. I remember arriving at Tannadice one night to play for the reserves, not long after I had signed. I was trying to get a bit more match fitness, having not played much at all in pre-season at Ibrox. Wee Jim thought a few run-outs in reserves would help, and he was right.

Janine came with me to watch that night, and as we entered the stadium and went upstairs, it seemed like Wee Jim was the only one around. He ushered us both into the kitchen, put the kettle on and made a pot of tea. He was chatting away to both of us and couldn't have been nicer. He was being the perfect host! Put him in a football dressing room after a match, though, and

226

he was like the Tasmanian Devil on steroids!

During their golden era of the Eighties Dundee United had a great reputation for being able to keep their best players at the club. Jim McLean only ever seemed to sell a player if he thought it was in his interests as the manager. I believe the seeds of this were sewn much earlier when he managed to secure all his top young players on long-term contracts, which meant they were never given the chance to exercise their rights under the new 'freedom of contract' legislation which came in 1980 (the year I left Dundee). In my opinion, without a doubt United did what they could in terms of keeping their top players happy. However, no matter how loyal or faithful the players were, you could not blame any of them for wanting to play at the highest levels in England and reap the financial security their talents deserved, and in financial terms United were always going to be a provincial club. A footballer only has one short career, and in my day unless you played for the very biggest clubs in England you did not earn enough out of football to secure your future financially.

The biggest problem for professional footballers of my era was the terms and conditions under which players' contracts were governed. Up until about 1980 the club had the right to retain a player's registration even if the term of the player's contract had expired. This meant a club could continue to keep you and treat you more or less any way they wanted. All they had to do was continue to pay your current wages and not pay you any less or you could walk out the door on a free. The bottom line was, unless a club decided to agree to your transfer, you were powerless. They could make you train whenever they wanted, however long they wanted, at any time and on any day. This was grossly unfair, it was highly restrictive, penal and downright immoral. Fortunately for Jim McLean, it was the main reason he was able to originally tie up some of his best players on long-term deals to

227

stop them leaving the club. The pay structure at Dundee United was such that it made it very difficult for players to hold out on signing punishing long-term deals or extensions. Typically at United, Wee Jim would be pressing you to re-sign an extension to your existing contract when you still had two or three years of your present one to run.

When I was there a young player had broken into the first team and Jim was already pressing him into signing a long-term extension of his existing contract. When the only incentive the player asked for was a small signing-on fee he was not given one, but was only guaranteed a first-team wage. The player refused and was immediately dropped from the squad and put back onto the basic reserve-team wage. Knowing that the player had liabilities and was trying to save up to get married, he knew he would not be able to afford to live on his reserve-team basic wage. Sure enough, after a few weeks the player went back, cap in hand, and was tied up on a long-term deal that meant the best part of his career would be over before he would ever have the right to move under 'freedom of contract'.

Actually, before the initial 'freedom of contract' rules came in, footballers to a certain degree were like virtual slaves. Clubs could do all sorts of things to you without any recourse. Thank goodness the players' union came in and began to work on changes that removed some of the more draconian measures. Nowadays players make so much money and have so much freedom that it can take a much more sophisticated type of man-management to get the best out of a top player. The highly paid players of today can turn round and stick two fingers up to a club or manager without fear of losing anything financially. Some say the lunatics are now running the asylum and that is possibly true. Today's footballers owe a huge debt of gratitude to Jean-Marc Bosman, who was responsible for the ultimate abolition of a club's right to demand any compensation by way of a transfer fee when a player's contract expired. Unfortunately this, along with the bloated salaries, did not fully come into play until I was well out of football on the playing side. Timing being everything!

During the Eighties, apart from the rare exceptions, Wee Jim was renowned for keeping players at Tannadice until he was finished with them! It was not a case of players not wanting to play for Dundee United, it was just a case of players wanting to nail down and secure their financial future. Who in their right mind could blame them for that? When I signed for the club United had some players that were among the best in Scotland. At that time that really meant something, as the standard generally was so high. United's Scottish internationalist, central defender Dave Narey, was world class and typified the ability of Jim McLean to hang on to his best players.

For a short while I really didn't think I was going to last very long at United. Initially, I was not made to feel very welcome in the dressing room. Bearing in mind there was a tremendous amount of insecurity about money at the club, I suppose it was no real surprise. Coming from Rangers didn't help as many of the players in that dressing room were not exactly Rangers fans. I also think the fact that I had played a part in some of the major Cup final disappointments a lot of these players had suffered at Hampden against Rangers during that era didn't help the initial bonding process.

When I first joined United, Jim McLean was very ably backed by his assistant, Walter Smith, who was a real Rangers man. His dream came true when in 1986 he left United to link up with Graeme Souness under the new Murray/Souness revolution at Ibrox.

My initial lack of form and my frame of mind were causing

me concern in those first months at Tannadice. I even pulled out of a European tie in Ireland because I felt so down about things I just couldn't face the travel and all the inevitable hassles and pressures I would've felt with being the new player away with the team. Much as I enjoyed the build-up to European games, I would sometimes try to find my own space to get away from the added tension of having to pay extra attention to what was being said. For me this could be mentally tiring. If I was just with one or two players I could relax more because hearing was much less of an issue than it was when I was with the whole group.

I occasionally also used to pull out of national squads because of this and, unless I was sure of getting a game from the start, I just didn't see the point of putting myself through all the usual hassles of having to try that bit harder to keep up with what was being said. When in a squad I found some voices and accents much easier to hear and understand than others. Some were a nightmare. Sometimes when being spoken to I would just nod but in reality I didn't have a clue what was said to me. I don't think many people outside or inside football could possibly understand what it's like to be hard of hearing in a football dressing room. Sometimes there are no prisoners, and if you don't have your wits about you or aren't able to stand up for yourself then you just get eaten alive. Naturally, most footballers are at their happiest and secure when they feel they are part of the group.

I think my biggest regret is that I allowed my own fears and insecurities about who I was in football to sometimes get the better of me. To put it bluntly, my mental core was not what it could've been. Sometimes that made it difficult for me to perform consistently to the standard I was easily capable of. I think it could also explain why it always seemed to take me a while to settle in anywhere at a new club.

Professional football is very intense and demands are made on you day to day, week to week. The season lasts typically around nine months. It's a mental and physical grind, especially when things are not going well and you are struggling to find form. If a club pay big money for you then you are under pressure to perform from day one. I was already an established player at Rangers, having played 250 games for the club. The fee Dundee United paid for me was not huge but nonetheless the supporters had a right to expect me to deliver from day one. Often if players don't produce the goods straight away, things just never get off the ground and so you find yourself on your way again before you've even settled your Pickfords invoice, and I'm not talking ninety days either!

My early performances with United were not great. My fitness and stamina levels were very poor. So with things not going too well and feeling like I was struggling, I realised I needed to talk to the manager. He had been beginning to get on my back a bit by this time, though once again I had come to the same conclusion I wanted to fight for my career. I wanted to prove to Jim McLean I was committed to the club and capable of doing a good job for him. Unannounced, I went to his office after training one day, chapped on his door and asked to speak to him. As he just sat and listened to me, I told him I was frustrated with my form and lack of fitness. I then put the ball back in his court by asking him to tell me what he thought I needed to do to get myself back up to the fitness levels I was capable of. I told him I was prepared to do whatever he thought it was going to take. Sometimes with me it was just a mental thing. Yes, I had been grieving again but I was being a bit self-indulgent. I had allowed myself to wallow in it. If I wanted to get my career back on track again it was time to get back to work! Jim McLean was great about it and suggested a specific programme of track work in the afternoons

231

on top of the morning sessions. He said initially it may affect my performances but that he would allow for that and as long as I kept going at it things would improve. I honestly think that day was the turning point in my United career and I'm sure Jim McLean began to see me in a new light.

Richard Gough, who was still at United at this time, was a player whose attitude I admired. I first remembered Richard as a chubby, shy teenager when we had been in the national Under-21 squad together. He worked tremendously hard at his fitness and within a couple of years he was unrecognisable. You would always see him in the gym or pounding the track regularly after squad training sessions were over. I began to join him, working very hard to improve myself. I really wanted to show the club I wasn't just there for a jolly! Me being me, it may have taken a bit of time to come to this conclusion but now I really wanted to play for United and win some more trophies!

As much as Wee Jim could be your worst nightmare he was without doubt a brilliant football coach who knew and under-stood the game better than anyone else I knew in football. Genius is not a term I would use lightly but during my whole career I believe I worked with two: Davie Cooper at Rangers and Jim McLean at Dundee United, who were both complex characters. During this era Jim McLean was doing things that were way ahead of the vast majority of other coaches and managers. No one lost the plot more than he did in the dress-ing room on the Saturday, but come the Monday morning he was back to meticulously preparing for the following game. If he was unhappy with a performance he wouldn't compound things by flogging you on the training ground as a punishment like so many other managers used to do. Jim McLean tended to hit you more in your pocket with fines instead; it was maybe less tiring but much more annoying! Wee Jim's training sessions at

United were the best I ever had in my entire career. They were always well organised, high-tempo and brisk, with everything done to the clock. Yes, you worked your socks off at United but it was rarely, if ever, a slog! The way we trained was the way he wanted us to play on the Saturday; every rehearsal was for a specific reason. That reason being to maximise performance when it came to game time.

On the coaching side, his great strengths were that he was acutely aware of what his squad needed and acutely aware of what your strengths and weaknesses were. In all my time at the club I cannot recall him ever asking me to do something he knew I would not be capable of doing well. People talk about how he was a nightmare to work with; I disagree completely. He was the only manager I ever played for that entrusted me to get on the ball in midfield and be a playmaker. He was the only one who encouraged me to drop off and get myself on the ball, especially when we played against top European opposition when possession became nine-tenths of the law! Actions speak much louder than words and whenever any manager demon-strated his faith in me, I thrived on the responsibility of it. Jock Wallace was the only other manager apart from Wee Jim who gave me this. Under John Greig at Rangers I always seemed to be second fiddle to Bett and Russell in this department, admit-tedly they were both great players. The downside, of course, was that when Wee Jim trusted you to do a job, you dare not let him down or then you really did see the bad side of him! That Dundee United team was easily the fittest team I ever played in. There were several real athletes – Gough, Narey, Bannon, Milne – but all had world-class engines. Sometimes Ralph used the wrong petrol in his, though!

As my first season at Tannadice progressed, I began to feel the benefit of Jim McLean's training regime. I felt my form getting better and my confidence levels were much better too. The real turning point for me was when we went out to Switzerland to play against Xamax Neuchatel in the second leg of the second round in the UEFA Cup. Unfortunately we lost to a very late goal in extra-time, but I scored our only goal, having also scored a good goal in the first leg at Tannadice. It was exactly the type of European tie I seemed to thrive in. They were a good technical outfit commanded by Uli Stielike, the former West German internationalist. They also had some full Swiss internationalists, they were high-calibre opposition.

Having been very narrowly defeated in Switzerland, we came back to play against my old club Rangers at Ibrox in the league on the Saturday. It was my first trip back to Ibrox since I had left. Apparently some of the Rangers directors couldn't believe how fit and sharp-looking I was. Wee Jim played me up front that day, and if it hadn't been for the combination of Rangers keeper Nicky Walker having a particularly good game and me not being clinical enough in front of goal, I could've easily scored four or five goals. Unfortunately the game finished 0–0, us having totally dominated the proceedings. I was lean and fit, my sharpness was back and overall I was very pleased with how well I was playing! It was annoying for me not have taken any of my chances that day because it really would've underlined things right in front of my old club! Maybe I have just hit the nail on why it didn't happen that day. I was just overly keen to score.

The great thing about form is that when you are in it and playing to levels you know you are realistically capable of, you don't need anyone to tell you. When confidence surges through your veins, it's the best feeling you can have as a professional sportsperson.

After the game Jim pulled me to one side and told me he was delighted with my recent performances, but he also told me he didn't want me to tell anyone about how I had managed to get myself into such good condition again. I think he was sensitive about his methods getting out into the public domain. Being a genius wasn't easy for him!

By the autumn of 1985 Janine and I had bought a new house up on Golf Course Road, Rosemount, Blairgowrie. This was normally outwith Wee Jim's permitted perimeter boundary, but again being accommodating and reasonable, he knew I belonged more from this area and appreciated I wanted to live nearer to where my family interests were.

On the pitch there were no mind games, my head was clear and I was very focused on my football again. Having played previously for Dundee and Rangers, it was never going to be easy winning over the United fans. Generally, though, you tend to get what you deserve from football supporters, although you have to balance the fact their praise and criticisms can sometimes be a bit over the top. Basically, if you do it on the park, no matter who you are, they will accept you and begin to get behind you. At United that's what was beginning to happen to me.

As a team we really should have feared no one in Scotland, and despite not winning the league in 1985/86, we gave a good account of ourselves. I could feel myself really beginning to enjoy my football again, and despite his reputation as being difficult to get on with and work for, Jim McLean was largely responsible for helping me to turn my career around again and getting it back on track. At the end of my first season with United I was largely very satisfied with how things had developed and with that I was able to look forward to a nice holiday and relish the start of 1986/87.

By the start of season 1986, although the great United title-winning team had begun to lose its shape a bit, Jim brought in players that gave the team another dimension. He signed Jim

McInally, Dave Bowman and my former teammate at Rangers and Dundee, Iain Ferguson. Goalkeeper Billy Thomson, who was signed in 1984, had also begun to stake his claim more and more, and so United legend Hamish McAlpine moved on, having served the club magnificently playing not far short of nearly 500 games. Local league championship-winning legends Davie Dodds and Ralph Milne also moved on, Ralph finally moving to Charlton Athletic in 1987, having been out of favour for most of 1986. I think it must've been hard for the fans to see such great servants of the club leave, but sometimes players need a fresh challenge and a fresh start to reinvigorate themselves. The new players, I think, added experience, skill and a bit of steel, and plus the fact Iain Ferguson and I had both won in major Cup finals at Hampden, so maybe it was thought we could help with exorcising the Hampden Park hoodoo demons!

It was good to meet up with Ferg again. I teased him that he was stalking me because everywhere I went he just seemed to follow me! We knew each other's games instinctively and I think we respected each other as players. With his right foot, he was the best striker of a football that I ever played with, or against for that matter! He knew how to get goals and had a proven track record. Jim McInally and Dave Bowman both came from having spells in England, both were ball winners with a never-say-die winning mentality. Typically they could also play a bit too. Rarely did Jim McLean sign anyone that wasn't at least decent technically. In our opening game of the league campaign we beat Aberdeen 2–1 at Tannadice, with me scoring a very good headed goal from a Richard Gough cross and Richard scoring the other one himself.

1986/87 was also a huge year for my former club Glasgow Rangers. Big Jock, having not made any real impression, moved on to pave way for the Murray/Souness revolution. This was really what kick-started a massive decade or so for the club. Souness, with what seemed like a blank chequebook, brought in a whole new calibre of player to Rangers. Players such as England internationalists Chris Woods, Graeme Roberts, and none other than the England captain Terry Butcher. This type of transfer business was unheard of in Scottish football. It was obvious that Rangers now held a massive advantage over all the other bigger clubs in Scotland.

In Souness's first ever league game in charge at Ibrox in August 1986, we were their opponents. It was a game I will never forget, for various reasons. The atmosphere at Ibrox on that warm summer's day was absolutely electric. It was a warm afternoon and on the pitch it felt like a cauldron. It was a game that just reeked of the big occasion. As expected, Rangers came out of the blocks with all guns blazing and took the lead in the first half, before scoring again by half-time, both goals coming from none other than Ally McCoist, who was now just getting into his stride as arguably Rangers' best ever goal-scoring machine. We hadn't really done much wrong and were perhaps a bit unlucky to be two goals down, but our dressing room scene at half-time was one to behold. As usual the players never spoke, you never did until Wee Jim was finished and that was rarely before the buzzer went for the start of the second half!

On this occasion, however, Wee Jim told us that he was sick to death of us all and that, as far as he was concerned, he'd thrown in the towel. Slightly over the top since it was only the second game of the season and particularly because we'd beaten Aberdeen in our opening game of the season! Without any further ado, Wee Jim went on one of his rants; he basically told us all he was sick of the lot of us and that as far he was concerned we could go out and just do what we wanted in the second half.

With that he stormed out of the dressing room, slamming the

door on the way out and leaving the rest of us all sitting in silence, not knowing what to do or say. First-team coach Gordon Wallace and some of the other back room staff tried to lift the gloom that had now descended upon us all. I don't think there was anyone in that dressing room at that moment who thought none other than a real 'gubbing' was on the cards in the second half.

Ibrox is a very intimidating place when it's full of hungry Bears who can smell the blood of a wounded prey. Before we went back out on to the park, we'd regained our composure and accepted the difficult situation we were in, just as the Samurai warrior who goes into battle without fear because he has accepted his fate beforehand whatever the outcome.

Taking the park for round two, we seemed to throw off the burden of fear and anxiety and replaced it with a devil-may-care attitude. Okay, so if we're going to go down we'll do it in style. Remarkably though we scored three goals in that second half. Up-and-coming talent Kevin Gallagher scored twice to bring things to all square. With the score at 2–2 and the clock ticking down to the last seconds of the match, we were awarded a free kick out on the right-hand side. Paul Sturrock and Eamonn Bannon stood over the ball and it was funny because before they had decided on who was taking it, I wandered over and told them just to deliver the ball into a certain area and if they did I'd get on the end of it. Again I was in the frame of mind that I just wanted a goal so badly!

Eamonn Bannon maybe wasn't as naturally talented as Davie Cooper but if you wanted a player to run his heart out, get crosses into the box and score goals himself, he was right up there with the best of them during this era. Eamonn was a qualified PE teacher and I think he did like to show he was a bit of an academic but in truth he was also hilariously funny, and very good for team morale. He took loads of stick from the manager and would often joke that he took the pressure off some of the rest of us – that was no joke! In my opinion Eammon also scored the best goal ever scored by a Dundee United player. It came against Borussia Mönchengladbach in the UEFA Cup at Tannadice before I was a United player. He ran with the ball almost the full length of the pitch, leaving about five Borussia Mönchengladbach players in his wake before calmly slotting it past the keeper. It was just about as good an individual goal as you will ever see.

As the referee blew his whistle for our free kick to be taken, Paul released Eamonn down the right flank. Eamonn then checked back with the ball before swinging in the killer cross with his left foot. Not quite as stylish as Davie Cooper but just as deadly! Somehow, as was often the case in these situations, my survival instincts had taken over and I simply got to the ball before anyone else. I made good contact and the ball glanced into the back of the Rangers net. 2–3. Game over!

I can remember my forward momentum carried me into the Rangers net and for some reason I grabbed onto the back of the net liked a caged lunatic. I suddenly let out this huge burst of pent-up emotion. The referee almost booked me for inciting the Rangers fans, who were almost within arm's reach. They were going bonkers at me! I suppose I had a bit of chip on my shoulder, having left Rangers on such a low note, and here was me back at Ibrox getting one over them. I can't deny the satisfaction I took from scoring that winning goal! There is a great photo of the moment, where you can see the expressions of the Rangers fans in the background behind the goals; it's priceless!

Janine and her dad had gone to the game that day, but the complimentary tickets given to us by Rangers were in with a load of rampant blue-nose Bears up in the back of the stand. With us being 2–0 down at half-time, the prognosis was not good for the second half. So in view of all this they decided they would be better listening to the second half on the radio in the car park! In the end we had really outplayed Souness and his team of all-stars and deserved to win the match. I felt within myself that day that this team I had become part of was capable of much more than anyone seemed to think or realise. I was thinking that if this United team could shed itself of its inferiority complex, then it was without doubt a unit capable of beating teams of the very highest calibre. I was sure of it. But would its creator and mastermind Jim McLean also become one of its biggest obstacles?

Jim McLean's anxiety levels and uncontrollable temper, in my opinion, were never far away from undermining the excellent coaching skills that he also possessed. It's funny looking back on what he did that day in the dressing room. I don't think he was any use to his team when he lost his temper in such a way. In retrospect, walking out of the dressing room and out of the way was the best thing he could've done that day. Maybe he should've stayed away from the dressing room on match days and just concentrated on coaching.

Wee Jim was, to me, like a cross between Arsene Wenger and some sort of wee devil! His ability to blend good players into a team was second to none, but in my opinion, his biggest problem was himself. I think he constantly off-loaded onto his players because he couldn't control his pent-up anger and frustration, perhaps because he had some sort of inferiority complex and constantly needed to prove himself, or maybe he was just consumed by the competitive urge. I thought there was also a tendency to pick on the more creative players of the squad. Players like Ralph Milne, Eamonn Bannon, Paul Sturrock and myself were never far away from having a layer or two removed by the blowtorch! Maybe in players like us he expected more, or maybe he just recognised their true potential and wanted to make sure he was doing everything he could to get them to fulfil their promise. As a player with Dundee he himself had been the fans' target for abuse and apparently it got so bad that his own fans once actually booed him when he scored a goal. Now that has got to hurt but perhaps it also inspired him to go the extra mile and have the sort of success as a manager that he had wanted as a player. I can only really speculate on this but somewhere in the darkest recesses of his mind perhaps lay the reasons why he seemed to feel it necessary to vent in such a verbally violent manner. It was a great shame he seemed unable to control his emotions and frustrations after games. It was the only real flaw he had (albeit a large one) because on every other level he was simply the best.

8

BARCELONA

Jim McLean was such a strict disciplinarian, had he known what Iain Ferguson and I did the night before our away leg at the Nou Camp, we might never have played in what turned out to be probably the most memorable night in my whole career! Season 1986/87 had started well in the league with good wins against Aberdeen (2–1) at Tannadice on 9 August, a game in which I scored what proved to be the winner from a Richard Gough cross, and then of course that memorable game against Rangers at Ibrox when I again scored that late winner.

I really began to feel this team had a bit of belief about itself. There were no real prima donnas, just down-to-earth, good basic footballers, all with differing strengths and weaknesses. In goals we had Billy Thomson, in my opinion the best goalkeeper in Scotland at the time. At the back we had the composure of Malpas and Narey, and the heading ability and defensive qualities of Paul Hegarty. Richard Gough on paper was a big loss to the club but in truth I don't think we missed him as much as we thought we would. He'd been unsettled for some time, so by the time he moved on I think all realised it was in everyone's best interests. In midfield we were very strong, with the ball-winning tenacity of players like Dave Bowman and Jim McInally. Jimmy Mac without doubt was the most compatible

242

midfield-playing partner I ever played with, and as the season went on we developed a great understanding of each other's games. Our contrasting styles really began to gel and complement one another. Although mainly a ball winner, Jimmy Mac's skills were underrated; he very seldom gave the ball away and rarely got flustered in possession.

I remember him saying to me when he was first picked for Scotland that he thought I should've been in too. Jimmy was as honest a pro as you will ever get; he had no chips, issues or hang-ups, and I believe there was mutual respect between two ex-opposing Old Firm players, Jimmy, of course, previously having played for Celtic. When I left United I never again felt part of such a good team of professionals.

Then there were the 'play anywhere' utility men like Billy Kirkwood and John Holt. Holtie was another out-and-out Dundonian. He was as hard as nails and would've run through a brick wall if it meant a chance to win possession. When playing for Rangers I had some real physical battles with both Holtie and Billy Kirkwood. On the creative side in midfield we had the running power and creative attacking skills of Eamonn Bannon who, on his day, was an absolutely top-class midfield player. Eamonn, if playing today, would be well suited to playing at the highest levels in the Premiership. Finally in midfield we had the passing, play-making ability and added goal threat of myself. Jim McLean was the only manager who seemed to have the faith to play me in this role and I think I rewarded him by proving that this became my strongest position. I believe I also proved to a lot of people through my European performances that continental football was most definitely suited to my style of play. A shame I never got the chance to play for Scotland because in my United role I was more than capable of it, even though there were some real top-class Scottish midfield players during this era.

Up front we had the best striker in Scotland, Paul Sturrock, who looked and trained like a sack of potatoes, but put him on a football park and 'Luggy' was as good a front man as there was in the game – some said a wee bit like Kenny Dalglish. Yes, in some ways he played like Kenny Dalglish: he could take the ball into his feet whilst tightly marked and spin away from defenders, making even the best of them look silly! He could also score goals and did regularly but spent most of his time moving and creating for others. For attacking width we had the young Kevin Gallagher, who could catch pigeons up and down the touchline. Kevin went on to fulfil all his undoubted potential with Blackburn and Newcastle, not to mention becoming a full internationalist. Ralph Milne had exceptional pace and skill, was a wide attacker or winger but only played twenty-two times that season. I think Kevin was beginning to force Ralph out of the picture for a starting slot in the team. The enigma of Milne was to remain so and his days at United were becoming numbered.

As a pure finisher we also had just about the best in the business of his generation in Iain Ferguson. His critics called him lazy and selfish, but not in my opinion, Ferg was the very arrow tip of this United team. He had the killer touch in front of goal. Built for strength with those big heavy legs that were never going to do the type of scurrying around a park that the likes of a Gallagher or Strurrock could and would do. Ferg was a penalty-box poacher, a Gerd Müller-type of player, but he could also score many goals and did regularly from outside the box, as he could generate more power and accuracy with his right foot than almost any other player I have known. If you trawl YouTube you can find his 44-yarder against Hearts, quite simply as spectacular a long-range effort as you will see. Wee Jim knew it, too. Ferg was probably the only player in that team who could get away with not grafting his nuts off. But as I said, effort is

relative to what the end product is and every good team needs
a prolific scorer and Ferg was ours. In that season 1986/87 he
scored twenty-eight times from fifty-one appearances ... That,
to me, says it all. A good team is all about having the proper
balance of skills.

Jim McLean was a master of being able to blend players and
mould a team, very much in the way the great Brian Clough did
at both Derby County and Notts Forrest. We didn't have a massive squad and had to rely on all of us staying fit. Fortunately, in
general that season we did. I do not recall any major long-term
injuries to that team. Actually, incredibly for me that season,
only Billy Thomson made more appearances (sixty-one), though
I ran him close with fifty-nine – but there were a good few others
who were not far behind.

Some also would say this United team I played in were maybe
not quite as good individually as the title-winning one. But the
new additions, such as me, Iain Ferguson, Dave Bowman and
Jim McInally, gave the team another dimension of skill, steel
and experience. We had all played for bigger clubs and were not
overawed by big-occasion games.

At the start of our now legendary UEFA Cup run, having
overcome very tough obstacles in earlier rounds against Lens
of France, University of Craiova of Romania and Hadjuk Split
of Croatia, momentum was clearly building in the squad. Nothing, though, could've prepared us for the excitement of who we
were drawn against in the quarter-finals! There was a huge buzz
of anticipation around Dundee, as we were in amongst some of
the very biggest names in European football. So when the draw
came and we'd been paired to meet European giants Barcelona,
the feeling was simply awesome. They were one of the biggest
and most famous club sides on the planet. Now I am sure had
we drawn them in the first round we would not have been as

confident of having to beat them in serious competition but our confidence levels had grown considerably along with our performances in the competition.

I think it was Jack Nicklaus who once said something along the lines of: 'Achievement comes when expectation levels and belief levels rise at the same time in the knowledge and assurance of your own capability.' Well we had just beaten three strong sides to reach the quarter-finals of the UEFA Cup and we were also in the quarter-finals of the Scottish Cup. We'd also reached the semi-finals of the League Cup and were still in outside contention of winning the league. Sure Barcelona were a big mountain to climb and we knew it would be difficult to progress further, but we were determined not to be overawed or intimidated. Barca had some great players, and a real British flavour to them at that time. With Terry Venables (El Tel) recently installed as manager they had signed Gary Lineker from Spurs and Mark Hughes from Manchester United. In that pair they had two of the best strikers in Europe . . . but we had Paul Sturrock and Iain Ferguson!

The whole of Dundee was buzzing in anticipation of the tie, and on 4 March, in front of a packed stadium at Tannadice (21,000 fans) we played out the first leg but in the dressing room before the game it was amazing how calm we all were. There was no special build-up to it. With games flowing thick and fast, I'm sure Jim McLean was right not to make a particular issue of it, just because it was Barcelona. He was right, after all it was still only the quarter-finals.

The atmosphere that night was fantastic. Tannadice was just a small ground but the terracings were very close to the pitch and when the stadium was full it generated an incredible atmosphere for big-occasion games. And there were none bigger than playing Barcelona! We were beginning to get a lot of press and media interest for interviews, etc., so it was decided that we would pool all the money from this together and divide it up at the end of the season. Looking back, it was peanuts in comparison to the game these days but to us it paid for a holiday or contributed to a pension fund but we for sure weren't retiring on it!

I'll never forget the hairs on the back of my neck rising as we walked out onto the pitch that night to face the aristocratic giants from Spain. I always knew I was going to play well when I felt this way. I was directly against Spanish national captain, Victor. I had watched him play for Spain in the 1986 World Cup. He was small but very strong and tough, with an engine that never quit. He looked like he had no neck at all, just his head atop a very wiry, steely frame. There were not many who could out-stamina me over ninety minutes at that time, but in Victor I had more than met my match. He just kept running non-stop and by the end of the game I was getting tired just matching him. Overall I think honours were shared. We'd both given as much as we could and I remember feeling utterly exhausted late in the game but still somehow managed to keep my legs going. Victor, he just kept going on and on, like the Terminator!

I can honestly say there were few games in my career that I enjoyed every second of but this match was one of them. Others were to soon follow. The pace and tempo in the first half was incredible. We settled in quickly and were moving the ball around at speed and getting some joy. There were no signs at all that we feared the opposition.

Lineker and Hughes were getting it a bit from our fans. Nothing more than was to be expected, really! I was impressed by the strength of both Barca's Brits; they were world-class athletes. I took a hard challenge from Hughes in the first half and felt the juddering power of his tree-trunk legs. He was a tank of a player but struggled to win over the Spanish fans and was having a harder time settling in Spain than Lineker. Lineker, though, missed a sitter in the first half that could've changed the complexion of the game but the razor-sharp reactions of Billy Thomson, our goalkeeper, prevented him. Big Thomo was like an extra man for us in defence – it's funny how many of the players in that team just got better and better as the season continued and he exemplified that. Success breeds confidence and confidence breeds success! I also truly believe you cannot be a great team without a great goalkeeper and Billy Thomson was most certainly all that.

With play raging on, we took the lead quite early on in first half, thanks to a Kevin Gallagher 'wonder' goal! Yes, we all still wonder if he meant it! Kevin had cut in off the wing and moved onto the ball before slicing in a cross that took Barca's goalkeeper completely by surprise. Tannadice erupted as the ball hit the net, and you could visibly see the Barca players thinking that this was not in the script!

As expected, they came back strong, trying very hard to break us down, but again we were a very solid defensive unit. Billy Thomson the big 'blonde Adonis', as Eamonn Bannon described him in the *Fair Play* film that was made in honour of our achievements, was virtually unbeatable, as again we held on without giving anything away. We all ran our hearts out that night; there was not a weakness in the team. Players like Jim McInally and John Holt covered more ground than a couple of bloodhounds on the scent of a fugitive!

In some ways, as a player you never want these games to end but when the final whistle blew we had beaten Barcelona 1–0. No one in our camp, however, were under any illusions. This was only half-time, as there was another tiny little hurdle to over come. That would be our night of destiny in the Nou Camp for the second leg! Before flying out to Spain for the game in midweek we had to put away Forfar Athletic in the quarter-finals of the Scottish Cup.

A lot is made today of sports psychology. But Jim McLean was a very forward thinker and was probably one of the first managers of this era to poke a stick at it. He decided that with our pending appointment in the Nou Camp for the second leg we should be exposed to the brain-bending power of a hypnotist! Luckily for us, he decided on a dry run first, so he invited this guy into the dressing room a few days before the Forfar game. He had us all sat as a group in the home dressing room after training. We were told to imagine a black box, and into this black box we were each to deposit all our negative thoughts and simply make them disappear or file > delete! Just as well Wee Jim wasn't involved, as the hypnotist would've needed to call and ask the council waste disposal to deliver a skip to contain all his negative thoughts! Seriously, I admired Jim McLean for having the foresight to do this. This was typically innovative of the man.

On 14 March, five days before we played the Barcelona return leg, we were sitting in the dressing room ready to take the field in our Cup tie against Forfar. Our psycho guru was there too and so we were all put into a pre-match 'trance'! As was usual on match days, Wee Jim was like a coiled-up cobra just waiting to be hissed off and the big problem was our hypnotist had forgotten to pre-order his metaphorical skip!

On paper Forfar represented no threat us, but this was the Scottish Cup, we were their Barcelona and Tannadice was their Nou Camp! And with the fixtures coming hard and fast, all we needed was a replay, but a friggin' replay is what we got and with no small thanks to Iain Ferguson's very late penalty equaliser! We had come so very close to being knocked out that day and that would've represented disaster. It was fair to say at this point our manager was none too happy with the input of our newly acquired psycho guru: 'HYPNOTIST, IS IT? A'LL GIE YE ALL FUCKING HYPNOTIST, YOU BUNCH OF SHITEBAG BASTARDS!' – or words to that effect! Actually, our hypnotist was more like a magician that day because he very quickly vanished, never to be seen on Tannadice Street again!

It had just been one of these days when we didn't focus on the job. Understandably, we only had the Nou Camp on our minds. We could hardly be blamed for that! Saturday had not been the best preparation for our trip to the Basque region of Spain, and even Jim accepted the Forfar game had been a big distraction to us. But, as said, luckily we got away with it and were still in the Cup and Forfar were put very firmly on the backburner for the time being.

Well we flew out to Barcelona without the psycho guru and, as I recall, our hotel was somewhere in the city centre. The atmosphere of the place was fantastic; it is such a vibrant, pulsating city. We first sampled what we were about to experience in full Technicolor with a training session at the Nou Camp. This is, of course, mandatory for the away team. Some of our fans had arrived at the stadium to watch us train. It was such a thrill just training on the pitch, never mind doing it for real a couple of days later, and we really began to soak up the atmosphere. As always, our sessions were light and brisk and I can remember just how much we all seemed to be relishing the challenge that awaited us. Wee Jim knew we had turned the corner and were on the home straight of a very long, hard, demanding season so there was no point in overworking the legs at this stage. As well as how we trained, what we ate, what we drank and how we slept was now more critical than ever.

On the eve of the match as usual we were free to relax and do whatever we wanted, but drinking, in the manager's book, was strictly taboo. There was also always a curfew; so as long

250

as you were in bed by curfew time there was generally never a problem. That squad were angels compared to others I had been part of! My roommate and pal Iain Ferguson had a glint in his eye, though. We'd had our dinner and decided to go for a walk to see some of the city and pass some time. After a mile or so, I'm not sure who suggested it but we decided to have a beer. In hindsight this was genuinely a great way to relax, so we sat in a bar watching some music videos and enjoyed a few beers, maybe three or four at the very most. As 'newcomers' we didn't appreciate that, as much as we were totally focused on the job in hand, if Jim McLean had caught us having even one sip of beer that night, neither of us would've played the following evening! Luckily there was no problem and we slipped back into our hotel in time for curfew.

The next day was just a case of limbering up in the morning and passing the day until it was the pre-match meal and off to the stadium. I always liked to go to bed in the afternoons before an evening match. Two or three hours' sleep before a major event is a great way to pass the time and energise in the process. You have to watch and not burn up too much nervous energy before the start or you can feel leggy and sluggish. When it was time we took the short journey by coach to the stadium and everyone was no very much in focus.

When we arrived at the Nou Camp it was awesome; there were people milling about and what struck me was the sheer size and stature of the place. I have played in some fabulous stadiums, including the San Siro, but nothing compares to the sheer size and splendour of the Nou Camp. It even has its own chapel! That was not much good though to ex-blue-noses messrs Redford and Fergsuon! I think had we tried confession before the match we would've been struck down by lightning or Jim McLean!

The training ground within the Nou Camp complex was as big as our 'compact but bijou' little Tannadice stadium! The dressing rooms looked like the size of small five-a-side football pitches and the bath was like a swimming pool. When it was go time we filed out of our luxury dressing room, ready for the long walk before the steep climb up the stairs to pitch level, like a bunch of gladiators preparing to do battle in the Colosseum. Maybe some felt we were being fed to the Lions that night but our hearts were as big as a lion's as we took to the pitch.

The preparation and the build-up had been superb and what struck me, looking back, was how calm we all were standing on the stairs waiting to take to the pitch. Our captain, Dave Narey, who led us up the stairs and onto the field that night, looked like the calmest person in the whole arena. He not only looked like it, I'm sure he actually was!

Our manager and his assistant Gordon 'Stubby' Wallace, having watched Barca a couple of times, had got our game plan precisely right. There was no point in trying to totally defend a one-goal lead. The plan was to keep it tight, defend as a unit, stay on our feet at all times and try and force them backwards or sideways but not through us. It was critical also not to give away fouls around the penalty area, if we could at all help it. But when in possession, keep the ball as long as we could and counter-attack whenever the opportunity arose. We knew things had not been going well for them and that the crowd would turn on them the longer things continued in our favour.

The first half went to plan and all was going well until just before half-time, when Caldere hit a drive that was deflected into our net. You could see the relief among the Barca players, it was almost as if they were thinking, 'That's it. We're through.' Our precious advantage was gone, it was back to all-square but we were a long way from Dundee. Now as a team we knew

252

we had to go and beat them in the second half or we were out. Although we had lost the goal there was little recrimination at half-time, remarkably even from Wee Jim! There was still calm and there was still a belief that we had what it took to win the tie.

In the second half we really started to play some good football by keeping possession, breaking forward, and were beginning to give them problems. Paul Sturrock was superb that night, the whole team were but his scurrying movement up the left was really hurting them. I felt as if my game was really flowing and just couldn't get enough of the ball. I was loving every second of it. Playing passes, breaking forward, linking up with our front men. The more the second half went on the more we felt this tie was still well within reach. We rode a bit of pressure from them too but kept probing and plodding away at them till eventually the big breakthrough came.

With one down and only five minutes to go, Paul Sturrock again won a foul on the left flank just outside the box. With our big players now piling into the box, I knew this was a real chance to create a goal. I steadied myself, taking time to visualise what type of ball flight I wanted to deliver into the danger zone. I was fairly proficient at dead-ball situations, i.e. corners, free kicks and penalties. The key, in my opinion, to a good outcome is to focus on the target and make good contact with the right part of the ball. I would always try to take a mental picture of where exactly I wanted to deliver the ball. I knew if I could put it into the right part of the box at the right pace and trajectory, we had players capable of getting on the end of it. I made sure to connect with the equator part of the ball, to ensure it wouldn't fly too high. I wanted to cross it in with pace at head-height. Sure enough, I whipped in a beauty. It curled tantalisingly into the box and was met by the United hulk John Clark, who duly despatched it via his head into the back of the Barca net. It was now 1–1 but we were ahead again on aggregate and they need to score twice within a few minutes.

That night we were without the injured Eamonn Bannon. He was a big loss but BBC's Archie Macpherson's gain as Eammon co-commentated on the match. Later, when watching the highlights, Archie referred to Eammon as simply 'Bannon'. Hilarious!

This was no lucky break. We deserved to be back in front through our general play. Here we were, a team of local Scots lads from a provincial 'corner shop' out Barcelona-ing Barcelona in their own backyard! Hard to believe, I know, but it was true! This was no backs-to-the-wall, park-the-bus rearguard action, hanging on for grim death. No, we took the game to them and played them in the manner they tried to play us but we were simply better than them at it. And for me, that was as good as it got!

The home crowd were really beginning to get on the backs of the Barca players. As an ex-Ranger I know how hard that can be for a team when that happens. All of a sudden players hide and don't want the ball, confidence evaporates and if team spirit and harmony is weak, it spells disaster! Mark Hughes had evaporated. Even Gary Lineker had supposedly mentioned to someone on the park (to paraphrase), 'This lot are not up for the fight and will throw in the towel.' We now also had away-goal advantage so we knew Barca had to score twice.

With literally a couple of minutes to go, I took the ball for a walk, but got forced into a change of direction and funnelled into a wall of Barca defenders, so I pivoted round, keeping the ball tight to my left foot and slipping a pass out wide to Paul Sturrock, who gave it back to Jimmy Mac. Macca then deftly split two defenders with a pass that released Paul again, right down to the byline, but this time with acres of space. Paul picked out

254

his target perfectly, finding Iain Ferguson, at the back post with a super cross. But Ferg was never going to miss this one, even though it was with his head, GOAL! 2–1. That was it, Barcelona now needed three goals but they knew it was game over. We knew it too and so did our fans!

I was totally exhausted but can seldom remember feeling so elated or satisfied with myself and any team performance I had ever previously participated in. I don't think anyone wanted that night to end. I think we all just wanted to savour it forever. I honestly cannot remember anything our manager said after the game I was on such a high. The Spanish press were very complimentary of my performance and one journalist in particular said, 'Holt, he is like a tiger. Redford, he is magnifico!' In reality the quality of all the players in that team made it easy for me to play my role well. They just gave me the ball when I was available and I kept play flowing and kept us in good possession. John Holt was indeed awesome that night but so too was my main playing partner in midfield, Jimmy McInally, they fought like true warriors. Hunting down our opponents, winning the ball and feeding the likes of me and Paul Sturrock, who was simply awesome. Above all this was a team performance of the highest calibre. There were no stars, no prima donnas, just a bunch of quality footballers who worked and played for each other.

After such a huge encounter, we again had very little time to rest on our laurels as we had Rangers at Tannadice just three days later, followed in midweek by wannabe giant killers Forfar in our Scottish Cup quarter-final replay. It was hectic to say the least! The big problem with such an adrenalin rush as we'd had in the Nou Camp was always going to be coming back down to earth in a very short space of time, but in football when you are having success it goes with the territory. I could never sleep after a big midweek game. Quite often I would have a few beers to calm me down and finally knock me out.

Back at our hotel in Barcelona, it was party time but it was curtailed by an 11pm curfew. Some of us were reluctant to adhere to it, and I remember our club doctor getting a bit upset about it. I think it showed how little he understood about our emotions that night, and whilst I take his point that we had another big game coming up in a matter of days . . . we had just beaten BARCELONA in the Nou Camp stadium! It's hard to describe in words just how good that felt!

9

MOMENTUM BUILDING

My form was just getting better and better. I still have that 'magnifico' quote from that Spanish journalist because it was not an adjective often used by the Scottish press when referring to me! Not that any of this seemed to matter much any more, the way I was now feeling. At last I felt as if I was beginning to convince at least some of the doubters within the Scottish media. Speaking of my performance in the Nou Camp, Patrick Glenn of *The Observer* wrote at the time: 'In no player is the influence of McLean and the United phenomenon more marked than in Ian Redford, the midfield man whose intelligently creative shuttling of the ball from no man's land into the heart of the enemy defence made him, for this observer, the outstanding contributor.'

In the frame of mind I was now in, the better the opposition the more I wanted on the ball to enjoy and show I could hold my own against the best. I was totally relishing the responsibility Jim McLean put on my shoulders. He gave me more confidence than anyone ever did by the sheer virtue of that fact that he trusted me in the role in which I trusted myself!

I was nothing if not a grafter on the park and in that United team I was surrounded by grafters. We ran and worked for each other. Our manager was second to none at blending our various strengths and weaknesses to ensure we maximised our performances. Jim McLean had this United team playing the type of football that in this era was only really typically seen on the continent. Getting myself back up again for the big games was never a problem to me. Motivating myself properly against lesser opposition where there was little to no atmosphere was. It was not that I didn't care; I probably cared too much. I think I was more fearful of playing poorly against weaker opposition than not being able to perform against top teams. This was especially so whilst I was a Rangers player because the levels of expectation were always so great. Maybe that could explain why I was sometimes seen as a bit of an occasion player. That's difficult to explain or rationalise, but confidence is just another word for 'present' or 'the now'. Big-occasion games do not allow your mind to drift from the task at hand compared to lesser games where sometimes it is much easier to allow your thoughts to time travel either back or forth.

However, I nearly always thrived on the excitement and build-up of a big European game or generally any big game where it was hard to take the 'eye off the ball'. European Cup football was so refreshing compared to the repetitive rigours of the Scottish Premier League. The games were coming thick and fast, with each one seemingly more important than the other. Inevitably fatigue was going to play a big part in our season. Being a small provincial club, we did not have the luxury of being able to really rotate our squad. If you were out of the team there were only two possible reasons why. One, you were injured. Two, you were dropped. Rested was just not an option.

Tannadice was packed out again on the Saturday as we faced Graeme Souness and his team of all-star Rangers. My confidence was so high that tiredness had yet to become an issue with me. This was a game I absolutely relished and it couldn't come quick enough. Disappointingly, the game ended 0–0 but my good

258

form continued as I dominated again in the midfield. Graeme Souness was getting narky and began trying to knock me off my perch. Later that same year, in the following season, he tried to sign me and take me back to Ibrox. I must have done something to impress him that day!

Much as I would've liked to have gone back to Ibrox to play a part in the Souness revolution, what I thought my game needed at this point in my career was European-style football every week. Ideally a move to the continent was what would've suited my style best of all. Playing in that great United team was fantastic but unfortunately they were obviously still confined to playing in the Scottish Premier League. It meant playing against the same type of opposition every other week. I was envious of the likes of Murdo MacLeod, John Collins and Paul Lambert, who all got great moves abroad and came back much more rounded footballers. My midfield-playing partner at Rangers, Jim Bett, also used to tell me about his experiences of playing continental football. It was where I thought my game needed to be to really go to the next level.

When at my best, not only could I play well with a ball at my feet under severe pressure, I had good awareness. I think I subconsciously developed this because of my deafness. When I was on the ball, I needed to be aware where everyone was because if someone shouted for a pass I would have no idea where they were by their voice. I don't think I was ever a dirty player but very few, if any, ever got the better of me by intimidation. I was never afraid to look after myself on the pitch when required.

It was also around this time that I at last found myself selected for the full national squad to play against Belgium in a European Championship Qualifier. It was such an honour for me to be picked. I had played for Scotland at practically every other level and was always very proud to pull on that dark blue Scotland jersey.

Having overcome Forfar comfortably in the Cup replay (psycho guru nowhere to be seen) we were now into both the semi-final of the Scottish Cup and UEFA Cup and were still not out of the league, although it had to be said we were now long shots on that one. Our success, though, was making our fixture schedule more and more punishing, and within the space of four days, between 8 April and 11 April, we had two massive games to play. We had the first leg of the UEFA Cup semi-final to play against German giants Borussia Mönchengladbach on the Wednesday, then on the Saturday it was the rip-snorting derby against our big rivals Dundee at Tynecastle in the semi-final of the Scottish Cup. Who said it's tough at the top!

But I was enjoying my football so much I just couldn't get enough of the big games. Incredible to think that within the space of under only two years of my dad dying, my career was resurrected to the point where I was on the brink of playing in a major European Cup final, another Scottish Cup final and breaking into the full national squad, It was a shame that he missed all the excitement of the 1986/87 season. Despite the tension between us, I know how much he would've enjoyed seeing me play in these big European games. Having felt we were just getting to know each other again shortly before he died, I would've loved him to have witnessed it all.

On the week before Borussia came to Dundee for the first leg of our UEFA Cup semi-final, along with teammates Malpas, Narey, Sturrock and McInally, I met up with the Scotland squad for the Euro '88 Qualifier match against Belgium in Brussels. The experience was both exciting and very disappointing for me because, although it was great to be included in the squad, it was hugely frustrating to watch from the bench as all my teammates were included in the starting eleven. I was bitterly disappointed not to get a starting berth, as I knew I was more than ready for it. I was playing as well as if not better than anyone in that squad at that specific time. I was appreciative of Jimmy Mac, who actually said my form was better than his, and believe me, his form was superb.

Unfortunately Scotland blobbed and we got hammered 4–1 in a match in which Nico Claesen got a hat-trick. I came so close in that second half to asking Andy Roxburgh to put me on and give me a chance but, alas, he put Pat Nevin on instead of me and left me sitting on the bench twiddling my thumbs. It was a strong Scotland team but we were very poor on the night. Ally McCoist and Jim Bett, who I knew well from my Rangers days, also played that night but I just never seemed to get the nod. Success in sport and in life, I suppose, is so much dependant on being in the right place at the right time. I was in the right place at the right time but didn't get the chance to show what I could do.

I really wish I had played alongside my United midfield partner Jimmy McInally against Belgium. I honestly think I would've done well and gone on to win a few caps. European football suited me down to the ground and no one would've been more committed on that field than me in a Scotland jersey. I just couldn't understand why Andy did not at least bring me off the bench, even if it was just to give me my debut. I mean, 4–1 down with ten minutes to go, what have you got to lose? I suppose if there was a positive about not getting that elusive cap in Belgium it was that it gave my legs a break and a chance to recover from all the games I'd played up till then. During the season I'd hardly missed a game and had already racked up over fifty appearances. My fitness had never been better than it was under Wee Jim at United. I had him to thank for that, without a doubt.

Next up was our first leg semi-final versus the German giants Borussia Mönchengladbach. The atmosphere inside Tannadice that night was again amazing. Our supporters could be forgiven for getting used to this type of stuff. It was truly amazing for such a relatively small club to be continually producing such good football. I think the fans were being bred on it because as long as I can remember they have always appreciated good football. The game itself was one I thoroughly enjoyed from start to finish, although it ended 0–0. I was so unlucky not to break the deadlock in the second half with a great left-foot pile-drive that hit the keeper's right-hand post. I felt myself growing stronger in that match as the game went on. It was one of these nights again when you just didn't want the ref to blow his whistle to end the match! Iain Ferguson must've especially felt hard done by that night, as he had two goals chalked off in the second half in a very spurious manner by the ref.

I tell you! Jim McLean did not realise how lucky he was to have the kind of pros there were in that dressing room at United. There were very few finger-pointers in that team. There was no need. When it came to finger pointing we had a manager who was second to none!

The way the Germans were celebrating on the park after that first leg, you would've thought they had already gone through to the final. Maybe they genuinely believed a 0–0 draw was good enough but had they not learned anything from our defeat of Barcelona in the Nou Camp? It appeared not.

We were every bit as good away from home as we were at home, in fact better. We were a classic European-style counter-attacking team that defended well in numbers and attacked with pace and precision. We also had the killer touch in front of goal. What other attributes does a good team need? Towards the run to the end of the season, we had so many big games coming at us one after another. Literally within three days of our first leg versus Borussia, we had the no small matter of playing our local arch-rivals Dundee FC in the Scottish Cup semi-finals on the neutral ground of Tynecastle, home of Heart of Midlothian. It was an absolute firecracker of a match, probably the best Scottish Cup tie I ever took part in. It had everything from start to finish. Dundee FC were no mugs at that time, and when I think of some of their players that day and compare them with the Scottish players of today, that whole team would've been playing for either Rangers or Celtic today.

Dundee were 2–1 up at half-time and had the edge but we were nothing if not an extraordinarily gutsy and determined bunch of individuals. Ferg, as usual, was among the goalscorers for us, scoring our counter in the first half then getting the equaliser in the second. The pace of the game was unreal and I remember guys like John Brown, Robert Conner, Jim Duffy and Tommy Coyne, all quality players, playing their hearts out. Our midfield was exceptionally strong and again I could feel our stamina and sheer willpower getting the better of Dundee.

Late on in the match whilst perched at 2–2, I remember someone throwing in a cross towards the back post. I took a gamble and got myself into the box. As I attacked the ball I remember thinking, 'I'm going to score.' I jumped, was just about to knock yet another last-minute winner into the net, when Paul Hegarty had decided it was his ball. He had wings on his feet when he jumped and there was no more focused an individual on that park that day. He of course got to the ball before me and did only what I was surely going to do myself, and that was score the winner. Paul, I'm sure, would've taken me, their goalie and the ball into the net along with himself if need be. Anyway, who cared? We were 3–2 up with minutes to go and heading for another Hampden Park final. Dundee still didn't see it that way, though, and with literally a couple of minutes to go, they were awarded a direct free kick on the edge of our box. Dundee stalwart John Brown stepped up and hit a cracker of a free kick but its quality was matched only by the sheer class of save by our goalkeeper Billy Thomson. It had been an incredibly physically demanding match but there was real joy and satisfaction in that dressing room after the game.

Within days we were back on the big stage again for the return leg of against Borussia. The atmosphere in Germany that night, at the then Borussia Bökelberg stadium (later replaced by the now 55,000 capacity Borussia Park), was just fantastic! It was hairs-up-on-the-back-of-the-neck stuff again! A footballer just cannot get enough of this type of atmosphere; it's just like a drug. I mean, the high you get from performing on a big stage like that is very hard to describe. There is no way you can experience such highs in your life and not miss them when they are all over. It wouldn't be human.

Our metaphorical rocket fuel without doubt was the way in which the Germans had thought they had done enough in Dundee to ensure they would go through. We started the match in determined fashion. Our mental and physical resilience showed how tough a nut we had become to crack. Quite often in the first period of a game things are a bit tighter because legs are fresh and full of running and mistakes less frequent. Sometimes it's harder to get that extra bit of space required to create and make something happen. I remember the first half being like that, with not really anyone giving much away. However, much to the German's dismay, we took the lead just before half-time. We won a corner on the left and Paul Sturrock took it. He swung the ball into their penalty box. It was half cleared but broke to Eamonn Bannon in the air. He could've made a goal attempt himself but he was a bit hindered, as he partially had his back to goal. Unselfishly, he nodded it on to Ferg, who once again was lurking at the back post and managed to squeeze another headed goal into the corner through a melee of defenders and their goalkeeper.

Ferg's goals were so crucial to us that season and as I am taking this trip down memory lane I am appreciating more and more just how valuable a player he was for us that year. Shame he never got a cap because, in my opinion, he was good enough to play at international level. Scotland had some good strikers in his era, players like Ally McCoist, Charlie Nicholas, Frank McAvennie, Mark McGhee, and of course our own Paul Sturrock, but in terms of pure finishing ability, Iain Ferguson was better than all of them. Albeit in my slightly biased opinion!

In the second half, just as we had expected, they came at us a bit and we had to ride our luck as they hit the post, as well as Thomo pulling off some great saves, but you could not hope to be able to progress in a major European competition unless you could sustain a bit of pressure. We were becoming masters at soaking it up.

As the game wore on, legs began to tire and we began finding holes in the German defensive ranks. Ferg came close with a header and really should've scored. I broke through twice, narrowly missing once and trying to lob the goalkeeper in another attempt in which frankly I should've done much better. Borussia were now running out of time, as they needed two goals!

Late on in the match our manager brought on young Kevin Gallagher to give us some much needed fresh attacking legs. With the clock literally ticking down to seconds, Kevin duly broke free up the right and was homing in on goal. I was completely knackered by this time but had decided I desperately wanted a goal and knew this would be the last chance in the match. Somehow I managed to make another run up the middle of the park to support him in a two-versus-one situation. Kevin, like all good strikers should be, was a bit on the selfish side but I somehow got my legs into the box, in the clear and available to finish the job off.

To his credit, Kevin saw me in the much better position unmarked and slid the ball square across, but it was slightly behind me. I was aware of their goalkeeper trying to shut me down quickly and my only thought was to try and take the ball wide of him. The ball bobbled as it came to me, making my first touch look a bit clumsy as it got away from me slightly. I think that actually helped me as it gave their keeper hope that he could get to it first and so he was totally committed to the ball. As he dived in I steered the ball away from him, to my left, into the empty space and to create an angle. I was now looking diagonally at an empty Borussia net! My legs were totally exhausted but all that remained for me to do was knock it into the net. Suddenly a nanosecond became an eternity again as I kept my composure and slotted it home. Immediately I was aware of all our fans directly in front of me and behind the Borussia goals. They were going mental. I used the only remaining energy I had left to raise my arms and salute them, a bunch of crazed Dundonians who were now realising the 'corner shop' team, Dundee United, had just got to the final of a major European competition.

Everyone back on the bench by this time were on the pitch, jumping up and down, because the referee had blown his whistle for the end of the match. There was a brief moment when I actually wondered if my goal would be disallowed because it was over time!

When back in the dressing room Wee Jim just couldn't contain his 'excitement' and 'joy', so he did what he did best at these times, he went ballistic, his target being big Thomo for giving away a free kick and nearly costing us a goal! Thomo was in no mood for it, though, and more or less ignored him and headed for his bath. Normally that would've cost him two weeks' wages and his place in the team, but even our manager wouldn't drop the best goalkeeper in Scotland when he was in the form of his life.

My own performance that night was just about as good as anything I had ever produced. In the second half I felt physically and mentally at one with myself. In all the years I was a professional footballer I can count on just about only one hand the times I felt that confident or in so much in the present. Now even the local press were recognising this. The Sports Editor of the *Dundee Courier* wrote on 23 April, the day following the match: 'Their place in the final was secured with a second successive win on foreign soil – remember Barcelona – through goals by Iain Ferguson and my outstanding performer of the night, Ian Redford.' It continued: 'I have to dwell first on the Errol lad's contribution. He played in midfield, and at the back, and as a wide player, and as a striker. He was back. He was forward. It was a piston-like performance seldom equalled by what used to be called a wing half.'

One of my prized possessions is a letter I received not long after this match. It is also dated 23 April 1987. Written by a Colin MacDonald on an old-fashioned typewriter, it reads:

Dear Ian Redford,

I have not written to a footballer since I was a boy (with dreams of playing for Scotland) away back in the early 1960s. But after Dundee United's performance in Munchengladbach [sic] last night, I feel compelled to put typewriter to paper.

The team performance was a joy to behold. But above that, I thought your own contribution was inspirational. Your battling, controlled play in midfield took me back to the days of Billy Bremner and Jim Baxter.

I've seen you play many times over the years, for Dundee, Rangers and now United. I think your game has developed so much in the past year or so.

I have a son, who is almost two years old. Should he have dreams of playing for Scotland when he grows up, I will show him the videotape of last night's game, tell him to watch you, and copy!

Good luck in the final. I'm sure you'll do it.

Yours sincerely,

Colin MacDonald

Over the years I've kept things written about me but I can honestly say this letter meant more than anything that has ever been written about me regarding my football career. This was not written by a paid journalist, this was someone who simply sat down, watched the match and felt strongly enough about my performance that he took the time to write to me. This was someone who only judged what he saw on the pitch. To be honest, over the years I cannot recall if I ever replied to it but I sincerely hope I did!

I found this quote recently, on a Dundee FC forum, thanks to a very helpful Dundee supporter: 'Ian Redford's energy and get-up-and-go in games, particularly in his early career, was the most remarkable I have seen in fifty-five years of watchin' the Dee!' I was touched by it.

And more recently still, I received the following praise from Dundee United supporter Jim O'Neill: 'I am a fifty-three-year-old Arab fan, and unlike fans of many other clubs, I have been blessed by the gods of football in witnessing so many incredible occasions. I have seen some of the finest players Scotland have ever produced – Bannon, Sturrock, Narey. I have seen trophies won and so many trophies cruelly lost . . . But on 22 April 1997, in the North Rhine, I was lucky enough to have been there to see what I'd describe as the most complete performance from any player I have seen pull on the Tangerine. Not just *that* goal where you [Ian Redford] take fourteen minutes to round Uwe Kamps. I am talking about the lot – ninety minutes of someone at the absolute peak of what they do. Never in any match I've ever been to has one player stood out so much. A privilege to say, "I was there", and to this day no player has pulled on our shirt and matched what you gave us that wonderful night.'

Even though it has been such a long time since I played football, it really does amaze me just how much the genuine fan still likes to recollect or perhaps indulge in a trip down memory lane.

Although predictably, with the weight of all the fixtures we were enduring the league slipped away from us, but an interesting statistic emerged from that season. We actually finished with 60 points, four more than when United actually won the league in 1982/83, and a point more than the Aberdeen team that won the league in 1984/85. Celtic were runners-up on 63 points and Rangers were champions under the first year of Graeme Souness with 69 points. I think 60 points in the league that year, all things considered, was incredible!

That United team I played in became exceptional psychologically, just through winning football matches. That season we accumulated 60 points in the league, we got to the semi-final of the League Cup, and we got to the final of both the UEFA Cup and the Scottish Cup. Winning Cup finals is all about having the right frame of mind and the right approach. It's a bit like match play in golf, where you only need to be better than your opponent by one hole. In a Cup final, as long as you score one more goal than your opponent you lift the cup. You don't necessarily need to play that well and nobody really cares as long as you win! Winning a league, however, is totally different. It's all about consistency of performance, over a long period of time. That's why Jim McLean liked players who were reliable if unspectacular and why he would crack up at players that gave him vast differences in the parameter of consistency. How many majors did Jack Nicklaus win by playing solid if unspectacular golf? Find the fairway, find the middle of the green, then two putt or sometimes one putt, whilst letting the rest of the field blow up trying to do it differently, the end result being consistency leads to success over a long period of time.

There was also a lot of talk about the Hampden 'hoodo' which gripped United during this era but this was rubbish in my opinion. In the main only good teams get to Cup finals but only one out of the two can win it. Jim McLean was very superstitious. There even came a point during that tremendous run when he wouldn't change his shirt, and it even got to the point where he had to see my father-in-law standing outside the stadium before the game. He seemed to view him as some kind of lucky charm! United were a great team during most of the Eighties. They got to loads of finals but in my opinion should've won more than they did. If you go into a final fearing defeat the chances are defeat is what you'll get.

I think if Jim McLean had possessed the same type of motivational skills like the late Brian Clough, then his record as a manager in Cup finals could've been much better. Yes, the players can do it in spite of the manager, but overall the results have to be better when the manager and his players are in harmony and working together.

The demons that drove Jim to become one of the all-time great Scottish managers or coaches were also, in my opinion, responsible for restricting or capping his success. I think possibly when it came to domestic Cup finals, the fear of losing was too strong at United. Players need to go into a Cup final, almost mentally accepting every possible outcome before a ball is kicked. Then just go and enjoy it and do the very best they can on the day! The result then takes care of itself. If I ever became the manager of a team playing in a major Cup final, the only thing I would tell them would be to not be afraid of losing it. I honestly think had Jim taken more of this line with his squads then Dundee United would've bagged more trophies than they did.

With the climax of the season approaching, we had three Cup final matches to play in May, all within in the space of two weeks. This on the back of an already long, hard, punishing season. Our league season still hadn't ended so there were other games to squeeze in the lead up. On 6 May we had the first leg of the UEFA Cup final, our opponents being Gothenburg of Sweden. Then on 14 May we had St Mirren in the Scottish FA Cup final, then on 20 May we had the return leg of the UEFA Cup final back in Dundee. Seldom can any Scottish club have ever been involved in so many big games in such a short space of time. Although we were the fittest team in the country, inevitably a price would have to be paid for such a long, hard, demanding season. Mental tiredness was becoming more of a problem than physical tiredness, in my opinion. There are only so many massive adrenalin rushes a body can take before fatigue begins to play a part.

The squad flew out, full of anticipation of the biggest pending event in the club's history, to Gothenburg for the first leg of the UEFA Cup along with friends and family. The friends and family stayed in one hotel and the players in another. There was a very relaxed atmosphere about the whole proceedings and I even recall Wee Jim having a smile or two in the build-up to the game.

There were two things that disappointed me greatly about that first leg of the final. The first was we were to be without Iain Ferguson as he was suspended, picking up yellow cards in the previous rounds. Ferg was a vital cog in our wheel and his goals throughout the competition had proved to be invaluable. The second was the state of Gothenburg's pitch. Not easy to go from playing on the surfaces we had played on in the previous rounds against Barcelona and then in Mönchengladbach against Borussia, to the less dry rutted surface we found in Gothenburg. You would expect that having got to the final, one of the most important aspects would be the playing surface!

But a pop concert had been allowed on the park literally a few days before the final. When we trained on it we knew it was awful. I also realised that on this surface we would never be allowed to play our quick-passing, counter-attacking style of football. The pitch was rutted all over, making a good first touch virtually impossible. The manager had also taken the decision to play me up front as a target man in Ferg's absence. He had played me as a striker on more than one occasion. In particular, he liked playing me up front against Willie Miller and Alex McLeish when we played Aberdeen. He joked that I was the only one stupid enough to try and hold the ball up against them. It's possible that he decided that playing me in my usual playmaker role would be a waste of time because he realised I would not be able to play my usual passing game on that surface. It is sad to think that, with all the effort and preparation that went into the success of our European run, the first leg of the final was played on such a poor surface.

The one thing Jim McLean could do nothing about was the state of the opposition's pitch. In my opinion this is what cost us victory in the final, even more so than the fact Gothenburg were as fresh as daisies, having just begun their season whilst we were jaded and largely burned out from being at the opposite end of ours. They were a big, powerful, physical team, and playing on that rutted park suited them much more than it suited us. They did not possess the range of skills that we did but they more than matched us in physical strength and running power.

It was a lovely, warm, balmy evening in Sweden as we took the field in front of all our friends and family, and our well-travelled and hugely loyal United fans. There were 50,000 fans in the Ullevi stadium that night for the final. All the ingredients were there for another classic United European performance, but in all honesty the whole thing was a massive anti-climax because of that pitch.

That night in Sweden in my role as main striker I played directly up front against Glen Thysen, who later went on to play for Liverpool. He was a big, strong and very powerful defender. As a team we really struggled to get anything going that night but I very nearly scored with a drop volley on the turn inside the box. It was about the only effort I had at their goals in the entire match. Our outstanding goalkeeper, Billy Thomson, nearly lost an ear when Petterson broke through and he dived, saving at his feet, but Petterson followed through and caught him, completely unintentionally. This really rattled Billy and he was very dazed to the point of concussion. Shortly afterwards they won a corner-kick, which normally Billy would've come for and dealt with no problem but unfortunately didn't. Their man rose above Eamonn Bannon at the back post and headed the ball firmly downwards, and with the rutted ground like concrete the ball bounced more like a Thunderball than a football, and it shot straight up into the roof of our net! No way would that have happened on a decent surface and no way would Thomo have allowed that cross to get away from him had he not been dazed and injured. Predictably, the game ended 1–0 to Gothenburg. There were also serious signs that we were now becoming emotionally drained by it all.

In what probably was the most amazing season of the club's

history, it is unbelievable to consider that nine players in that team played a minimum of fifty games each! The tally was as follows: Thomson 61, Redford 59, Gallagher 57, Bannon 57, Malpas 57, Narey 54, McInally 51, Ferguson 51 Sturrock 50. I think that is an amazing statistic and I wonder how that would compare with the average appearances of a regular first-team player today. I look back on that statistic with pride and I cannot emphasise enough the quality of the players in that team.

I think by this stage Wee Jim's bottle was really beginning to go, with being 1–0 down from the first leg of the UEFA Cup final, knowing his team were beginning to show signs of exhaustion, a Scottish Cup final beckoning and the Hampden hoodoo again threatening to rear its ugly head! There was also a small matter of having to play our last league game of the season on the Saturday after we came back from Sweden. As to be expected, it was a very below-par performance. However, with nothing at stake and two more Cup finals still to play, you would've thought the manager would've accepted that? Not on your life! In the dressing room after the game he went ballistic again and ordered us all in on the Sunday morning for a track session because he reckoned we weren't fit! What made matters worse was that beforehand he even gave some players, me included, the option of not playing. Stupidly I declined his offer and opted to play! We were all very down about this, particularly in view of the fact we knew we had not done ourselves justice in the first leg of the UEFA Cup final.

On a personal level, I was pulled into the manager's office early in the week and told that I needed to prove my fitness by having a breathing test. Fifty-seven lung-bursting games later that season and I needed a 'breathing test'! Knowing how vola-tile Wee Jim could sometimes be and thinking my Scottish Cup final place was at stake, I took the bull by the horns and went back to the manager's office early on in the week. I reminded him of the games I had played. I told him that he needed me at Hampden in his starting eleven as I was a proven winner in Cup finals and on big occasions. He then put the onus back onto me by asking if I could guarantee him a performance in the final with no excuses. I looked him straight in the eye and told him he could rely on me 100 per cent. As I came out of his office I took a deep breath; I knew what the consequences would be if I didn't deliver! Well, at least I now knew for sure I was in the team for Hampden on Saturday for the Scottish FA final against St Mirren.

On paper St Mirren were no match for us. But we did not like playing against them at all. They were a tough physical team with players like Billy Abercrombie, Brian Martin and Brian Hamilton. They also had a very young up-and-coming Ian Ferguson and Paul Lambert. Having said all that, as a team they were no mugs and no matter who the opposition, it was down to us to beat them.

I can remember sitting in the dressing room at Hampden and looking around at some of the players I was about to go into battle with to try and win the Scottish Cup. It gave me a real sense of security and confidence. In my mind at the time I was thinking there was just no way we were going to lose this match. Hampden hoodoo? Bollocks!

Call it bad luck, call it exhaustion, call it whatever you want, but lose the match is what we did! There is no doubt at this stage we had gone more than a bridge too far. The spark in the team had gone. It was nothing to do with nerves or bottle because that season we had evolved into a team that believed we could beat anyone. There was no fear in that team – that was a fact!

Sadly, I don't think our manager helped our frame of mind that week. After our last league game he should've told us all to go away to rest and relax and not come back till the Thursday before the final. A big call, maybe, but one I think should've been made. Instead it seems hard to believe some of us, me included, had our arses run off on the cinder track on the Sunday morning following that last league game and only now, a few days before the Scottish Cup final. Jim I think was panicking at the very time when it was crucial to maintain calm. Not easy, I know, but it was as if he'd already forgotten we'd just beaten teams of the calibre of Barcelona and Borussia Mönchengladbach. Having built a great team out of nothing, was this possibly more to do with the 'Hampden hoodoo' than anything else?! No one could really influence Jim McLean. Gordon Wallace, who'd taken over from departed first-team coach Walter Smith, was as knowledgeable as anyone in the game; I'm sure he must've thought Wee Jim was nuts to be doing this to us after so many games and with two such vitally important games to go. In my opinion, if Wee Jim had just a bit more belief in what he himself had created, I have no doubts he was as good as anyone in the game. Alas, however, his temperament got the better of him. Key players were being upset and dropped at a time when all I think was required was to let them get on with being how good they were. Great loyal players like Paul Hegarty I felt at times had their heart and soul ripped out of them. Guys like Paul never asked for much but repaid the club a thousand times by becoming such great and loyal servants.

That day at Hampden on 14 May will go down as one of the most bitterly disappointing days in my career. We were clear and outstanding favourites and if any team deserved to win something that season it was us. I think I would rather have lost to Rangers or Celtic that day, but to lose to St Mirren was about as gut-wrenchingly hurtful as it could possibly get. I can't totally explain it but I somehow always had a feeling that when I really had to I could pull something out of the bag. When I said to Jim McLean I could guarantee him something in the final, in my own mind I truly meant it and more importantly believed it too!

The final itself unsurprisingly was another poor one, like so many finals at Hampden. Why on earth did they always seem to roll that park till the surface became so hard it was like trying to control a golf ball on concrete! There was not very much to recall from the match itself as we slugged it out with them and as time wore on predictably it ended 0–0 after ninety minutes. This was exactly what our already dying legs needed ... extra-time! We were totally out on our feet but I was determined to make something happen.

Dave Bowman, who'd also played a good number of games that year, was a hardman of a midfield player ('Psycho' our fans called him, for some reason!). Bo could play, though, and he slipped a pass through to me after I made a diagonal surge to wide left, managing to break away from the St Mirren defence. I drove to the touchline with the ball before sweeping it with my left foot right across their danger area.

Kevin Gallagher probably should've left it to Ferg, but went for it and missed. However he was not offside when Ferg, who was lurking behind him, knocked it into the empty net. Goal! 1–0. Or so we thought! Sometimes in a Cup final it can take just one moment like this to turn things your way. We had desperately needed a break or a bit of luck. But the referee saw things differently and disallowed the goal for being offside. I have looked at that goal on video many times and to this day I still cannot see why that goal should not have stood. We were totally gutted and protested vehemently to the ref but he was having none of it and booked me for persistently protesting. Now for the first time I was really beginning to wonder if United's Hampden hoodoo was for real!

From that moment on you did not need to read the script to know what was going to happen next. Literally minutes later in the first half of extra-time, St Mirren's Ian Ferguson, latching on to a through ball, broke away from John Clark, and thumped it past Thomo into the net. That was it, we had played our last ace but it was St Mirren that dealt the final blow!

I have never felt such deflation in a dressing room. There were players in tears, me included. We'd come so far that season and had so much success and yet so far everything had eluded us. Every professional athlete knows how it feels to give everything and lose out in a major event. As I sat in that dressing room, mentally and physically exhausted, I could hardly even speak. No one really knew what to do or say because, yet again, within a matter of only a few days we somehow had to try and lift ourselves from the heartbreak of defeat in yet another major Cup final. This time the second leg of the UEFA Cup final v Gothenburg at Tannadice.

Thankfully there were no recriminations this time from our manager. He certainly didn't say it but I'm sure he understood exactly how we were all feeling, as he must've been totally gutted himself. Despite his wobble after the first leg he was acutely aware of how exhausted we all were. Incredibly, however, within a few days Tannadice was once again electrically charged on the last night of our magical European adventure! It was a truly marvellous occasion for the club, but tragically, for the fans, and everyone who had played a part in that great year, we just didn't have anything left in the tank. As always we tried our best and had some good moments in the match, but Gothenburg were a very powerful team and were obviously much fresher than us. I have no doubts had we been even a bit fresher and played them on a good surface then we had enough within our ranks to have beaten them. Even our own playing surface that night wasn't good but it was pretty much the same with all Scottish football playing surfaces come the end of the season.

Amazingly, though, lifted by our incredible support, we set about trying to restore the deficit. I was back in my more familiar midfield role but this game was played more like a traditional Scottish Cup tie than a technically orientated European encounter. It was high-tempo stuff with not too much silky skill being played. Having gained a bit of momentum, the wind in our sails was all but snuffed out after only twenty-two minutes when they took the lead. Effectively, that was more or less game over because it meant we now had to score three goals to win. With all the best will in the world I don't think anyone believed that was going to happen given how mentally and physically exhausted we all were. We kept trying, though, and pushed as hard as we could. We did get one back in the second half through big John Clark – actually, it was a stunning strike from the bulky, versatile defender – and we did have several other close calls, but it was just not to be.

And so the most amazing footballing season of my whole career was over. Looking back, I do so with enormous satisfaction but with more than a tinge of sadness that such a good team did not have a trophy to consolidate it all. I think we became victims of our own success, to a certain extent. However, I do still have the satisfaction of knowing I played a role in one of the best runs any Scottish football team has ever had or known. Sure there was heartbreak, sure there was disappointment but would I have swapped that for winning in the Nou Camp or scoring that last-minute goal in Germany against Borussia? Not a chance! These are the kind of memories you just don't forget.

The most abiding memory I have of that final, final night in Dundee was not of the match or how I played, which wasn't actually that great, but rather of how brilliant our fans were when

Gothenburg were presented with the trophy on our pitch at the end of the game. Not only did they cheer us and support us through and through they also were big enough to give Gothenburg a good, honest round of applause. This great sporting moment not only set a precedent, but it actually earned the club a large sum of money from UEFA for the Fair Play Award. I think Dundee United were the first ever recipients of this award. I think the amount was £25,000. They had been with us all the way.

What promised to be of great consolation to me turned out to be another major disappointment. I was again selected for the national squad to play in the end of season International Rous Cup, with matches scheduled at Hampden against both Brazil and England. They just don't come bigger than that, but I had picked up a knee injury at Tannadice in the second leg against Gothenburg. However, being desperate to make my Scotland debut, I joined up with the squad along with a few of the other United boys who had also been selected. I knew I was struggling and tried to hide it as well as I could, somehow managing to get through the training sessions without it being obvious I was injured. Eric Ferguson, the Scotland phsyio, knew me from being the physio at Dundee FC when I played there. He was treating me between training sessions but I think he also knew I was struggling.

Scotland head coach Andy came to me a couple days before the game with the news I so desperately wanted to hear. He told me I would be making my debut against Brazil and would most likely also be playing against England in the other match. The knee, though, was getting worse and worse in training. It was swollen. I think I had overstretched the main cruciate ligament. It felt very weak and unstable. But I was so reluctant to pull out for fear of Andy leaving me out in future altogether. It had taken me long enough to get picked in the first place and I was determined that I would give myself every chance of making it onto that park.

The day before the match, however, I realised that not only would I be letting myself down, I would also be letting Andy and the team down. This I couldn't do. I went to Andy and explained the situation. He seemed to be okay with it but I was ruled out of both matches. This was another terrible disappointment to me as I had so longed to get that elusive full cap. My play that season had deserved it but once again luck was just not with me. My chance to make a name for myself as a Scotland player had really gone, as later on that year Andy called me and told me he was leaving me out of the squad and replacing me with Ian Durrant of Rangers. His reasons were that he felt Durrant was better than me at playing in front of the ball.

Inevitably season 1986/87 was going to be a tough one to follow, but we still should've tried to build on the success of it. That magical UEFA Cup run we'd had may have been history, but for the next season, as far as I was concerned, it was all about building on the success of the previous one. I am not sure just how prophetic Jim McLean really was, but not long after that season, instead of him saying he expected my career to keep improving, he told me that I had probably reached the pinnacle and would most likely not achieve as much ever again. In truth, what he said shattered my optimism and unsettled me.

No giant-killing runs this time. We took an early exit out of the UEFA Cup, losing in round two to Vítkovice, of former Yugoslavia, having beaten Coleraine easily over two legs in the first round. In my opinion, Jim McLean, having assembled and created something really special, maybe wasn't prepared to allow himself the luxury to quite believe it. Yes, if you measure success in terms of decades then United were, or indeed are, a smaller club, unable to compete long-term with the much bigger Glasgow guns. Wee Jim was maybe a bit like Dr Frankenstein. He created life out of nothing but it grew to the extent where he perhaps became afraid of how powerful it could be. There is no doubt he could be a very difficult man to work for, and I am the type of person who can only put up with it for so long.

I had heard rumours that Borussia Mönchengladbach had been interested in taking me to Germany. They had been impressed with both my performances against them. To be honest, this unsettled me, as I had long harboured a desire to play European-style football on a regular basis. A move to German football at that time in my career would've been a dream come true. In Scotland, United were as near to giving me this as any other club, but it takes two good teams to make a good football match and there were not many teams who even tried to play that type of football in Scotland. Although I loved playing for Dundee United in that era, they still played in the Scottish Premier League, so apart from the big games against Rangers, Celtic and the derbies versus Aberdeen and Dundee, having had such great experiences it was now only European football that really did it for me. Wee Jim had got wind of my discontentment and was immediately on my case.

I had started the season really well but pulled a hamstring against Rangers early in October, and apart from trying to make a comeback much too early against Falkirk where I limped off, I was out till virtually the New Year, when I managed an appearance against Arbroath in our opening Scottish Cup campaign. Again we went all the way to the final, beating Dundee in the quarters then Aberdeen in the semis, after a reply in which we were down to ten men, club 'psycho' Dave Bowman receiving a red card! In the replay again we were the better team but thought our luck was going to be out when Davie 'Psycho' Bowman was sent off! That night we again showed why we were a side that could go to somewhere like the Nou Camp and win. Our work-rate, our character and desire, along with the ability to keep possession despite being a man down, was exceptional. I was very satisfied with my own performance, but once again Ferg finally put the Dons to the sword with a late second-half goal that once again sent United to another Cup final. Heartbreakingly for me, though, I had earned a yellow card that took my points tally over the limit and so again missed the final through suspension. I was so gutted I didn't even go to the final. I did not really enjoy being away in a group for any length of time when I knew I was only going to be a spectator!

At least Jim McLean didn't force me to go, as other managers would have. I watched the final versus Celtic on TV at home that year, but I just hated it. On the one hand, if we had won, I would've felt worse from my own perspective because of missing out. On the other, if we lost, I would be gutted for the team and our fantastic fans. As it turned out, it was the latter. United again had lost another final at Hampden ... hoodoo? What hoodoo?

Season 1988/89 was to be my last at United. I just seemed to be getting one rollicking after another, and whether I played good, bad or indifferently, it made no difference. It was no wonder some players found that type of stuff hard to deal with. It was just pure and utter rage. It was a great shame because it seriously undermined his other managerial skills, which were second to none. Eventually there were other major incidents involving media and press that possibly contributed to Jim McLean moving out of management and upstairs to the boardroom. There was an incident when we were at an airport when coming back from a game when a cameraman ended up on the carousel! Later on, not too long after I had left United, there was, of course, the famous one when Jim attacked a television interviewer in the middle of an interview after a game.

I was growing ever more tired of playing against the same type of opposition week in, week out. The Premier League for me killed football from a purist's point of view. The new ten-team league structure bred more fear and more negativity. Managers became more afraid to trust young talent and so would opt for the 'seasoned' high-plains-drifter-type of footballer, who wasn't really going to make the game any better or more attractive. The days of players like the naturally gifted Andy Ritchie of Morton, or as I would refer to him now, 'the talented Mr Ritchie', were becoming a thing of the past. Unless you could run all day and tackle like a Pitbull Terrier, there was not much hope for you playing in the Scottish Premier League. There were, of course, odd exceptions, but it seemed like all the natural talent was slowly but surely being squeezed out of the game.

Quite simply, I knew I was getting to the age when I had to try and make something happen otherwise I would be too late. My unrest and disillusionment came to a head one day not long after I had come back from a minor knee injury that I'd picked up playing in a local derby match against Dundee. After a furious exchange in his office in which I also lost my temper, I stormed out, nearly taking Wee Jim's office door with me. I decided then to officially inform the board that I wanted to leave. I wrote out a letter and more or less put it to the board that I could no longer play for Jim McLean.

When news of my transfer request broke, it was all over the national press. Then, right out of the 'blue', I got a call from Walter Smith, assistant to Graeme Souness at Rangers. As said previously, I had worked with Walter at United in the early part of my time there and got on very well with him. He went about his business in a quiet, efficient manner, but he was also not a man you would try to get the better of. I respected him as a person and as a coach, and I believe he went on to prove this by becoming a top manager.

'Reddy, it's me, Walter Smith. How would you fancy a return to Ibrox?'

There was a stunned silence at the other end of the line. Finally when I had picked myself up off the floor, all I managed to blurt out in reply was, 'You are FUCKING right I would.'

All thoughts of playing for Borussia or in Europe faded to grey as I licked my lips at the thought of being part of the new Rangers/Souness revolution. At the time, Graeme Souness and David Murray were to Glasgow Rangers what Mikhail Gorbachev and a JCB had been to communism and the Iron Curtain! The old 'Politburo' had gone and Rangers were at last becoming the club I think John Greig had visualised but unfortunately had not been given *carte blanche* as Souness had.

'Okay, sit tight and don't say a word to anyone,' said Walter. 'Graeme is trying to do a deal with Wee Jim to bring you back to Ibrox. I'll call you back when I hear more.'

That was actually the last I heard from Walter until the next development.

The writing was really on the wall for me when I made it clear I no longer wanted to play for Jim McLean. It was sad because Jim had done so much to turn my game around and get me playing back to something like my best. Having got injured against Dundee in a league game on the Saturday, I missed out on the first-round away leg of our Cup Winners' Cup campaign against Floriana of Malta. But after a scrappy first round I was fit enough for the return leg and played in the match. However, Jim went totally mental at me in the dressing room after that match as the team had not played well and struggled to win convincingly.

After that match, mentally I was finished with playing for Jim McLean.

In the next round of the UEFA Cup, it was back to Romania, this time against Steaua Bucharest but, not surprisingly, Jim dropped me and was beginning to give me the 'treatment' he reserved for insubordinates! It backfired on him big time though in the away leg, as he took me with no intention of playing me. I was out of favour and we both knew it. It was a crazy situation because at the time I was the playmaker of the midfield and if any game was suited to my style of play it was a European-style Cup tie.

Having lost at home in the first leg, we were up against it back in Bucharest but it was not beyond the grasp of the squad there was at Tannadice at that time. I sat on the bench and had to watch as we went a goal behind, but he still would not put me on the field. Eventually with no more than a matter of a couple of minutes to go he stuck me on – what a waste of time. He knew the game was over and so did I! Sadly for me, that was my last appearance for Dundee United.

The fans who I felt had really grown to support and value me were not happy about Jim McLean not playing me. They knew how well equipped I was for playing European-style football. Jason Thomas of *The Times* said of me in an article not long after we'd got to the final of the UEFA Cup: 'Like Narey, a Rolls-Royce of a central defender, and Sturrock, the best striker in Scotland against man for man marking, Redford is well suited to European football.'

On the plane home again, as it was a chartered flight there were maybe a hundred or so fans travelling with the squad. They were all sitting up the back of the plane and had been having a few drinks to drown their sorrows. The team were down at the front of the plane with the management and press somewhere in the middle. Not too long into the flight, but long enough for the alcohol to have kicked in the fans began chanting, 'One Ian Redford. There's only one Ian Redford. One Ian Redford . . .' Apparently Jim McLean's face was crimson with rage, the players around me could hardly contain their laughter and, of course, it was all right in front of the press, who were sitting right in front of the chanting fans. It was a long flight home and for the manager there was nowhere to hide!

I have never forgotten that moment and was grateful for the supporters who chanted my name. They let the manager know how they felt about him leaving me out of the team. This gave me a big lift and it was also of great amusement to the rest of the squad! I think the fans' actions that night on the plane contributed greatly to Wee Jim finally letting me go. Not long after this event, I got a call from the office to say they had agreed terms with Ipswich Town and it was now up to me to decide whether I wanted to go or not. A familiar story here?!

Ipswich were not in the English First Division at the time, and not the club I would've chosen to play for or country I wanted to go to, but I figured I needed to get away from the boredom and repetition of the Scottish Premier League and just had to get away from Jim McLean for the sake of my sanity!

There was only thing still stopping me now from moving to England and that was Rangers. Walter Smith had not phoned me back since his initial call and I really wanted to have one last attempt at trying to resurrect their interest before leaving Scottish football. I managed to get hold of Walter but he told me that the deal was off. Ipswich had offered more than Rangers were prepared to pay for a player they had let go only a couple of years previous for £70,000! It was another disappointment. I'd had my hopes raised about going back to Ibrox to join the revolution but then dashed again by Jim McLean's reluctance to sell one of his top players to another Scottish club, especially Rangers! But I suppose, to be fair, if indeed Ipswich were the club coming up with more cash, then who could blame him, apart from me!

I did say to Walter that I would be prepared to go back to Jim McLean and flatly refuse to move unless they agreed to sell me to Rangers. In hindsight, that would probably have meant my early retirement from football. However, I don't think Graeme was prepared to be dragged into a bidding war for me and would simply now look for other options. Looking back, it was just not going to happen for me and so I had little choice but to join Ipswich Town!

So in November of 1988 my days of playing for Dundee United FC had come to an end. I was so sorry to be leaving the best team I ever played for in my career. It was great to have played for Dundee United alongside so many top-class players. If I had to pick only two who I think said more than anything about Dundee United it would have to be Narey and Sturrock. They were both as good as it got!

As for Jim McLean, well, I am the first to thank him for reviving my career at a time when I was really low and actually could've quit football for good. He was one of the best coaches the Scottish game has ever known. I am sure if he ever looks back there will be things he regrets. Especially but not exclusively, in the heat of the moment in the dressing room after games.

I look back on that magical spell of my career at Dundee United with enormous pride and satisfaction. Jim McLean, commenting in an article in the *Dundee Courier*, once said of me, 'He is a treat to work with. His hunger and desire to do what we are asking is an example to everyone. I am hopeful that it has rubbed off on other players, young and not so young. Of the people who have come to us [from other clubs] Redford equals the best we have ever had in attitude and determination.' He then went on say, 'He has already scored eight goals for us – not one from the penalty spot – and that is fitting reward for what he has put into the game. Whatever he achieves he deserves.'

That's good enough for me!

10

THE TRACTOR BOYS

As usual it was all done in a hurry. Janine and I were flown down to London on a Sunday afternoon in November 1988 to take a look at our potential new club. A fee of £200,000 had been agreed between Dundee United and Ipswich Town. All that remained was for me to agree personal terms.

Ipswich manager, John Duncan, came to meet us in our hotel that night for a chat. I'm not sure what I was looking for from John, but whatever it was I just didn't get the vibes. Maybe I was hoping for someone to inspire or motivate me. In truth, a good pro should not need to be inspired or motivated by others. That need or desire has to come from within. There are far too many tough obstacles and barriers ahead to rely or depend on others to see you through. The ones who play at the top the longest are generally the ones who are self-motivated and have that inner-bred desire to perform in every game. I think by the time I'd left United, most of mine was gone. My drive, enthusiasm and passion for the game was no longer a driving force in me and mentally I was just not prepared for the type of football I was about to be asked to play. What I was about to discover was that the English First Division was not much different than the Scottish Premier League.

As a younger player I had the running power and legs to back

290

up my enthusiasm but the game in Scotland had changed so much by the time I had got to my late twenties. Managers and coaches were beginning more and more to look at the physical attributes of a player as opposed to his skill level or talent, the obvious result being a huge decline in the entertainment and enjoyment factor.

John Duncan seemed very non-committal about where he wanted me to play, and that I think was the initial problem. I think what I wanted was an assurance that I would be asked to get on the ball and make passes and score goals. Just as I had done for Dundee United. This at least would've given me a platform from where I know I would've fitted in. This would've helped me to believe Ipswich were the right team for me. Disappointingly, I never got any real indication of what he wanted or expected from me. This I thought was very odd for someone that was prepared to pay a fee of £200,000 for me.

I should've heeded both Janine's and my initial instincts but the problem was I had burned my bridges at Dundee United, going back to Rangers died a quick death thanks to Wee Jim and that elusive move abroad was now just a pipe dream. There was no going back, so despite the initial misgivings, in the end I signed for Ipswich Town FC. Without doubt they were a club of good pedigree and reputation. At least, I assumed it would be a chance for me to play English football but any thoughts I had of being able to play the type of football I enjoyed very soon evaporated.

Ipswich Town, at that particular time, were a poor team, struggling to get out of the old English First Division. The big plus was that sleepy Suffolk is a lovely part of the world to live and Ipswich was a cosy little family-type club. The people were very friendly and the weather was much better than it is in Scotland.

I think success in professional football, like most other things too, is about being in the right place at the right time. Apart from the obvious things like dedication, talent and determination, you need to have that knack of arriving at the station just in time to catch the train before it leaves the platform. If I wasn't getting on the wrong train, I was arriving at the right station but going to the wrong platform – only to see the right train pulling away with me left standing there!

At Glasgow Rangers I had been in the right place but at the wrong time. At Ipswich, it was more or less the same thing. They had been a great team under Bobby Robson, winning the league, the UEFA Cup and the FA Cup. I remember them coming to Glasgow to play a pre-season friendly against us in my Rangers days. Some of their players were world class. The names roll off the tongue: Butcher, Osman, Brazil, Wark, Mills, Beattie, Thysen, Muhren. One of the big stars of that team became a good friend to me at Ipswich, Glaswegian and Rangers fanatic John Wark

John and his wife, Suffolk girl Toula, were a great help to Janine and me when we moved to Ipswich. Warkie was a great midfield player. Today he would've been very much in the same bracket as Frank Lampard in terms of his ability to score goals as a midfield player. His penalty-box instinct was like nothing I'd ever seen before. My goal average for a midfielder was pretty good, but the difference between Warkie and me was that he would make three runs into the box, get on the end of three and probably score one or two! Typically I would make six or seven runs into the box and be lucky to get on the end of three and also be lucky to score one! You simply cannot teach or coach the type of goal instinct a player like John Wark possessed.

The writing was on the wall for me as early as my Ipswich debut, when my new manager put me straight on the bench, with little explanation. My immediate interpretation based on how little communication there had been between us since our first meeting? He'd just spent £200,000 on a player used to playing at a much higher levels, yet somehow was only good enough to sit on the bench! Youngster Jason Dozzell was John Duncan's playmaker at the time. Jason was a talented player, all right, who eventually went on to Spurs, but we were similar in style, and perhaps not suited playing together in midfield. It was almost as though John had needed to make a signing to prove something to the fans. Having signed me however, it was as if he didn't know what to do with me. When I did get a start he began playing me wide on the left, a position I hated as I got older, quite simply because I no longer had the legs to get up and down the park the way I had so easily done for Rangers and United. Also, as I was getting older the game was getting faster and faster and much more physical. Young players like Town's Dalian Atkinson typified the new breed of player becoming more prevalent in the game in both Scotland and England: big, powerful and extremely quick.

Even in the odd game when John Duncan did play me in the middle of the park, he mostly wanted the back players to bypass the midfield and launch it long up the park. Only Jim McLean could've made a team out of that Ipswich squad. John Duncan seemed an inexperienced manager at this level of the game, and I think, as a relatively young manager, he was maybe a little out of his depth at Ipswich Town. His type of management was much more suited to lower-league football. Ipswich were a bit like Dundee United. The fans through the Bobby Robson era had been bred on good football.

On one occasion at Fratton Park, in a midweek league game against Portsmouth, Duncan decided to play me in the middle of a midfield four alongside Warkie. On paper it was a good pairing because Warkie was also comfortable on the ball and although his legs had gone he could read the game brilliantly and never got flustered. The conditions that night didn't help as the pitch was dry and crusty and it was windy too. Not long into the first half, Duncan was out of his dugout screaming at me. He didn't want the ball down, he didn't want any touches, all he wanted was the ball one-touched forwards: 'KICK IT, RED-DERS. JUST KICK IT FORWARD.'

I was thinking, 'I've had enough of this SHIT!' The next time the ball came anywhere near me I just deliberately booted it straight into the stand like a rugby player playing for touch, much to the amusement of both sets of supporters, who must've thought at that point I had totally flipped.

Duncan came rushing out of his dugout and I expected him to be roaring words to the effect of 'What the fuck are you playing at!' Instead, unbelievably, he shouted, 'THAT'S IT, REDDERS, WELL DONE, MY SON!'

Warkie and I agreed after the game that we'd played more like Bruce Lee and Jackie Chan than footballers with all the constant high kicks we were doing. Playing in midfield for Ipswich at that time was also a bit like being a plane spotter, where everything of interest is going on over and above your head. The omens were not good for me in that first season at Town. In fact, within weeks of me being there I went to Duncan and basically told him to make up his mind what he wanted from me. To paraphrase: 'Look, John, I am in the process of buying a house and relocating to this part of the world, and you are not exactly giving me good cause to feel I am doing the right thing. Could you please let me know where I stand, as I am not prepared to move to the opposite end of the United kingdom to sit on my arse for a struggling team.' I was thinking that my honesty might have provoked John one way or another into either accepting this was not going to work out, or putting me in the team in my proper position and having the confidence to let me get on with what I could do. Big mistake, as John did neither and I found myself largely out of the team. It was a very frustrating time in my career. Whenever I talk about my time at Ipswich, I usually say it was a great experience apart from only one thing – the football!

Early in 1989, however, John Duncan went out of the box and became the first British manager to sign a player from the former Soviet Union, the player being central defender or sweeper Sergei Baltacha, captain of the former Soviet Union and the great Dynamo Kiev, a player who was a national hero, having played in World Cups, European championships and was part of the great Dynamo team that won the European Cup Winners' Cup. Further, as part of the deal, it was agreed that Ipswich would go to the Soviet Union to play some exhibition matches. This type of transfer was unprecedented. As a publicity stunt it was great PR for Town because it got huge coverage nationally. Things were so different at that time under the old Soviet Union but under new leader Mikhail Gorbachev things were changing.

When Sergei arrived in the UK with his family – including wife Olga, a former Olympic Pentathlete, children Sergei junior and daughter Elena – Sergei's salary apparently had to be paid to the Russian Embassy, who then in turn gave it to Sergei. The family also had to report to the Soviet Embassy regularly and 'officials' would come from London to Ipswich to check their accommodation to make sure they were living within their means. Incredible to think of that time and that communism in the Soviet Union was only a year or two away from crumbling into oblivion.

I felt so sorry for Sergei on his Ipswich debut (Stoke City at home). Like me, he was getting on a bit, although still incredibly fit for his age. Of course, true to fashion, John Duncan again inexplicably did not play Sergei in the very role that had made him a world-class defender. It was as if the publicity of the Baltacha transfer was more important to the club than he was to the team. Subsequently, one of the best sweepers in the world made his debut for a poor Ipswich Town FC playing wide midfield on the right, with me playing wide on the left. In modern football there is no more demanding a role physically than playing wide in midfield. For that reason most modern wide midfield players are very fast and strong runners and, above all, they are young!

Creating width is one the best strategies in football. Without width, it's difficult to get in behind teams and exploit their defences. José Mourinho showed this when he set up his Inter Milan team to take advantage of Barcelona's only weakness, that being a tendency to play more narrow and through the middle as opposed to trying to get round the back of defences from wide play down the flanks. Mourinho obviously encouraged all his defenders to funnel Barcelona's wide attackers in towards the middle, making it very congested, to the point where even the great ball players of Barca struggled to make room and space to create.

In hindsight, it said much about John Duncan's tactics or strategy, putting two of his oldest and least mobile players out in the areas where the highest degree of running power and mobility was required. Unbelievably however, Sergei scored the only goal of the match, but it was also about the only kick of the ball he got in the entire ninety minutes!

It wasn't till I got to really know him, and when he could express himself in English, that he was able to explain what he'd also been thinking that day. In short summation, roughly translated, 'What the fuck have I just let myself in for!'

It's hard, on reflection, to recall a single game that I really enjoyed during my time at Town. It was a shame because Ipswich are a great family club. It's a pity they have never quite been able to recapture something like the standard previously set by the former greats, managed by the late Town and England legend Bobby Robson. Now he was a motivator!

In pre-season 1989 we toured Russia as part of the aforementioned agreement between Kiev and Ipswich, over the signing of Sergei. Again as a PR exercise it was great but in terms of preparation for a new season it was a nightmare. Ukraine at the time was annexed and controlled by Russia as part of the old Soviet Union, was not a place for an English club to prepare for a new season. The travelling conditions were very basic, as was our accommodation, and the most important thing of all for a team in pre-season, the food was very dodgy to say the least!

We had flown from London to Moscow from where we then had to take a train to Kiev, which was a twelve-hour nightmare trip! Eventually when we got to Kiev, Sergei was there to meet us. Our base was in Kiev and from there we flew to most of our scheduled games, via Aeroflot or Russian Airways, which at the time had one of the worst flight-safety records in the world! On one occasion I remember we flew to Lithuania from Kiev. When we were taking off one of the passengers in front of me virtually ended up on his back as his seat literally toppled over as the plane took off. For some obscure reason it had not been bolted down. I have heard of economy class but this was ridiculous! Coming back from the match, the flight captain or pilot decided to participate in the frivolity among some of the tour officials, so we had the frightening situation where he was sitting up the back seemingly enjoying a vodka or two! Meanwhile, there was what appeared to be smoke belching out from somewhere in the galley kitchen or catering area of the plane. No harm done, I think someone had just burnt the toasties!

Nearly all of the squad had food poisoning. I was really ill and lost ten pounds on that trip and it cost me my fitness for the start of that season. No wonder we got off to such a bad start! I don't think this was the place to be going for a pre-season tour, putting it mildly! As pre-season preparation for a club of the status of Ipswich Town FC, intent on gaining promotion to the Premiership, it was poor. Our very loyal fans weren't pleased by our performances on the pitch at the beginning of that season!

My good memories of Ipswich – and there are some good ones – were more to do with the people and the area. Janine and I used to enjoy trawling the antique shops of Long Melford or taking a drive to the delightful villages such as Woodbridge or Lavenham. They are among the most charming villages or small towns you will find in the UK. Suffolk is Constable country and no one has since quite captured the charm and beauty of the area such as the great artist himself.

There was also one other very memorable event. Janine and I celebrated the birth of our first child, Natalie Christina. She was born on 11 October 1989, at 9.05am, eight hours after Janine went into labour. Typical woman, always late!

Having come from the hospital on cloud nine, I was brought back down to earth by having to play for the reserves in the afternoon. On the football front things were not great. I didn't enjoy the travelling aspect of playing in England. Quite often we'd leave for away games on the Friday night. After the match it was straight on the bus and back to Suffolk. The bus was always well stocked with booze and by the time we got back home to Portman Road, there was always a few that were well sozzled. Poor Sergei had no idea what he had let himself in for!

Sergei indeed looked lost in the beginning. It was at this time that we befriended him and his family. The first time Janine and I invited them over for dinner at our place was honestly a struggle, as they spoke very little English, but it was clear they were grateful for the invitation. Sergei's kids, Sergei junior and Elena, were very smitten with our dogs Monty and Sidney and they played with them. Elena was around only four years old and Junior was around seven. Obviously they had both inherited the sporting prowess of their parents. I remember Elena as a very plucky, gutsy kid who got very keen on tennis from a very early age and with her obvious sporting family pedigree it was no surprise to see her eventually become Britain's number one. Her talent and determination were very evident even from such an early age. Unfortunately, Elena appeared to have some bad luck with health problems that perhaps seemed to hold her back from fulfilling all of her undoubted potential.

Occasionally we'd all go round to the Warks' on a Sunday afternoon. I still have some good photos of us all out playing football or cricket in the garden with the kids. This was the good part of being at Portman Road and that town squad were like the League of Nations. We had Frank Yallop and Craig Forrest from Canada, Mich d'Avray from South Africa, Romeo Zonder-van from Holland, Sergei from the Soviet Union and, of course, Warkie and me were the sweatys from Scotland (sweaty socks = Jocks).

On paper we looked like a good enough team but we just didn't gel. I'm not sure our manager, John Duncan, really under-stood the strengths and weaknesses of his players. I can almost guarantee that someone like Jim McLean would've at least got that Town squad into the play-offs. It was also the case that a lot of the players in that squad had peaked and were getting a bit on the mature side. Namely myself, Sergei, Warkie, Mich d'Avary, and Dutch internationalist Romeo Zondervan. Interestingly, Romeo must be one of the very few professional footballers who actually qualified as a pilot during his career as a footballer. He was a typical Dutch player – good technically, comfortable with the ball.

By the end of my second year at Town, John Duncan had at last departed. It came as no surprise. In fact, I think it was a big relief to the club, purely from a professional point of view, of course. I know John; he is a very decent, well-meaning guy, but I just don't think he had the personality required to be a top-grade football manager. He was naturally dour and negative and was not a motivator. To be a good manager I think you must be either a great motivator with strong personality or have exceptional knowledge and understanding of your players.

I think it was clear the pressures of managing a top-level club were beginning to show. I'm sure John too was no doubt hugely disappointed at not doing more for the club.

David Sheepshanks, formerly of the FA, who was the chairman of the club at the time, taking over from Patrick Cobbold of Tolly Cobbold the brewers, was someone I liked and respected and who I think had a good understanding of how to get more out of individuals. With the departure of John Duncan, Ipswich appointed ex-West Ham legendary manager John Lyall. He was well respected in the game and had built his name and reputation at the West Ham United Footballing Academy as a football purist. Or so I thought!

Unfortunately for me, and some others, it seemed Lyall's idea of getting out of the First Division was more akin to the old-fashioned Wimbledon-style kick and rush. It was also thought that Lyall's appointment would be great for Sergei and that he would be given more of a chance to play in a role more suited to him but, surprisingly, Lyall had not long arrived at the club before he decided to let Sergei go. In truth, I could see where Lyall was coming from, it's just that he, like myself, no longer had the legs to play the type of up-tempo, pressing high up the field type of game. It requires fit young legs. The good news was that Lyall decided to give me a chance as a striker because of my performance in a pre-season game at Southend United. He took me aside and told me he liked me as a front player because I could 'frighten people'. Not sure what he meant by that, but okay, fair enough! Anyway, I got my chance as a target man and it paid off, particularly in the early part of that season.

Although I couldn't run any more, I could take the ball in to feet, bring others into the game and get into the box and score goals. Under John Lyall I probably enjoyed my best spell at the club. That's not really saying much, though, and all good things of course come to end and I can put the end of my playing career at Ipswich Town under John Lyall, down to one match and one man.

In the 1990/91 season we were drawn against Southampton away in the fifth round of the FA Cup. In our pre-match tactical team talk Lyall instructed me to mark their young unknown striker. A lad called Shearer, Alan Shearer! I think had Lyall any idea of just how good this young player was going to become I would've got a bit more sympathy. As it turned out, I took the blame for the defeat as Shearer got to the ball before me twice in the penalty box at set plays and converted each time and we were out of the Cup! I reckon I hardly kicked another ball for the club from that day. It was also the first time I had ever seen Matt Le Tissier play at close quarters. He reminded me so much of Morton's big Andy Ritchie – what a talent – but like big Andy he sometimes looked like he played the game at walking pace – that was until he had the ball at his feet!

Actually, I can remember one enjoyable game for Town. It was also an FA Cup tie in 1989 against Brian Clough's Nottingham Forrest. Cloughie was like Wee Jim in many ways. Clough was a great manager who did things his way and who liked his teams to play good football. He very kindly described Dundee United's feat of getting to the final of the UEFA Cup as the greatest relative achievement of any British club. When Cloughie praised you, it meant something! We were beaten 3–0 but it was a game in which I felt at least able to get a touch on the ball and to make passes.

Life at Ipswich Town wasn't very much fun for me after new kid on the block Alan Shearer roasted me in the penalty box at the Dell. From then on I was virtually frozen out and playing with the stiffs [reserves]. For a professional footballer there were few things more depressing than being exiled into the reserves. Nowadays it must be so comforting for the players who earn so much money from their basic weekly salary they don't need to worry financially. When a manager makes it clear you are no longer in his plans you just feel like you are no longer part of the club. The most horrible feeling in the world for me was not being in the first team on a Saturday. It was a horrible conflicting feeling of guilt because on the one hand you want your team-mates to do well and win, but on the other you are hoping they lose because if they are winning then you are not getting back into the team and the manager has proved he is right to have left you out. To put it bluntly, it was a mind fuck!

I got to loath the training at Ipswich because Lyall's weekly training regime was based purely on high pressure, closing down the opposition and tackling. He deliberately set out exercises that would promote aggression and confrontation. I think he believed this was the only way to get the club out of the league, and he could well have been right. This was maybe against the grain of his true philosophy on football but he believed it was what was required for the club at the time. At that stage in my career this was just not for me at all. All this high-tempo, physical stuff was more akin to army training than football.

Unsurprisingly, Sergei also did not fit in to the John Lyall boot camp survival football strategy plan and with his contract coming up at the end of the season it was looking more and more as if he would have to return to Kiev with his family. Sergei had wanted to play as a deep-lying sweeper, typically behind two centre-backs. He was not used to playing in a flat back four and squeezing the opposition back up the park, as this made him vulnerable to the diagonal ball over the top. We would joke sometimes that Sergei liked to play so deep that he suffered from the bends! During this time our families had become good friends. We knew how difficult a time it was for the Baltachas, with trying to fit in and not knowing what was coming at the end of the season. They had few other friends in the UK and were not enjoying the prospect of having to go back to Kiev. Ukraine was still under Russian rule as it was part of the Soviet Union but things were definitely changing.

Not long before the end of the season Sergei was officially informed that his contract was not going to be renewed. Lyall had decided he was not part of his plans for the future. We had grown fond of the Baltacha family and wanted to help. They were in a real predicament because without a contract Sergei could not get a work permit and without a work permit they would have to leave the country. St Johnstone manager Alex Totten, who'd been Jock Wallace's assistant manager at Rangers during my time there, was beginning to get a real name for himself as manager of the new revolutionised St Johnstone FC. Well-known local Perth businessman Geoff Brown owned the club and had not long built a brand new stadium, having sold Muirton Park to developers, and the place soon became an Asda supermarket. Alex had been a hyper, enthusiastic coach under big Jock at Ibrox and a genuinely likeable good guy. His personality, however, was different as a manager. I called him on the phone one day and told him all about the Sergei situation. I told him that he was a great player who'd been totally wasted and played out of position. I explained that his contract was due to expire, the family's predicament and how keen they were to stay in the UK. Alex initially expressed real interest in Sergei and so I managed to persuade chairman Brown and Alex to meet with the player and his family. In his sponsored Lada, Sergei and the family headed north to meet with St Johnstone. Meantime, Janine and I had already headed north to Perthshire for the close season. I had managed to persuade Alex and Geoff to put Sergei up in a hotel for a couple of nights whilst they had the chance to meet and hopefully agree terms. They had of course obviously checked out his pedigree, but apart from that, went purely by my recommendation. In between there were of course the transfer negotiations which included haggling with Geoff over how much Sergei was going to be earning.

Sergei was about to show Geoff Brown that he wasn't the only one who could be hard when it came to negotiations. Geoff had built a reputation for being a tough, no-nonsense, self-made businessman who treated every pound as his prisoner, but when Sergei learned initially what St Johnstone had to offer he was none too pleased. He was, of course, grateful to me for setting the whole thing up but he was not about to sell himself short, even though he was not exactly holding too many aces. Initial discussions and indications from Geoff Brown had been cautious and guarded. Although I was still optimistic, Sergei was a bit peeved at Geoff's initial figures. When we arrived at the stadium for final discussions, Sergei was understandably nervous. He had psyched himself up for what was a crucial meeting for him and his family. I was taken aback though when just as we were about to go into the meeting, he said to me, 'Ian, now you this leave me.' I knew what he meant!

As we sat down I could see Sergei had the hump big time! He was in no mood to be soft-soaped into signing for St Johnstone

304

for peanuts. Sergei basically told Geoff, in his own brand of Russian/English, to pay him a wage that reflected his worth. Geoff Brown was angling initially to get the player on the cheap. After all, in Geoff's eyes, despite Sergei's reputation he was largely unproven in the UK and his work permit was about to run out. Geoff was no mug; he knew held all the aces. Why should St Johnstone pay top money to a player under those circumstances?

Sergei told him to look at his CV, then those steely-blue, piercing Soviet eyes narrowed, locking on their target! 'Okay, now you listen me. Look, I top player. I no second-rate player. You pay me good money, I play for you. I do good job for you. You agree now or I go home Kiev.'

Geoff's expression was like that of a boxer that had just landed his very best punch only to realise it had not inflicted any damage whatsoever to his opponent. It was an education for me just to witness that conversation. The deal was done there and then and, to be fair, Geoff Brown gave Sergei a very good deal, under the circumstances, to play for his up-and-coming St Johnstone. The irony had not escaped me. Here was my new pal from Soviet Russia signing for the first club I ever supported!

I remember Sergei telling me that Olga and the kids were in Kiev at the time of the Chernobyl meltdown in 1986. Elena was not much more than a baby, Junior no more than four or five. Sergei had been away with the Soviet squad somewhere and I think he had known more about it from Western media reports. When he found out what had happened, he called her immediately and told her to tape up all the windows and stay inside. We will never know the true cost of this disaster but there are still families paying the price for radiation fallout today. Chernobyl is only something like 70km from Kiev and I know there are still massive health problems in Ukraine today related to the fallout from one of the world's worst ever nuclear disasters.

The signing of Sergei Baltacha in 1990 was a very big deal for St Johnstone FC. It was only later on when I began going to Kiev on business I discovered just what a big star he was in his homeland.

Janine and I left Sergei and his family to settle in Perth as we headed back south for what would be my last season as an Ipswich Town player. I was glad to play my part in bringing Sergei Baltacha to St Johnstone, where he became a firm favourite of the fans and was Saints' answer to David Narey. I am also glad to say that in hindsight I did my bit for British tennis too!

Meanwhile, for me it was back to the purgatory of a new season at Ipswich under John Lyall. In truth, I was no longer enjoying being a professional footballer. If I'd had the wealth that most people seemed to assume, then I would've retired from playing football there and then. The game was changing so much, you had to be a physical machine that could run and tackle all day long. At one time I could certainly run, and although tackling was never one of my strong points, I never shirked from it. But in truth my legs were gone and at the age of thirty-one I was finished for top-level British football. Maybe if I had got that dream move to Europe, or even to America it would've prolonged my career at the top. The other irony was that all the extra money I was paid in England was basically lost on our property in Ipswich as we sold our house in Scotland just before prices started to rise and bought in England just as prices started to fall. We could not have timed things any worse. At the time prices had fallen by as much as 50 per cent! When we moved to England everyone but everyone told us to get on the housing ladder. Well, we did and when it came to moving back north we couldn't give it away, eventually having to take a massive hit on it. Ironically, from a purely financial point of view, if we had had stayed at Dundee United, we would've ended up much better off.

The last period of my time at Ipswich was particularly miserable. John Lyall had accepted offers for me, giving me the chance to leave, but I felt I should be entitled to some of the transfer fee in view of what Ipswich were being offered and by what I would also be saving the club by being off the wage bill. In short, I wanted the outstanding remainder of my contract paid to me up front before I left. Lyall dug his heels in but stubbornly so did I. Basically it meant I had to tough it out for virtually a whole season till my contract expired as I was frozen out completely by Lyall. It was without doubt the worst period of my whole career.

Fortunately, along came Alex Totten and St Johnstone, who made Ipswich an acceptable offer. It was not long into the start of pre-season in 1990/91. It was such a relief to get away from the nightmare of being surplus to the requirements of John Lyall at Portman Road. It was goodbye Ipswich Town and I was off back to the future to link up with Sergei and finally get the chance to play for the first club I had ever supported when I was a boy.

11

GOING BACK TO MY ROOTS

When I signed for Saints, it was a big thrill for me to think I would be playing for the first club I had ever supported as a kid. Initially it gave me a real boost. Coincidentally, I joined Saints not long after Raymond Stewart had also returned to his native Perthshire. St Johnstone manager Alex Totten had recruited Ray as a player-coach. For me personally it was good to be linking up with Ray again, but even better, I would be getting the chance to link up with Sergei, who was fast achieving legendary status among the St Johnstone fans.

With my new manager I guess the first clue I had that things were not really as they appeared was the first day I signed for the club. I had just come out of his office and had been speaking to some of the reporters who were milling around. Alex, of course, was also present. During the conversation I happened to call him by his first name, as I had always done in the past, and since I had known him so well, I naturally thought nothing of it. However, immediately he pulled me aside and told me that he expected me to call him 'Boss' from now on. At first I thought for a moment he was pulling my leg, but no, he was deadly serious. Had he taken me into his office and explained that he would prefer to be called 'Boss', as that was how the rest of the squad

308

referred to him, then there would've been no concerns at all. I was totally perplexed by it.

There's no doubt that Alex did a great job for Saints, getting them promotion and consolidating the club in the Premier League, but when I joined the club we struggled to improve on our situation. Now there are different ways of looking at that. You could take the view that a provincial club like St Johnstone should not really be expected to be anywhere higher than mid-table in the Premier League. Or you could ask why they were not able to improve when good money was being spent, strengthening the squad. Perhaps one of the reasons he was not quite the same person as he'd been with me at Ibrox was that he perhaps felt insecure in his position as manager. I wonder in hindsight whether he may have been pressured into signing me by club chairman Geoff Brown. Geoff was very much a hands-on chairman and I'm sure if he had an opinion regarding the team, he would not have been shy to air it to his manager.

I think one of the great strengths of good management is the ability to evolutionise but not necessarily revolutionise a club. Alex Ferguson and Jim McLean were great examples of managers who did this in the Eighties in the Scottish game. They were both masters at putting in solid foundations and building from the ground up. Alex Totten had some great success early on but his managerial style was one-dimensional, in my opinion. Taking St Johnstone out of Division One and getting them promoted was a fantastic achievement but instead of looking ahead, I think he was inclined to hold on to the past and not really accept he was in a different arena, an arena that required a different level of player and possibly a different approach to some games.

Getting out of the lower divisions is more about hard work and enthusiasm but that can only ever take you so far. If you look at teams that get promoted, quite often they seem to do well in year one because they are running on sheer adrenalin and enthusiasm because it's all new to them. Once teams get the chance to suss you out, you need to evolve and adapt into a different animal. I think this was the crossroads Alex was at when I arrived at St Johnstone.

As well as the first season had gone for the club back in the Premier League, the second season was not exactly a failure but the signs were that things were beginning to stall. It also appeared that Sergei was being criticised for his style of play. He seemed to be carrying the can for playing too deep and making the game too uncomfortably stretched for Alex and his assistant, Bert Paton. That said, I'm not sure Alex Totten really utilised the experience around him in the dressing room to the best effect.

During my first season at St Johnstone Alex did the unthinkable: he dropped Sergei! Results had not been going well and I am sure he was being pressured more and more by those assisting him into thinking that Sergei was the problem. This was not typical in Scottish football, to play with a traditional sweeper behind two centre-backs. In my opinion, pushing up to the halfway line is fine when you have defenders with real pace who rarely get caught with the ball over the top. But Sergei was a ball-playing defender who liked to make passes from the back and who no longer had the pace required to play this style of system. He was as rare as a dodo in the Scottish game!

The Monday morning after Sergei was dropped, he came to me in the dressing room with a copy of the Scottish *Daily Record*. In huge bold headlines on the back page it said: Baltacha Is Axed. Sergei, however, was still struggling with the language aspect and so wanted me to explain what this meant: 'Eean what is zees ax-edd. What does zees mean?' I of course explained, or tried to as best as I could. When the penny dropped you could immediately see his eyes narrowing. He was furious, because Alex had told him on the Friday before the game that he was 'resting' him. This he had understood! Knowing Sergei as I did, I knew what was coming next. The ex-Soviet was not a man who had any problems with confrontation and so he immediately sought a showdown with Alex.

It was a costly action as it effectively finished him as a first-team player with St Johnstone under Alex and Bertie. Sergei's outburst in their eyes merely vindicated their decision to leave him out. I too had hit the skids with Alex, and for the following match on the next Saturday Sergei and I both found ourselves still in the squad, but when the team was announced, neither of us was even on the bench. We were both sorely hacked off by this and jointly decided we didn't want to hang around and watch the game. We both felt strongly that this was a total injustice and that somehow Alex was being unreasonable, as if he wanted to ostracise the pair of us. There was no hard and fast rule that said players not participating had to stay and watch the game, but obviously it was not the done thing on a Saturday, to leave the stadium immediately after the team and subs were announced! There were some puzzled looks from supporters as Sergei and I made our way out of the stadium but I think we were also both getting to the stage and age where we'd had enough of this type of stuff.

Later that afternoon the word got out that we'd been spotted playing golf on Craigie Hill, a local course in Perth we both lived near to, and from where you could just about see into McDiarmid stadium! In hindsight this was probably not the right thing to do but we were similar creatures. But I'd been through far too much in my career.

I am actually the easiest person in the world to win over. Just give me some space and a bit of respect and I'll give you total commitment and respect in return. Eventually Alex was sacked later that season and it was rumoured that Sergei and I might have been in the running for the job. A couple of days after Alex left I actually called up Geoff Brown and asked him to give Sergei and I a chance to manage the club, at least in the short-term. I think Geoff gave may have given it some serious thought but in the end the job was given to an ex-Rangers teammate and former Irish internationalist John McClelland. But it was clear from the onset that we were both surplus to requirements.

I absolutely hated that second year at St Johnstone under McClelland, because I played only a few first-team games for him. The bitching and backstabbing that went on had to be seen to be believed and frankly I was growing ever more tired of the whole thing. I was much too old for this stuff now!

Without really knowing or properly understanding what my feelings were, I was reaching a crisis point because I knew my playing career was over. Physically my legs had gone for top-level football and mentally I was tired of the pettiness and repetition. I didn't know what I wanted to do, my career was over, as I saw it, and I was looking into a very dark tunnel. I knew I was not going to be part of McClelland's plans for the following season and also knew I didn't want to be. It was the most anxious and depressing time of my life apart from when I lost my brother.

Natalie, my daughter, was around three at this time and my son, Ian junior, was not long born when I finally felt there was something seriously wrong with me. It happened one day when we had gone to the pictures in Perth. Janine and I had taken Natalie to see a movie. Suddenly out of nowhere I had an overwhelming feeling of claustrophobia and my heart began pounding as if it were going to come out of my chest. My breathing also became extremely shallow. I was convinced I was having a heart attack. In fact, what I was really having was an anxiety or panic attack. It was terrifying. I quickly got out of the auditorium and made an excuse of needing the toilet. My underlying anxiety I think is something that has been with me virtually all of my life but it had started to come to the surface and for the first time had begun to manifest itself physically. The feelings of depression were much stronger too. I was not realising that the more anxious and worried I became the more severe the feelings of depression got. My appetite had gone and because I was still having to train every day and not really eating well, I was becoming exhausted physically too. It was getting so bad that it was becoming a huge effort for me just to get out of bed. There were times when I felt so bad that I don't know how I managed to get myself through the day, although it seemed that I felt worse in the mornings and a little better as the day wore on. Finally I decided to go to the doctor to see what he thought. I only ever go to the doctor when there is no alternative. I don't mind the dentist's, but I hate going to the doctor's. I always have.

The doctor, of course, told me what I already knew, that I was suffering from depression and anxiety. He prescribed me some antidepressants by the name of Seroxat and told me to take them daily and that they would not begin to work properly for at least a week or more. The pills he gave me, however, did not help at all; in fact, they made me much worse because I was beginning to lose touch with reality. At times I began hallucinating. It was like my mind started playing tricks on me.

At first it didn't click that it was the prescribed drugs because I genuinely thought I was going completely insane. I was feeling so ill that on the morning of my son Ian junior's christening I could not get out of bed and it took me all the strength I had just to get myself dressed. I scares me even now when I think of it, and may be one of the reasons why I simply refuse to allow myself ever to get into that state again, no matter what! Thankfully I decided that, as things were not getting any better the pills were not working, so I threw them all away. Although I still felt very depressed, at least I felt as if my mind was back to dealing with reality. I believe the problem with many of these drugs is that they are merely a chemical cosh but they don't give you a way back to health; they just keep you chained or trapped inside a mental maze. I believe anyone can come back from depression if the will to do so is there.

I am not in the position to advise anyone in a medical sense when it comes to depression, but what I would say is that taking antidepressant drugs was a disaster for me. Had I continued to take them, I'm not sure I would here today to relate my story. It actually scares me to think back to some of the very dark recesses my mind was in during this very difficult time of my life. The best thing that happened to me was going to see a psychologist. After two or three sessions of just talking everything through, I at least began to be able to focus my mind on wanting to get better. This was the turning point for me but it was a long haul because I reckon that from that last period of my contract with St Johnstone till at least another couple of years, I was more or less feeling very depressed all the time, with very little respite. I knew I had to find something to do to at least give me a reason to get out of bed in the morning, and whether or not it was divine intervention, something did come up and it proved to be the catalyst for me getting out of the very black hole my mind was in.

The phone rang one morning. It was Hugh Campbell Adamson, Chairman of Brechin City. He asked me if I would be interested in putting my hat into the ring for the vacant managerial post. Having not long gained my Advanced English FA coaching licence, it was a chance to go into management, albeit pretty much at the bottom of the ladder. I was not sure management was what I wanted but it was a job and opportunity to at least get on the ladder.

And so another chapter was about to begin!

12

BRECHIN UP WAS SO HARD TO DO

Not long before I accepted to the post of player-manager at Brechin City I was persuaded to take up an open invitation, along with my father-in-law, from my very good friend from Pawtucket, Rhode Island, Fred Andrews and his wife, Sheila. Janine and I had befriended them whilst holidaying in Bermuda in 1988. Fred had also become fond of Janine's dad and we all had fishing in common. Having been over to Scotland as my guest on our family stretch of the River Tay at Birnam Dunkeld, called the Newtyle beat, and also for the christening of my son Ian, Fred had promised to reciprocate and show us some good fishing, USA style. Now I was not feeling good at all but thought if anything it might help to dig me out of the black hole I was in.

One thing I had started to do, mainly since that terrifying experience of the panic attack, to the point of obsession, was to take my own pulse. I had managed to convince myself there was something wrong with my heart. So when it came time to go to the States, I was still in a right old state myself. But I began to check my pulse rate about every five minutes. I was being completely irrational in thinking I was heading for a heart attack. But this was all part of the anxiety side of my depression. These feelings were new to me and as yet, having not been to see anyone,

I was not able to understand what was really happening. In fact, I didn't realise at this time, but in truth I was heading towards a nervous breakdown.

When we got to the States I was still feeling very uptight and the more uptight I got, the more I would check my pulse, and the more I would check my pulse, the faster my heart rate seemed to want to go. I'm sure Fred and Sheila could see I was not myself, but they didn't say anything.

The whole thing came to a head again when Fred took Luigi and me to a shopping mall in Pawtucket. Suddenly I again felt as if my heart was going to come out of my chest, and I felt what I can only deduce was a massive rush of adrenalin going through my body. It was nature's fight-or-flight mechanism kicking in. My heart was pounding like crazy and again I was thinking I was having a heart attack. In fact, what I was having was another panic attack. I told Fred and Luigi I wanted to go to hospital because I was convinced I was going to die! Fred and Luigi were both very concerned and so we got to Fred's car and they rushed me to A&E in the Pawtucket General Hospital. There they wired me up and did a whole load of tests and, of course, diagnosed that this had been a stress or panic attack. After monitoring me they just gave me some chill pills called Ativan (from memory) and told me I'd be fine.

That evening we had been invited next door to Fred and Sheila's neighbours for a barbeque and it was so funny because within a few drinks, on top of the pills, I was wired to the moon – so much so that nobody could get me off the karaoke all night. God knows what Fred and Sheila's neighbours must've thought of me! Luigi was amazed, as he never thought I could sing ... well, I can't really, but I was sure as hell giving it my best shot and not giving a damn about anything. Actually, it was a great feeling, but like all great feelings, they don't last too long! I seemed to go through the remainder of my American holiday on autopilot.

Not long after I had got back from being a state in the States, I got that call from Brechin City Chairman Hugh Campbell Adamson. I was obviously not overly enthused and not really in a very good mental state but thought I really needed something to stop me from becoming more and more depressed. I think my initial core anxiety and depression had come from the tragic events and subsequent circumstances of my childhood. There were still many unresolved issues or baggage I had been carrying around for too many years. The insecurities I was feeling relating to my career were superficial in comparison to the very deep psychological seismic shifts I had experienced early on in my life. But still, worryingly enough, my football career as a top player was at an end, or so I thought, and I had a wife and two young children and basically no idea what I was going to do.

With the benefit of both hindsight and experience, the best way to tackle depression is not with drugs but a change of outlook and the psychological and metaphorical moving of the goal posts. In talking to a professional this was where I obtained the mental tools to begin not necessarily to cure myself but to be able to realise that though you may never completely get over mental trauma, you most certainly can learn to accept and learn to live with the many negative thoughts and feelings. By setting daily goals, giving myself self a pat on the back for simply just getting through the day, and trying to keep my mind in the present as much as I could, I kept telling myself no matter how badly I was feeling I was capable of turning things round and getting well again. I am so glad I made the decision to stop taking the antidepressant drugs because I think when you are in this state you need to be able to at least see the way back. With the drugs my mind was just a fog of confusion, and I could feel myself losing touch with reality. Sooner or later if your willpower is strong enough, you can beat it, but it takes real determination to overcome something that preys on those very things you need to beat it. In summation, quite literally all it took from me was just the sheer will to fight on and want to get better.

With nothing else in the offing, I took the job at Brechin City as player-manager in succession to John Ritchie, who had just got the club promoted to the First Division. I knew it would be a difficult task for such a small part-time club to survive in the First Division, but I didn't think I really had much to lose! What I wasn't told by the 'committee' was how little the club were able to give me in terms of money to buy players. I was literally being outbid by junior clubs, who could not only pay larger transfer fees, but were also paying players more in wages.

During the early days of that first season in charge, when I played for and also managed Brechin City, I barely knew what day it was I was so deeply depressed. How I got through some of the games I just do not know, but without that spell at Brechin City it may have got even harder to drag myself away from the darkness and, believe me, I was in a very dark place for a long period at this stage of my life. I'm not really sure what the committee and supporters of Brechin City were expecting from me, but in reality just managing to stay sane and in the league would've been a huge achievement for me. Thankfully I eventually achieved one of these goals, the most important one to me!

Looking back, the whole thing was a good experience and I had enjoyed the aspect of working with the players who I thought on the whole responded well to what I was trying to do. There were some, though, who preferred the previous lump-it-forward style and my second in command, John Young, had been part of the system. I got the distinct feeling John was not really in favour of the tactical changes I was trying to make towards playing entertaining football. But I told him we'd be playing football and not kick-and-rush, no matter what he thought. John was a decent enough guy but I never thought he was convinced. John was old school, just get it over the halfway line then push the defence right up as quickly as possible.

I was unlucky, because had I been able to find a goal-scoring striker I'm sure we could've survived in that league, against all the odds. Typically as a team we enjoyed lots of possession with good movement, relative to our standard, but without being able to convert the chances we always created. Winning the hearts and minds of part-timers who were not used to being asked to make a pass was also initially a problem. The players had been loyal to the previous manager, who had got them promotion, and understandably some were sceptical about the changes I was trying to instil on the pitch. Encouragingly for me, Ian Archer of the Glasgow *Evening Times* wrote on 1 March 1994 after we had played St Mirren: 'St Mirren looked decidedly average, but here's a thing: Brechin City, slap-bang bottom of the First Division, were an absolute credit to the Scottish game and it was a treat to watch them. They passed the ball as best they could. They even had a couple of players who liked to linger on it and caress it. Ian Redford, their player-manager, deserves to move on to bigger things.'

I cannot move on from this brief period of my career without mentioning one of the most embarrassing things ever to happen to me in football. It was at the start of pre-season in my second season with Brechin. I arranged through my coaching staff to do a fifteen-mile cross-country hike over Glen Clova. We all departed on the team bus to our starting point. The bus then dropped us off, and carried on to our finishing point, which was in the car park of a local hotel on the other side of the mountain. I had even recruited some of the local Brechin Road Runners

320

Society to act as our guides to ensure that no one would get lost. One of the guides was to stay with the leaders whilst the other one would stay at the rear, ensuring to pick up all the stragglers who would otherwise never find their way home on this incredible journey! About the only thing we didn't plan for was what happened next.

Club captain Bobby Brown and I had settled into a nice, good-going pace about fifty yards back from the leaders, with all the stragglers picking up the rear maybe 100 yards or so behind us. About an hour or so into the run, we had got to the top of the mountain and could clearly see the front runners not far ahead. Within seconds, however – and I mean seconds – the mist came down and I couldn't even see Bobby, who was literally standing beside me. In no time at all Bobby and I had no idea where we were and had begun to wander around, not having a clue where to go. Eventually we stumbled onto a stream and I decided it would be best to follow the stream downhill and get off the mountain ASAP, if we could.

Eventually we came to a track and found a small concrete shelter. It was beginning to get cold and we had long since stopped sweating, so shelter at that point was the best option! Well, we sat for hours waiting for that bloody fog to clear – however, not before the alarm had been raised and the mountain rescue team had been scrambled. It was as if Bobby and I had been abducted by a UFO. We simply vanished in the mist. Later on, by the time the mist had cleared, we found and followed a path down the mountain and eventually came across a couple of campers, who very thankfully offered to drive us to the safety of civilisation. Well, the next training session went down very well, when I was presented with a compass by John and the boys. Hmmm, I wonder how many managers have been able to say they managed to successfully lose themselves during a pre-season run!

The last straw for me at Brechin came not long after the start of that season and after a very heavy home defeat by Hamilton. I just felt I was on a hiding to nothing, and without any money to improve the squad things would not get any better with what we had, so I resigned. Maybe I should've stuck it out longer at Brechin and if I had maybe I would've found a bottom then bounced back from there.

Luckily for me, literally within days of my leaving Brechin City, I got a call from Raith Rovers manager Jimmy Nicholl. Jimmy, an old teammate at Rangers, had been pulling up trees with his bare hands at Raith. He offered me a cameo role for the rest of the season and also signed up Dundee United legend Davie Narey. Davie and I, of course, played together for three seasons at Dundee United and I knew him really well. In all honesty, though, I did not really enjoy being a bit-part player, even though the club were enjoying their best ever period. That season at Raith Rovers culminated in them winning both the First Division and League Cup. What an achievement for such a small club. Jimmy Nic did a fantastic job at that club and it will never be forgotten.

The League Cup final was very ironic for me for two reasons. The first was because it was played at Ibrox, my home as a footballer for Rangers for nearly six years, and the second was because our opponents were Celtic, the old arch-enemy. Celtic were managed at the time by Tommy Burns, and he had them playing beautiful football, in the tradition of how the Celtic supporters always want their team to play. But unfortunately for Tam, at the time they did not have a great cutting edge and were also being out-gunned in every department by a much more affluent and cash-rich Rangers. Well, it was years ago – how things change!

I started on the bench and don't remember too much about

the game apart from ex-Ger Gordon Dalziel scoring and Celtic equalising and the game going to extra-time. I came off the bench during extra-time but to no avail, as the game went from extra-time into penalty kicks to decide the winners. As a former penalty-kick taker this should not really have fazed me, but as I was not nominated as one of the five who would initially be designated as takers, I didn't relish the idea of being called upon. Remarkably, though, after each side had gone through their nominated five penalty takers, it was still all-square and went to sudden death!

I was now crapping myself, as for some reason I just did not fancy this situation one little bit. I think there were another two kicks taken before it was the turn of Celtic legend and superstar Paul McStay, after which it was to be me. Now, as anyone who knows Paul will probably tell you, he is a very hard man to dislike or wish ill of, but at that moment I wanted him to miss that kick more than anything in the world. Sure enough, Paul obliged and did exactly that; he missed the target and saved me the ordeal of another do-or-die Cup final penalty, in which my previous record was: one taken, one missed!

As a teenaged kid playing for Dundee, I would've grabbed the ball off anyone and stuck it in the back of the net without too much fuss. But after twenty years of being a pro and in the frame of mind I was in, I was no longer that young, self-assured player that I eventually became at Dundee. The rest is history but that late appearance for Raith Rovers was to be my very last appearance as a professional footballer. I'd had enough, I was beginning to feel better mentally again and I knew it was time to make the break from the playing/coaching/managing side of the game. One thing that did disappoint me was that Jimmy never used me as a coach or even as someone to help out with the younger players. I felt I did have a lot to offer.

Anyway, for me it was time to move on and seek new opportunities and it was with this in mind that I decided to qualify to become an official FIFA players' agent. Football agents were beginning to become more and more involved in professional football. There were already more than a few on the go but I felt that as an ex-player and qualified coach who had plenty of experience in the business, I would be well suited to advise younger players. Another new chapter was opening up but I hadn't factored in that I was about to be dealing with the Eastern European mafia!

13

FROM UKRAINE WITH LOVE!

Now that my playing career and brief foray into management were over, it was back to the big question of where do I go from here? At this time, players' agents were beginning to become prominent in the game. Governing body FIFA decided it had got to the stage where it needed to be regulated and so they made it that you had to apply to them to become an agent and, if successful, you were granted a licence to be a fully qualified FIFA players' agent. Mainly it involved posting a financial guarantee to the equivalent of 100,000 Swiss francs. Taking my own experiences into account and realising that more and more money was beginning to come into the game, it therefore seemed obvious to me that there could be an opportunity for me as an ex-professional player to get involved on the business side of football.

By this time Sergei had also come out of the game and was looking for something to do to generate an income. On 4 October 1993, Sergei and I sat together in his lounge and watched as the tanks shelled the Moscow White House. As president of Russia Boris Yeltsin used force to dissolve the Russian parliament, Sergei and I concluded this would be a time of opportunity for business in Russia and Ukraine and Eastern Europe generally. 'Coincidentally', not long after this Sergei was visited by an old acquaintance from Kiev who told him, 'I'm rich beyond my wildest dreams.' He had whetted Sergei's appetite by telling him about all the opportunities that were opening up in Kiev.

Sergei then went off to the Ukraine to try and find a way of continuing to support Olga and the kids. It was a very difficult time for him too because they had become settled in the UK and I don't think he and Olga wanted to go back to Ukraine at the time. Elena and Sergei junior had got used to life in Scotland and it would've been much harder for them to go back. It was being touted that Eastern Europe was the new frontier, like the Wild West had been. Typically, though, by the time we were all reading about it in the newspapers, the big stuff had already been sewn up, leaving the crumbs to the small prospector.

Having been away for a few months, Sergei contacted me and told me he wanted me to come and meet with his 'friend', who was apparently pulling all sorts of strings in Kiev. Naively I thought it would be a great chance to maybe meet up with some players Sergei could introduce me to and we could begin to do some football business. What I didn't know or understand is that things just don't work like that in Eastern Europe! However, it was in November 1995 that I embarked on my first trip to Kiev to meet up with Sergei and his contacts to see what potential openings there were. There were not too many licensed FIFA agents in Eastern Europe so I thought this would be a good chance. It's funny, the things you remember, but I was sitting beside an American chap on the KLM Amsterdam/Kiev flight. He never said anything to me the whole flight but as we landed at Boryspil Airport and were taxiing up the runway, he turned to me and said, 'Welcome to hell.'

Sergei was at the airport to meet me and take me to the apartment that he had been renting in one of the more upmarket areas of the city. It was good to see him again and on the first night he had some of his old Dynamo friends round and we drank vodka and I got very drunk. A sign of things to come perhaps! The next morning, feeling quite hung over, it quickly dawned on me that I was in a new world altogether, as when Sergei got out to his car, he began checking underneath for explosives ... what's all that about, I thought.

Initially Sergei had managed to get himself some work in coaching, with a local professional Second Division club. When I first arrived, he took me along to the training to meet with some players and staff. He introduced me as his friend and a FIFA licensed players' agent. The officials of the club indicated that they were keen to work with me. They wanted someone to represent them in Europe when it came to marketing, sourcing and selling players. This was my first agreement with a club as a FIFA agent. It was never going to be a money-spinner but at least it was a start of sorts. A couple of very promising young Dynamo Kiev players had been there on loan, and they were also showing real interest in me becoming their agent. They had dreams of playing for big clubs in the UK and saw me as the possible conduit, but as soon as the Dynamo Kiev president got wind of this he refused to allow the players to work with me. He was the boss!

My first meeting with the acquaintance who'd visited Sergei in the UK was an experience I have never forgotten. They had agreed we would meet at a hotel in the centre of Kiev. The hotel was, in fact, owned by this guy. Sergei and I were a bit early and so we sat outside in the car, parked on the street and waited for him to arrive. Sergei had a driver, an ex-Afghanistan War veteran called Petrovic, or Peter. He sat behind the wheel, with Sergei and me in the back. Suddenly we were aware of a huge limo with blacked-out windows breezing past us then pulling into park just in front of us.

Two doors quickly opened and out got two bodyguards,

armed with machine guns. They seemed to be in a high state of alert as they were obviously checking out the windows of the buildings across the street. They were also checking out other parked cars. They looked to me like they were ex-military, as they were both fit and athletic-looking. Sergei's 'friend' then emerged onto the street. We then got out of the car and went over towards him. The armed bodyguards acknowledged Sergei and were very suspiciously looking me up and down.

Sergei then introduced me to his contact. I can honestly say I don't think I have ever felt more uncomfortable in my life. His stare was very hostile and threatening. This was no friendly welcome to Kiev, matey! As we all made our way into the lobby of the hotel, the guards were running ahead, checking out every-thing in front of us. Eventually we got upstairs and I was shown my new accommodation. This was where I was to be staying in Kiev from now on, and I had little to no choice in the matter! The meeting itself was more of a general discussion to see if there were any areas where we could be of mutual benefit and to explore areas of trade potential. There were no specifics on the agenda.

When the meeting was over I was left wondering what it was all about. His 'friend' I felt was not really serious and gave me the impression he was just paying Sergei lip service. From the look of this guy I wasn't sure if he would be very interested in buying whatever it was I had to sell anyway. He did own some supermarkets, though, and it was agreed that I would try to source some UK products that would be of interest. At that time in particular, drinking water was a big issue in Kiev, mainly due to the pollution and after-effects of Chernobyl.

To me this seemed like a logical opportunity. Eventually we did manage to supply his chain of supermarkets with some containers of tinned foods and bottled water, sourced from a

328

Welsh spring! Nothing but nothing was easy, though, and there was always a hiccup or two in trying to get basic goods into the country. It seemed the tariff goal posts moved every other week, and it got to the stage where there was not much profit to be had from one container load. We really needed to ramp up the volumes to make it worthwhile.

After my initial visit to Kiev, I decided to form a company specifically for the purpose of Ukrainian business. I knew I needed to find someone in the UK who had some experience of doing business there. Eventually Sergei and I found someone and made him commercial director of our newly formed company. It was agreed I would return to Kiev with him to progress initial discussions and try to establish some business with Ukrainian companies. So I returned to Kiev with Terry Jones, our new commercial director. Sergei and I were expecting a go-getter and were optimistic given his supposed contacts. With Terry installed, we thought we had all the right ingredients in place. One of the big problems was trying to sift out the genuine business contacts from the ones who just promised everything but delivered nothing. We once had a meeting with a so-called serious businessman who turned up dressed in a Scooby Doo jersey! It was hilarious, all through the meeting I kept singing in my head 'Scooby, Scooby Doo, where are you ...' But then on the opposite side of the scale, we were told about another big company who'd heard Baltacha was in town and wanted to meet us for a general discussion. They were big metal dealers. Unknown to me at the time, metals are one of the biggest mafia commodities in Ukraine and Russia. People were known to be 'offed' when it came to metals. But Terry was confident he had the contacts to be able to do metals business.

On a bitterly cold, damp Kiev afternoon, Peter drove us through the streets of the city to an address on the outskirts.

Terry, along with his interpreter from Moscow, Tanya, Sergei and myself, were all in the car huddled together. We eventually arrived at a very dark, desolate-looking apartment block with no streetlights on outside it. Peter parked the car and we headed inside the building in pitch darkness. I was wondering what on earth was going to happen next!

As we all got to the top of one of the flights of stairs, Peter knocked on a door. Suddenly a slit opened and we saw some light. Something in Ukrainian was mumbled and then the door opened. To my utter amazement, inside was completely like a scene out of a James Bond movie. There were crystal chandeliers, luxurious leather settees, antique furnishings – it was totally surreal. Just inside the entrance of the door stood a waiter dressed in white jacket and white gloves. He was holding a tray of drinks. They were the most luxurious-looking lead crystal glasses of whisky I had ever seen. We were then shown through the lobby into a very plush office suite and were seated around a big oak table. Peter said quietly to me that the reason we were handed the drinks upon entry was so that they would take our fingerprints from the glass. He was deadly serious – what?!

After a few minutes the big boss came through and immediately recognised Sergei. We all sat down round the table but all talk was in Russian. Terry and I could not understand anything that was being said.

As commercial director, Terry, through Tanya our interpreter, went on to tell this guy all the things we were capable of doing and to me it just seemed like pure fantasy. I did understand the bit at the end when Tanya repeated the warning we were given about not to try to do anything that would interfere with this company's business. The threat was as menacing as it was real. In hindsight I think Terry was out of his depth. In reality we were never going to be able to compete in the traded metals business,

330

as it was sewn up and controlled by big mafia-type organisations. After all, that is where the big money was: aluminium and steel.

On the last night before Terry, Sergei and I were all due to fly back to the UK from Kiev, an important meeting was set up for us with a supposed very influential character. His name, funnily enough, was also Sergei. I called him Big Sergei, to differentiate between him and our Baltacha Sergei! It was becoming quite confusing! Big Sergei was apparently in charge of security at Boryspil Airport. He was up for business, that was quite clear, but the only thing that was not so clear in my mind was exactly what kind of business was he up for! The meeting had gone well, with lots of the usual promises of 'I can do anything and I can get anything.'

Afterwards, Big Sergei informed us that he would arrange to pick us up and take us to the airport the next day, and so he did, in his big top-of-the-range BMW. I have never breezed through an airport as easily as I did that day at Boryspil. Big Sergei was indeed the man, or so it appeared!

One area that we were trying to get into was the exportation of chemicals for the plastics industry. Terry knew someone who apparently advised there was a big market for this type of stuff in Europe. Between us we managed to agree to buy twenty metric tons of adipic acid from Big Sergei, as he knew the factory owners and was able to 'negotiate' a cheap deal on the initial twenty-ton order. Adipic acid is used as a monomer for the production of nylon. It is quite a common material and relatively non-toxic. The plan was to buy from Big Sergei at discount, ship the goods into Rotterdam and sell it on for a profit.

Well, it all seemed like a great idea at the time and when we again returned to Kiev, the big man had instructed us that we would be picked up from the plane, would bypass security and

331

be taken straight out into the arrivals hall. For some strange reason, however, that just didn't happen and so we headed with all the rest of the punters through the normal channels of entry. When we got out to the arrivals hall the big man was not a happy bunny. He wanted to know why we had taken so long. When he was told that in actual fact no one had come to escort us off the plane, he was totally embarrassed and mortified by the whole thing, as he had lost face. It didn't take him long to gain the upper hand again, though. He got hold of the nearest female security guard and absolutely tore her to shreds – in Ukrainian, of course, but it didn't take a language expert to realise this girl was getting the verbal beating of a lifetime. In fact, according to our Sergei B, her only crime was that she happened to be near Big Sergei at the time of his embarrassment!

Eventually we sorted out all the details about the arrangements for our shipment and it was agreed that we would pay Big Sergei for the goods, including his commission, as soon as we were in receipt of funds at the other end from our buyer. Now there really were periods when I wished I was back on the football field, and this was one of them! The good news was that our goods hit Rotterdam as per schedule. The bad news was Terry, having assured us everything was 'all sorted', still had no buyer for the goods and we were left holding twenty tons of adipic acid in the port of Rotterdam. Worse still, Big Sergei was getting twitchy and wanted his cash. This was fair enough but until we got the goods sold we didn't have the cash to give him. Patience was not one of Big Sergei's strong points, and I am so glad that all these problems did not really begin to materialise when we were still in Kiev. I somehow think getting through that airport and on to the sanctuary of a KLM or BA flight would suddenly not have been as straightforward. Ukrainians or Russians can go from being your best friend to your worst enemy

332

in a heartbeat. You are either loved or hated with little room for anything in between!

The days were going by and back home in the UK Terry still couldn't source a buyer for the goods. It was all getting too much for the big man back in Kiev, and it subsequently came to a head when the phone rang at the side of my bed at about two o'clock one morning. It was Sergei B, and he was talking very quickly in his broken Scottish-Ukrainian dialect. He seemed agitated and said something along the lines of: 'Eeyan, Eeyan. I need talk with you. It's Big Sergei. I ceenk he want treat us now.'

Well my first thought was that it was a very strange time to be calling me just to tell me that the big man back in Kiev wanted to treat us to something! Being that time of the morning, it wasn't till the fog in my brain began to clear before I realised that Big Sergei was now threatening us! This was all getting out of hand and I was beginning to think that this Eastern European venture was not all it was cracked up to be! Sergei Baltacha quickly decided that he needed to go back to the Ukraine to sort this out, once and for all. Quite honestly I for one was not really feeling like jumping on a plane and heading out to Kiev for a showdown with Big Sergei, who had just turned psycho, and I most certainly did not want him to be the first person greeting me at any airport upon my arrival!

Sergei Baltacha was a different kettle of fish, though, and being the well-known sports star he was, he had enough connections to ensure this would be no one-sided battle. Apparently it had got very heated between Big Sergei and Sergei Baltahca in an office somewhere in downtown Kiev. I know Sergei always carried a firearm with him for protection when he was in Kiev. Eventually, though, we managed to calm the big man's fears by assuring him we'd get a buyer for the goods. I think the problem was he had over-extended himself with the factory owners and maybe he wasn't quite as powerful as he led us to believe! Possibly his balls were being squeezed on the other side, if you know what I mean. Terry did get the goods sold in the end but we had to take a loss on the material to get it away quickly. Lesson learned. Peace resumed. Not sure where Quentin Tarantino got his ideas from but, let me tell you, there was an untapped well for him in Ukraine.

Without doubt, though, the most gruesome experience of my time in Kiev was when Sergei Baltacha went to the offices of the initial contact that we were supplying with tinned foods and bottled water. Apart from supermarkets, he had many other businesses in Kiev. He had a large head office in central Kiev, which was patrolled with armed security guards. This place was like Fort Knox! One morning Sergei had gone to his office headquarters. In the reception area there were some police officials milling around, and there were big pools of blood all over the floor. It turned out there had been an armed robbery. Two guards had been murdered, having been first drugged with laced vodka. Two rogue security men posing as shift workers had offered to share some vodka before taking the over murdered pair's shift. This had been a horrendously brutal and callous slaying of two security guards just doing their job. This experience brought home to me the potential dangers of doing business in Ukraine or Russia. It was maybe opening up to the West for business but it was a dangerous environment and you had to be very careful about who you got involved with.

In terms of making money, the Ukrainian venture was not going anywhere, as Sergei and I really were just two ex-footballers trying to do something neither of us we were really properly qualified to do. Having said that, doing business abroad is very difficult, even for those who are experienced and qualified. It is all about the right contacts. Terry, who we had hired as our commercial director, turned out to be pretty ineffective, as he was always very long on promises but short on results. It came to the point where I basically told Terry he had to go. He was just not able to come up with the goods and deliver commercially as promised. Meantime, Sergei and I had found some other contacts who we thought would be better and more experienced when it came to actually getting something done. The new partners, one from Hong Kong and the other from Indonesia, were both established and based in the UK. They had good contacts and were looking to gain access to the Ukrainian market. They agreed to put additional funds into the business to give us the best chance of being able to get things properly off the ground.

One of the new partners, Azir, had agreed to spend time in Kiev with Sergei, whilst I was to be based more often than not at home and working on organising the supply of goods from the UK. The other new partner, Nigel, was more of a silent partner and investor in the new business set-up. Things were slow to start but began to pick up a bit and we were doing some regular but small shipments. After a few months I agreed to go to Kiev for a two-week period to run the office in the absence of Sergei and Azir, who came back to the UK for a break. I had just arrived in Kiev and immediately was about to be given a baptism of fire!

The telephone rang in our office and I was quite literally summoned to the offices of the son of ex-president of Ukraine Leonid Kravchuk, the same Kravchuk who not too long before leaving office as president signed an agreement with the Russian president at the time, Mikhail Gorbachev. They decided to refrain from pointing nukes at each other, as there had been much tension since the break-up of the Soviet Union. I think Russia still very much saw Ukraine as its bitch and did not take kindly to the independent streak Ukraine had shown since the Soviet Union broke up. There was, of course, all the added

335

complications of who owned what. It was a bit like a couple split-
ting up and arguing over who owned the Celine Dion CDs and
who got to keep the cat!

Kravchuk junior wanted to know why his delivery of a container load of water was still lying in the port of St Petersburg.
The fact that I was a long way from home and Junior had a body-
guard that looked like he could crush golf balls with his teeth
meant I hadn't the heart, the courage nor the inclination to tell
him it had frozen solid in the port and was probably the biggest
ice cube the world had ever seen! He was none too pleased as
I went on to explain that, as he had insisted, the goods were
shipped via St Petersburg as opposed to the much milder and
further south, Odessa. It was not actually our fault. I left Kravchuk's office thinking, 'Crikey, am I now about to be gunned
down in the street or what?!' At this point I was already contemplating a taxi to the airport. 'Get me out of here . . . now!'

Those two weeks in Kiev were about the longest I have ever
spent. One of the highlights was when one of our customers,
another Sergei (funnily enough), who worked for our biggest
customer, invited me to play five-a-side football with his friends
on a Saturday morning. He also invited me to his flat to meet
his family and have dinner. I must admit, it did help to take my
mind off things!

Ukrainian hospitality really can be second to none. Initially I
took badly with all the vodka toasts at the dinner table. Sergei
and I were invited to dinner a lot, mainly by friends and potential business associates. I think part of the tactics of the potential
business partners were to get you drunk, then get you to make
a commitment to do something, or agree to something that
maybe you wouldn't otherwise do when you were sober! The
hospitality in Kiev, generally though, was hard to beat. There
was always far more food and drink on the table than you could

possibly consume. Even though effort was never a problem on my part!

When you are invited to dinner at someone's home in Ukraine, the food is laid out all over the table and normally there are lots of different dishes to try. It is viewed as good manners to lift whatever it is you intend to eat and sniff it loudly then exclaim that it smells really good! Typically it's the done thing for the host to make the first vodka toast, then the toast moves to the next person at the table and so on until you have gone right round the table. Only to begin the second lap and more! It's not the done thing to turn your nose up at something on the table, so you eat everything and pretend you like everything, even although you can feel your stomach churning at something you don't quite fancy.

The food I could handle, as most of the time it was delicious and I love to try all sorts of different foods when I am abroad. The vodka I could also handle in moderation, but the food and the copious amounts of vodka combined I could not handle. There were a couple of nights, especially in the beginning, when I spent the whole night literally hugging the toilet being violently sick. I was just not used to eating and drinking as much, both at the same time.

There was only one dish that used to make my stomach churn. It was called *piremeni* or what I would call 'floppys'. It was not so much the way they looked but rather the squelchy noise they made as you scooped them out of the dish. They were probably the Ukrainian version of ravioli. Having said all that, the food generally was wonderful so there was no way I was ever going to starve!

When I was on my own in Kiev, Sergei gave me the use of his flat for the two-week period. His mum would come round in the mornings after I had left for the office to cook me some dinner, all I had to do was reheat it when I came back from the office in the evening. It was dark when I got up in the morning. Dark on the way to the office. Dark in the office. Dark when I left the office. Not to mention dark when I went to bed – great if you were a vampire!

The best feeling in the world was when I stepped onto that homeward-bound plane knowing I had survived the two weeks. The beers on that flight home from Kiev never tasted so good. It's not that Kiev is not a nice place – actually, it is an amazing city – but when you are trying to do business there and money is involved, tension and stress are never far away.

By the end of those two weeks I had seen enough to convince myself that my efforts were not going to bear any fruit. We were essentially about three years too late to be doing what we were trying to do because the market was practically all sewn up. I went to Nigel and told him I thought we were wasting our time and that I just couldn't see any progress being made. Not long after this, Nigel and I split from Sergei and Azir. They wanted to continue on with the business. Nigel and I wanted out. In the end I got out without losing any money but I certainly did not have much to show for the all the stress and effort! It was like chasing the pot of gold at the end of the rainbow. All promises of wealth and success, when in reality big opportunity just didn't exist for small-timers like us. We just didn't seem to connect with the right people, or maybe even the wrong people, who genuinely were able to get things done! If I had received a pound coin for every time I heard the phrase 'no problem' or 'it's all sorted', I would not have needed to try and sell anything. I had no other option other than to put it all down to experience and move on.

Sadly, Sergei and Olga drifted apart and were headed for divorce. Sergei junior I think stayed in Scotland, but in any case, we began to lose touch with all of them. Our families had some great times together in those early days but, as always, life moves on and nothing stays the same. So, having withdrawn from the business in Eastern Europe, I decided and try to focus solely on becoming a successful FIFA licensed players' agent.

14

MY LIFE AS A FIFA LICENSED AGENT

Apart from the agreement I had with the Ukrainian Second Division side which, unsurprisingly, came to nothing, I had never really utilised my FIFA agents' licence for a year or so from when I first received it. I knew there were opportunities in professional football for players' agents even though as a player myself I never had any real experience of using one, except for when I gave pioneering football agent Bill McMurdo a whole load of my football videotapes to use as marketing tool. Incidentally, I never saw them again! There were very few players' agents around in the early Eighties but Bill McMurdo was one of the first.

Not long after the Bosman ruling, players had much more say and freedom with regard to what they could do when their existing contractual obligations were fulfilled. Not surprisingly, this led to an immediate upsurge in the amount of activity of agents within the game. Literally there were FIFA licensed players' agents springing up from all over the place. But with the Ukrainian business venture at an end, I decided to try and focus all my attentions on utilising my experience, knowledge and contacts in football.

I think, as in any business, initially you do need a bit of luck or something positive to happen to get the ball rolling. Fortunately

340

for me, my first real breakthrough came within twelve months of deciding to throw my lot into the agency business. Initially it was all about making contacts and I had managed to get myself in touch with a Liberian national living in America who was an associate of George Weah, the former Liberian internationalist and also former World Player of the Year. My Liberian contact, Emmanuel, was up for me trying to source clubs in the UK for some of the top Liberian internationalists. Well, you've got to start somewhere! His main client at the time was a player named Mass Sarr. Mass was playing for Hadjuk Split in Croatia. I had looked up some details about him and discovered that he had been at Monaco at the time Arsene Wenger was the manager, or coach, as they like to call them.

I decided to contact Wenger, who had recently become manager of Arsenal, to see if he would be prepared to talk to me about the player. To my surprise, he could not have been nicer and was very helpful indeed, taking time to talk, and giving me the pros and cons about the player. It transpired that Arsene's assessment of Mass proved to be totally accurate. He said the player was very talented but tended to be a bit lazy and could be prone to putting on weight.

After a few months of on/off negotiations with Hadjuk Split, I finally got a document from them giving me the exclusive mandate to sell the player. As I had already experienced, dealing with Eastern Europeans is never as straightforward as it often promises to be, and there are always obstacles put in front of you when you least expect them. The general manager of Split at the time was not initially giving me the mandate, perhaps because he wanted in on the deal. Eventually, though, he relented because I think the club wanted rid of Mass because they were desperate for cash, and so in the end they gave in and we made an agreement.

341

Having managed to tie up an agreement with Split, my task was now to find a club for the player in the UK. I knew Mass had the ability to play top-level football but I also knew that bigger clubs would be reluctant to take a chance on him. Eventually, though, I found the right club for him. Reading FC were being managed by ex-Celt Tommy Burns, who has since passed away. Tam was one of the nicest and most genuine people you could wish to deal with. Chief executive of Reading FC at the time was property developer Nigel Howe. He was no soft touch but I found him straightforward and good to deal with. Eventually after negotiations I think we both came away thinking a fair deal was struck all round. It had taken me months to get Hadjuk Split to accept a greatly reduced transfer fee of £158,000. I was paid a very good and fair commission for all the work involved. It had not been easy!

I watched Mass make his Reading debut and he totally electrified the whole stadium. Sadly he was unable to provide the consistency week in and week out. Whether it was down to injury or attitude, I'm not really sure, but if I had to put money on it, and based on my further experiences of Mass, I would say it was more likely his attitude that let him and Reading FC down.

The Mass Sarr deal was really what got me going and gave me belief that I could make a go of being an agent. I began signing up mainly younger players in Scotland and also began an association with ex-Newcastle United player Lee Payne. Lee was based out in Holland and had good connections. He, like myself, was very much a football man but had his playing career cut short due to injury. He was trying to do in Holland what I was trying to do in the UK. We hit it off and began an association that was to bring us some decent rewards over the next two or three years. Lee was also working with ex-Brazilian internationalist Mirandinha, who he had played with at Newcastle United. He was back in Brazil sourcing players for Lee for the UK market. We had also begun to extend our network into Eastern Europe and had made some good connections in Bulgaria.

One player we had managed to get access to was Bulgarian internationalist Svetoslav Todorov. He had come recommended, and so Lee and I got him over for trials in England. One of my first ports of call was usually to up-and-coming Preston manager Davie Moyes. Davie was just beginning to make a name for himself as a manager. We had some things in common. We were both ex-Old Firm players and we both gained our advanced FA coaching licences together at Lillieshall. I found Davie to be a likeable but tough no-nonsense type of guy. He was always approachable and keen to look at players, as he was always trying to improve his squads at Preston. When Lee and I took Toddy (Todorov) up to Preston for a trial, the weather was not very good, and the pitch was like a mud heap, but Toddy showed some skills that were way beyond the levels he was playing in that afternoon.

Lee and I were convinced that Davie would jump at the chance to sign the player and couldn't believe it when after the game he hummed and hawed about the player's work ethic and how he had shown a bit of reluctance to mix in with the others. I think Davie, in those early days, was a cautious type of manager. But purely from my perspective as an agent, it was frustrating.

In contrast to Harry Redknapp, who on seeing Toddy for the first time said, 'Yes, I'll have him.' Lee knew Harry Redknapp well and so when Davie Moyes decided not to take Toddy, we took him to West Ham. The deal was straightforward, all above board and we were treated very well by West Ham United FC. Taking a player on trial is very surreal. Normally he gets just ninety minutes to impress. For most foreign players that's little to no time at all to adapt to the conditions and new surroundings.

It's very much a pressure situation all round. UK football is a total culture shock to most foreign players.

Lee and I worked together more or less as partners for a couple of years and in that space of time we had a nice little business going and were beginning to build up some good clients. I was financing Lee. I gave him a BMW, paid his expenses and he was on a 50 per cent share of all the gross profits we made together. He was doing the business for me down south by covering games and picking up players. We'd then use our contacts to source clubs for them both at home and abroad. Initially it worked well, as we seemed to be on the same wavelength.

Looking back, there were some funny moments too! We once took this young Brazilian striker to Huddersfield for a trial and I will never forget us sitting in the stand together watching as this guy missed at least a dozen great scoring chances. We could see our investment going straight down the pan. I have never seen any player, never mind a Brazilian, miss so many clear-cut chances! The poor lad was devastated and on the next flight back to Brazil, never to be seen again! Worse still for me was that I had paid his return airfare! Never again!

In the end I was disappointed that Lee was restless and impatient to make more money and was beginning to make financial demands on me that I couldn't commit to. Eventually, we parted and Lee went his own way. He was ambitious and that was fair enough, but I felt had we stuck together for longer we really could've built something together. We were both ex-players, had a good understanding of the game and were capable of doing a very good job for our growing list of clients. It wasn't to be.

Having thought my hair-raising dealings in Eastern Europe were behind me, they were soon back on the menu again! Top Romanian club Steaua Bucharest had a young player called Marius Niculae. Niculae was only a kid of seventeen years but was already playing for the national team. I had spoken to Arsene Wenger about him and he told me he could possibly be interested in the player. Romania were due to play Italy in a World Cup qualifier in Bucharest and I had been invited to go by Steaua as their UK representative, with a view to watching the player, giving my assessment and making recommendations as to how best I could sell him on their behalf in the UK. Once more I managed to obtain an official agreement or mandate from Steaua regarding Niculae.

There was, however, one small problem. Niculae had a Romanian agent who seemed to control everything in Romania, never mind Romanian football, and he was not happy about the fact there was another agent (from the UK) trying to sell 'his' player to a top English club, when he already had a deal lined up with a big Italian club. The morning after the Italy match, my associate Steven, who had been instrumental in getting me an introduction to the officials of Steaua Bucharest, and I were both 'summoned' to the offices of Niculae's agent. It was clear within the first few minutes of our meeting that he was not happy with any foreign intervention!

Subsequently, out came the revolver from a drawer under his desk and along with him waving it menacingly in front of us, a lot of talk about what happens to people who double-cross him. As Steven and I were sitting at the desk looking at this revolver being waved around in front of us, my thoughts were really drifting towards, 'Where's the airport and what time can I catch a plane out of out of here!' Niculae's agent made it very clear that his player was going to Italy. It would, however, have been nice to know if the player himself had any input in this decision. Not that long after that Romanian trip, Niculae sustained a very serious knee injury that completely scuppered his chances of a big-time move. In all honesty, I have never seen a young striker give such great experienced Italian defenders as Nesta and Mal-dini such a tough time. Niculae was outstanding that night, and I'm sure Arsene Wenger must've come very close to making a move for him.

Funny how things come round, but a few years after I had got out of the business I read that Niculae was coming for a trial with Inverness Caley Thistle! I couldn't believe it. At first I thought it had to be another player of the same name. That boy had the world at his feet at the tender age of just seventeen. You need the luck of staying injury-free at the crucial times. I felt sorry that Niculae had not gone on to fulfil his great potential.

It was becoming more and more apparent to me that the market for foreign players was beginning to be controlled by mafia-type organisations or cartels. It was becoming virtually impossible for a small-time agent like me to get hold of a player and take him all the way to a big-money club without being muscled in on by a much larger group or 'organisation'.

By the late Nineties, due to all the easy money sloshing around in the professional game, thanks in no small measure to Sky TV, every man and his dog was trying to be a football agent. There are some I know who have made millions from doing nothing more than negotiating a transfer deal on behalf of a player or a club. I knew of several top managers in football who would only ever use the same agent and you simply could not get a deal done unless you were prepared to go through that specific agent. A small fry like me had to work smart and rely on doing more business at the lower end of the market where the fees were much less attractive to the big predators. I once was told the story of a big-name South American player who was due to sign a contract for a big English Premiership club. The player's agent had not even bothered to come to the UK with the player and that player was instructed not to sign for anyone

346

until a huge six-figure sum of money was agreed to be paid to his agent, for doing what? Absolutely nothing, apart from the fact he controlled the player.

The African connection was still good and I remember going out to Milan to meet with George Weah for a couple of days. I was a guest at the Milanero training camp of AC and thoroughly enjoyed the experience. George was initially stand-offish with me but came round and actually was a real gentleman. The manager of the training camp was interested to learn that I was an ex-player and indicated that he was glad there were at least some ex-players in the business of being agents. I was fascinated to know how long the Milanero camp had existed and was amazed when he told me it had been running since the Sixties. You need to see this place to believe it: nothing but perfect playing-surface football pitches about as far as the eye could see! Each player has his own private quarters or sleeping accommodation. They have doctors, masseurs, physios, psychologists, dieticians; they even have this beautiful nature trail where the players go walking when they are in recuperation mode from injury!

When I first signed for Glasgow Rangers, they only had the Albion, which consisted of just one grass park and one ash park! Come October the grass was gone and we were left with only two non-grass pitches to train on. And Rangers were one of the biggest clubs in the land. How on earth were we supposed to compete on level terms?

The Milanero experience was a great one for me and AC Milan could not have been more welcoming. I was given the chance to meet the likes of Paulo Maldini and Franco Baresi, who was retired from the playing side of things but who was involved in working with the young players at the time. I politely asked him if he remembered playing against me in that memorable Under-21 international match when we beat them in Italy 1–0.

He just smiled. Either he hadn't a clue what I was saying, or probably conjured up a vision of how we all looked that day in our shellsuits at the airport!

George Weah was obviously a man who had not forgotten his war-torn, poverty-stricken roots. I remember when we were coming back from Milanero to his apartment in Milan, we were stuck in the middle of traffic and there was a beggar who was going from car to car, holding out his hand in the forlorn hope that someone would give him something. Well the only person that I saw give this poor man anything that day was George, as he went into his pocket and gave this man a big handful of money. You should've seen the guy's face light up!

I tried hard to place some Liberian internationalists but in all honesty, they were the ones playing games with me. I was being given information from the so-called Liberian FA regarding statistics about international appearances, but what I didn't know until much later was that most of this information had been false! I was thinking I was bringing a fully fledged Liberian internationalist into the country when, in fact, most of the players I brought in, apart from Mass Sarr, were not internationalists at all. It is one thing being fed falsified information on a CV, but how on earth can you falsify the fact you are not a decent standard of footballer? Unbelievable!

I once had three Liberians staying with me at our home. In fact, these lads could've been gun-running terrorists for all I knew, because one thing was for sure, when I saw them play, they were not good enough to be professional footballers at any level in the game! You would be surprised to know how far some will go to make money in football from this sort of thing.

There was another very uncomfortable experience in Prague, where again my man Steven had got me a mandate to sell two Czech players (the names escape me). I travelled out to Prague one Sunday morning, as I had the mandate from Sparta Prague, who agreed to co-operate with me. I was greeted at the airport by a Sparta Prague official. He told me that I had very little time to do something in the UK, as the two players were almost on their way to Italy. I was taken for lunch with this guy, who also told me that the players had an agent but that he was being kept in check and that we were not to be concerned about his involvement. It turned out, though, that I was being completely duped and that this agent indeed was the power broker and he was using this club official to try and find out what I was up to with the players!

Later, when it was time to go to the match, I was standing just outside in the reception area of our hotel, waiting for my taxi to go to the game, when a big limo, windows blacked out, drew up beside us. Next thing out stepped Mr Big, the agent, who walked up to me and handed out a match ticket and told me I would be joining him for the match, as his guest! It was very clear I had little choice in the matter. On the way to the stadium Mr Big was chattering non-stop in pigeon English. Instead of trying to take in what he was saying, I was already making promises to myself that I just had to get out of this business and find something normal to do! I was not enjoying one bit being made to feel like I was being controlled by these people.

After the match I was taken back to the hotel and was joined for by my newly acquired friend for dinner. I was learning that it was almost impossible to do any kind of real business in Eastern Europe without having to deal with this mafia-type scenario. It was hard work being an agent and there was a lot of time, effort and expense only to find myself coming up against this type of thing more and more. The days of the small one-man-band-type agent were over and you needed to be working inside or for one of the big established agencies like Stellar Group, to stand a chance.

Another experience that left a bitter taste was when I ended up in Australia to represent my client Mass Sarr, for whom I'd fought so hard to get out of Hadjuk Split and into the UK to Reading FC. Mass had gained mass, as I had been warned and despite his great talent, he was just not doing it for the club. I felt really bad about this because I know how much the club did for him and for myself for that matter. I know Reading boss Tommy Burns was disappointed with him in the end. I'll always remember sitting in the stand, watching Mass make his debut for Reading. It was in midweek under the floodlights of the wonderful new Madejski stadium. He electrified the crowd that night, with some sizzling old-fashioned wing play. It was such a thrill for me sitting there knowing I had been the one who'd made it happen. Had Mass only knuckled down and worked harder he would've become a very wealthy Premiership footballer, without a doubt. In the end, though, it didn't happen. He disappointed the club and eventually when Tommy Burns moved on, new manager Glen Pardew handed him a free transfer. Mass then moved back to America, where his family were living. It wasn't long at all before he was back on the phone and looking for me to try and find him another club.

Through my old boyhood pal Stan Clarke, who had since emigrated to Australia, I was introduced to an Australian contact who was working as an agent. I told him about Mass and thought he would be ideal for Australian club football, as obviously the overall standard was not particularly high. Mass also seemed keen on the idea of Australia. My Oz contact did some spadework to see if he could come up with something. Within a short space of time we had a club who were very interested in the player. My big mistake was then to tell Mass who it was that was interested in him! By the time I had jumped on a plane and arrived in Sydney, Mass was way ahead of the game, having already made his own moves! My new Australian contact was also mightily pissed off. He too had been duped, not by the player but by a club official. I was absolutely seething when I discovered Mass had cut me out of the deal. Having tried to do so much, not just for him but for Liberian footballers generally, I couldn't believe this was how I was being repaid!

The meeting with his new club proved to be fruitless. There was no way I was ever going to get a red cent out of any them. Club or player! Even though I had Mass under contract, it was difficult to get anywhere without both the player and club being co-operative. What was I going to do, sue him? Mass looked very sheepish beside the chief executive of the Australian club as we all sat down at our meeting point, which was a café/bar in Sydney. This is where I can be very sympathetic to agents who genuinely work hard to source a club for a player or vice versa, only to get shafted when the player and the club get what they are looking for and discard the vital role the agent has played in putting the two together. At that moment I could've leaned across the table and gleefully smacked them both right between the eyes!

Having travelled halfway round the world only to be shafted out of the deal, I was not looking forward to a long, fruitless twenty-four-hour flight home. Meanwhile, Mass was enjoying his new life in Australia with his new club and a fistful of dollars! But I don't think it lasted too long before he was on his way again. Such a shame because what a talent he was and a likeable kid too, despite all his 'shenanigans'.

Another major talent I was involved with in his early years was Manchester United's Scottish internationalist Darren Fletcher. I had initially been given a tip-off from my French contact who said all the big scouts were raving about his performances for Scotland schoolboys Under-16s in a tournament in France. Fabrice, my French contact, worked very closely with

Lille FC and asked me to see if I could get him over to France. It wasn't long before I was on the phone to Fletcher's parents and introduced myself, I think they recognised my name and knew I was an ex-player. I asked if I could come and have a chat with them and of course young fifteen-year-old Darren. It transpired that he was already training with Manchester United, although he had not officially signed for anyone and they intimated to me he was still keeping his options open. I persuaded him and his dad to come with me to France to see the set-up at Lille and to see if it would appeal to him. It appeared Darren and his family were very keen and so agreed to travel out to Lille for a few days. We were very well looked after by the club, and what impressed me so much was not just the facilities but the philosophy of the club towards its younger players. The players were not only educated as footballers from an early age but they were also educated as people. They had live-in staff who prepared all their meals and generally took care of them. On the training ground it was all about developing skill and technique first and foremost, whereas in Scotland it had seemingly become all about how strong and fast you were or how tough you could be in the tackle.

The training facilities at Lille were also superb and it just seemed to be such an inviting environment in which to go and serve a football apprenticeship. I know I would've just about given my right leg to have been part of something as good as this when I was Darren's age. There's no doubt that Darren and his dad were well impressed with what they saw. It was hard not to be, but I think Alex Ferguson had got wind there was other strong interest in the player and had convinced the family that his future lay at Manchester United. Well, who could really argue with that? I do think Lille would have also been a great option for the player had he chosen it. I was very keen to become

Darren's agent but as soon as he opted for United it was game over for me.

There then seemed to be a spell where as an agent I just seemed to be coming up against one brick wall after another. By this time too my increasing deafness was threatening to become a major handicap in my life as the levels in my good ear began to deteriorate substantially – so much so that I was struggling to function on a normal, daily basis. Meetings were becoming a struggle and it was embarrassing for me to continually have to ask people to repeat themselves. Finally after much consternation I went to see an audiologist to find out what could be done.

Amazingly, I found that the new type of digital hearing aids were fantastic and I could not believe the difference it made to me. I think my pride was getting in the way initially but when I got over that my life opened up again to any possibilities. Suddenly I could hear things like the birds signing in the morning, and even the kids were asking me to turn the volume up on the TV! Despite now being practically totally deaf, there is no such thing as silence for me because I also suffer from severe tinnitus in my good ear. It's a constant buzzing noise in my head. It doesn't really bother me now as much as it used to. I guess over a period of time you get used to it, to a certain degree. Over the years as my hearing has continued to deteriorate, the technology has so far always been there to support me. I urge anyone who is struggling with their hearing to go and get tested and fitted with a hearing aid. I guarantee you will be amazed at what can be done.

The final straw for me as an agent actually came a while after I'd decided to call it a day. I got a call from a media/entertainment lawyer based in London who had been given my name. He was looking for someone with expertise and experience of both professional football and Eastern Europe to represent him on football matters in relation to discussions with a 'business syndicate' from Moscow who wanted to get involved in the UK football market. I was reluctantly persuaded to go with him to Moscow to meet with these people and see what they had to say or offer. I told him that I would only go on a consultant basis and only if he paid all my expenses, which he did. I also told him that I would give my honest assessment upon return to the UK and that no way would I be prepared to commit to anything over there. I'd had too many previous scary memories and experiences!

I flew to Heathrow and together we flew out to Moscow, along with a London-based Russian contact of his. Maybe I had become a cynical old git but I was not getting good vibes about this trip at all.

Upon arrival at Moscow, we were picked up and taken to our hotel in the city. It was here we were introduced to – wait for it – another Sergei, who it appeared was eager to become our Russian voice in negotiations. This new Sergei apparently was ex-Spetsnatz (special services) and an underwater specialist who also majored in unarmed combat, firearms and explosives! Apparently he could spend at least five minutes underwater without breath, but it was not long before I was wishing that he'd spend a lot more time than just five minutes underwater without breathing! He was the one who set up our meetings and it seemed like we were man marked by this guy from the minute we arrived till the minute we departed, about four days later. To give you an idea of what this guy was like, he took us to a café for lunch one day. After we'd finished our meal and got up to go, he'd decided to go off to the loo. We were all waiting in the car outside and were beginning to wonder what was keeping him. Suddenly he came running out and jumped into the back of the car, telling our driver to move quickly away. I could clearly see the bleeding and bruised knuckles on one of his hands. He was in real pain. When I asked what on earth had happened, he explained in his best English accent that he'd been accosted by a gay man in the loo and had quite simply knocked him out, or worse, I feared!

On the second day we were due to have our first big meeting with this group who, from what I could gather, seemed to want to set something up with a UK company or agency that would enable them to begin doing business in the UK. The alarm bells were already ringing in my head! We were driven to an area of Moscow beside a large river where boats were moored. We pulled up beside a large boat with a big gangplank. As we got out of the car we were met by patrolling guards, or more like soldiers, and they were all armed to the teeth.

From there we were ushered onto the boat and into a large room, where there was a big circular table. It was laden with all sorts of traditional Russian dishes. By the time we had all sat down, there were about ten people around the table as we began to eat. I was already thinking that, with all these people round the table, any future commissions would be pretty well diluted! I hadn't a clue what was going on, as no one was speaking English. Sergei, our newly self-appointed spokesperson, seemed to be the only one doing any talking on our team's behalf. The lunch went on for what seemed like ages but then the discussions dragged on for what seemed like forever.

I think it began to become apparent to Sergei that I was not really playing ball – not that I even had a clue where the ball was! I was showing very little interest or enthusiasm. Not hard when you have no idea what is being said or what you are even supposed to be doing there in the first place! I think my lawyer contact was perhaps naive and didn't really know or understand who these people were or who he was really dealing with. Sergei knew I was not really comfortable with any of it and he took me aside on the last day and told me what he did to people he worked with that would not co-operate or do what his people wanted. He then did a fairly impressive impersonation of some-one hosing people down with a sub-machine gun. It was all very high-tempo stuff, but I did not show much by way of emotion or understanding of what I knew he was trying to convey. I was tired of this type of threatening innuendo. I'd seen it all before. I simply regretted agreeing to go in the first place, it had been another waste of time.

I didn't know at all what my lawyer friend was thinking, but I had said to him I would let him know what I thought when I was back in the UK. His other Russian contact also travelled back with us, but I never spoke with either of them on the return flight. When I picked up my bags and was ready to go and catch my connection up north, I simply said to the lawyer, 'Whatever it is this lot are wanting you to do for them, count me out.'

I have no idea whether anything ever progressed from that trip, but I would've been surprised if it had. It was high time I learned to trust my instincts more. There was no way I would ever have dreamed of doing business without knowing who or what I was letting myself in for. For all I knew it could've been money laundering, drugs or anything. It certainly did not seem to be much to do with football! What also didn't really help the ambiance and flavour of that trip was the fact that in that short space of time of me being in Moscow, a beautiful but dangerous place, there was a car bomb explosion, an assassination outside a McDonald's and some Chechnyan rebels took some hostages in one of Moscow's main theatres. Tragically, when a special services team were sent in to rescue the hostages, it all went wrong and a lot of people ended up dead.

I was sitting alone in the departure lounge at Heathrow, waiting for my connection back up north, when my phone rang. It was the other Russian contact. He told me he was disappointed to learn from his lawyer friend that I did not want to be involved. He did, however, tell me he looked forward to coming to Scotland to visit me some time. I simply said, 'Cheerio, it was nice meeting you.' Never say never again! I mean NEVER AGAIN!

So after twenty-seven years of working in the Beautiful Game it was now time to move on and begin the next phase of my life.

15

REFLECTIONS

Over the years many people have asked me the same question: do you wish you were playing today and making the big money that players are earning now? Of course it's difficult to deny it would've been wonderful to have earned the kind of money that even very average players are paid today. To put it into perspective, my record-breaking transfer to Rangers in 1980 in today's terms would've made me virtually a teenage multi-millionaire overnight! Yes, it would've put me in a great position financially, but I'm still not so sure it would've made me any different to the way I am.

The problem for me growing up in football was dealing with the perceived wealth my family supposedly had outside of the game. I am also not going to deny that I was in a more fortunate position money-wise than most in my era – on the face of it, at least. But what should've been a cushion or nest egg to me I think, in fact, became more of a burden. I have learned over the years that having assets are no use unless you can make them work for you. Nothing was ever straightforward in my family, and there were always complications. There was also almost a sense or feeling within that I had to try and live up to the way I was perceived, and that is just not me. The only thing that matters is how you see yourself. Trying to live up to the expectations of others – even your parents – is fruitless, and will lead you down the wrong path.

What I did earn, entirely through my own efforts, was a decent playing career and a reputation as a good football player, despite the hearing handicap and emotional difficulties I had to overcome as a young child. In fact, my reputation as a footballer is what has kept me believing in myself as a person far more that any amount of money has ever done.

It's good that I am writing this chapter looking back as a man in my early fifties. With the benefit of hindsight and experience, it has enabled me to take a more pragmatic and philosophical outlook. I must add that it was my choice to feel the way I did about what others said or thought. Internally I just didn't deal with things very well. Yes, there were reasons, but there are no excuses; it was down to me. I think we all need to recognise and take responsibility for our own actions. As hard and as tough as it can be sometimes, it's the only way you can truly learn and move on.

Knowing what I know today, of course I would've dealt with and handled things completely differently. The important thing, I would say to any youngster nowadays, is firstly, external things only affect you if you allow them to. Secondly, if you have a good core philosophy of who you are and how you feel about yourself then nothing gets in your way. Ironically, I was far more insecure about money when I was younger and had more assets. I have never seen myself as a gambler but, without doubt, I have always thrived on taking a risk, albeit a calculated one. At least in my own mind! I wonder if possibly, in some way, part of me is still looking for that next high. Professional sport is like a drug and once you are hooked it's hard to break away from it.

I think what I have also learned and understood is that

sometimes choice or options can be a bad thing. It certainly was in my case, because over the years I have tended to hedge my bets instead of focusing my efforts, whilst continuing to move forward.

When Dad was alive I think I was actually driven by the fear of knowing that working for him could never be an option. Maybe when he died I initially lost that drive and focus. In some ways I think Jim McLean became my metaphorical father and was the one who drove me on at United. Looking back, after I left United I don't think I ever quite felt the same way about playing football again.

I know I can pretty much learn to do anything that I put my mind to, but going completely deaf I think made me tend to shy away from areas or situations where it would involve groups and me having to hear well. It could possibly explain why when I took up golf I became completely obsessed with it – so much so that a couple of years ago I got down to scratch and decided to give up my amateur status to become a senior 'professional'. In virtually the first event I played in – which was a lesser non-senior pro-tour event in Spain, but still a very high standard with some well-renowned players in the field – I actually made the cut and earned some pocket prize money! This was a huge thrill to me. I will also never forget slam-dunking a hybrid rescue club, from 175 yards into the wind, for an eagle at a par four and chipping in twice from off the green!

My son Ian is also a professional golfer, having turned pro two years ago at the age of eighteen. Golf is very solitary, and although obviously conversation is nice and something I enjoy, there is no pressure on that side of it for me with golf. Only a strong wind on my hearing aid makes it hard for me when out on the course. Apart from anything else, when you are playing in a pro tournament, you normally find most playing partners are only interested in concentrating on their own game. There are exceptions, though!

I so enjoy caddying for my son Ian in pro tournaments. He has such a talent for the game and is working hard to make his way. I know and understand it's brutally tough to make the breakthrough, as it is now in any sport. The 'development' tours do not pay good prize money but the organisers rake in a fortune in expensive entry fees and few overheads, and they don't give much back to aspiring young professionals. I think this is sad because I know many great young talents are lost to the game because of this. However, it's been great experience for both of us.

I think the fact I had such a difficult relationship with my father has helped me to be more understanding and patient with my own son. I certainly don't judge him as a person by how good he is at golf, but I am not slow to criticise when I see any areas that I think can be improved. Importantly, I know and understand every emotion he goes through, because I have felt the lot! I try to tell him that all that matters is effort. You can live with all else as long as you are giving all you have got. In my mind, there is no such thing as failure, merely varying degrees of success, as long as you are trying your very best!

Going back to football, I think the biggest problem most players of my era had to deal with when they retired from the game, or rather the game retired them, was what to do next. Many were not fortunate enough to get decent jobs in the game or a media punditry slot. I have also been asked so many times why I have never done TV or media work within sport. Today I would have no problem, at least as well as my hearing would allow. But it has taken me a long time to get over my self-consciousness about being deaf.

Believe me, I know it is very difficult to accept that the

excitement and adrenalin rush is over. Ally McCoist I believe once said, 'I'm going to play for Rangers as long as I can then spend the rest of my life being depressed.' The psychological aspects don't necessarily go away with money either. When you have played in big games and tasted the highs, the downside is sometimes a feeling of emptiness that cannot be fully described. I'm sure Ally knows what I mean!

Very recently I attended the funeral of my former Rangers teammate Colin McAdam. There were many ex-Rangers of my era who were also there. Afterwards, when we all went back outside the crematorium, there was a real sense of almost relief at seeing each other. I think when you are older you begin to appreciate different things. Priorities change. Although I spent some of my Ibrox career feeling like an outsider, here I was feeling very much part of the soul of one of the biggest football institutions on the planet, a club that is now almost unrecognisable from what it used to be. You see, in my mind, it's about people, but when the heart and soul gets ripped out by so-called 'business' men, that becomes hard to replace.

I felt proud to be there, paying my respects to a former Ranger and a teammate. Outside I stood alongside other former teammates – Ally McCoist, Bobby Russell, Peter McCloy, Alex Miller, John MacDonald and Gregor Stevens, who I must confess to not recognising without hair! We reminisced over big Colin and some of the outrageous things he did. He was a warrior on the pitch and feared no one.

Today is the age of corporatism and the money side of things just gets worse. I am in no position to be judge and jury here, but when I see what has happened to a mighty institution like my old club Glasgow Rangers, it makes me both sad and angry that the pure-bred football fan seems, to me, to be taken advantage of. There's no doubt that the fan is paying more and more and getting less and less. If you think about it, it's cheaper to watch all the live games in the comfort of your living room, on the big screen, with all the pre-match hype, glitz and glamour. The ordinary football fan often cannot afford to actually go and watch his own team from the stands. And sometimes, even if he can afford it, some of the games are kicking off now on a Monday night, or seemingly any night. It's amazing: sometimes you look at a Saturday fixture list and there's maybe only one game on!

Rangers, to me, always transcended football in as much as they are an institution. I have no doubt because of their sheer size they will make it back again, but how galling to think that a set of individuals have treated the club with such disdain and disregarded the very thing that made the club great in the first place – the genuine fan!

16

INJURY TIME

I am also often asked what I have been doing with myself outside of football over the years. In some ways I think I have tried to follow in the footsteps of Dad. He was very much a self-made man, a successful entrepreneur, but who unfortunately had his best business years taken from him, because of the family tragedy both he and Mum had to bear. Dad was very shrewd and was getting into things in farming before anyone else. Then, as everyone else was piling in behind him, Dad would be getting out and moving on to something new. He was one of the first big soft fruit growers in the Carse of Gowrie in Perthshire, and did very well for a few years before getting out when he saw the changes coming when the UK joined the common agricultural market, or EU. So over the last decade I have tried various pioneering ventures that have seen me travel a lot, particularly to North Africa. Like Dad was, I am a great believer in trying to find things for the future. The one aspect for me that stands out is our environment and how technology can improve it. Not only can but must!

There are those who would argue we are so far gone that nothing can reverse the process of damage we've inflicted on this great planet of ours. I led a delegation to Colonel Gaddafi's Libya and met with government officials to try and market some plastics recycling technology. It was, or still is, a process that converts all types of plastic waste into powder that is then moulded by a heat process, which then converts into various materials used for the construction industry. I mean, why take all the plastic we use and dump it into a great big hole called a landfill when we can use that wasted material to build and construct things? Great ideas really only become great ideas, though, when they are adopted into commercial use, and unfortunately getting the bureaucrats to move on it and make a decision proved very difficult for me in countries such as Libya. Despite the obvious opportunity, Libya also has such a beautiful coastline, with such great potential. Whilst there, I visited the very famous ancient Roman site, Leptis Magna. It's such a shame these countries never seem to be able to maximise their potential. It seems to me, though, the foreign policies of Western governments have not helped where it matters most, and that is seeing people thrive.

I had a similar experience with technology for the pharmaceutical side of the agricultural industry. In a way, this one was almost like going back to my roots. Along with my fellow investor/friend Stuart Anderson, we acquired a licence for North Africa for synthesised formulated organic compounds called terpenes. Terpenes are naturally produced by a large and diverse variety of plants. Very cleverly, the various formulated technologies involved an encapsulation process with time release when coming into contact with water. Ingenious stuff, and great for the environment, not only that but much cheaper than the standard, horribly toxic pesticides and fungicides.

Following discussions with the Egyptian Agricultural Ministry, we successfully treated Botrytis on strawberries with our 100 per cent environmentally-friendly formula. Imagine me, an ex-professional footballer, doing a presentation on this to a bunch of Egyptian government scientists. Phew!

I was very disappointed to have to give this up, as I know it is something North African agriculture would benefit from greatly. As luck would have it, though, pending EU approval took about four or five years more than it was supposed to, and then the Arab Spring put paid to any further trips back to Cairo, a place I love, with so many wonderful and helpful people. What's happening in Egypt now saddens me greatly.

Although great learning experiences, these ventures, as well as a serious investment in some technology in the biotechnology industry, did take their toll on me financially. But I'm not whining! It's not that I can't take a defeat, because I have probably lost far more battles than I have won over time. But usually I seem to always find a way to come back again.

You will find me on Twitter as @MrBHogan (after the late, great Ben Hogan, one of my all-time heroes) and my Bulldog, Mr Hogan! I am also available for after-dinner speaking.

I suppose you could say I am a bit of an activist. I strongly believe our Western governments, particularly the US, have at best misled us over the state of the global financial system. I do think we are nearing the end of a system that has been built entirely on paper IOUs and debt. I now believe only in things that are real and that I can hold in my hand. I strongly feel a large transfer of wealth is coming from those who hold paper promises to those who own physical gold and silver, or any other precious metals.

Anyway, life is much too short to dwell on negatives, and I've always believed that when one door closes another one opens up. I look back on my playing career with some great memories and I experienced some things that not many people get the chance to do. In terms of ambitions, I am always on the lookout for a new challenge, as I love to be busy. Over the years I have lived my dream, to become a professional footballer, made the cut in a proper professional golf tournament and now, at this later stage in my life, I have become an author. Something that for a long time I have also wanted to do.

Who knows what the future will bring, but whatever comes my way I will be up for the challenge and treat it as such. Despite some bad experiences, I always try to stay optimistic and keep an open mind and be ready for any possibilities or opportunities that may still arise.

APPENDIX: YOUTUBE LINKS

The following links correspond with individual stories from the book.

Rangers v Inter Milan, 3–1, Ibrox 1984
http://www.youtube.com/watch?v=d9XDeGifhOE

Motherwell v Rangers, 2–2, 1982
I score the second goal
http://www.youtube.com/watch?v=6KbYh1Q2kN4

DUFC v Barcelona , UEFA Cup, 1–2, 2 March 1987
http://www.youtube.com/watch?v=SKdF_UyZ7Pk

Inter Milan v Rangers, 3–0, San Siro 1984
http://www.youtube.com/watch?v=d9XDeGifhOE

Rangers v Cologne, Ibrox 1982
http://www.youtube.com/watch?v=TfQFFUDIMcg

Cologne v Rangers, 1982
http://www.youtube.com/watch?v=RTnvN5ygNz4

Rangers v Celtic, 1–0, 1984
http://www.youtube.com/watch?v=2yZQ8gyj8_w

Rangers v DUFC SCF, 1980/81

Penalty miss

http://www.youtube.com/watch?v=vMsT2Kqoy8Y

Rangers v DUFC LCf, 1981/82

Last-minute winner

http://www.youtube.com/watch?v=UQQYyaeC7Eg

Rangers v DUFC replay, Davie Cooper final, 4–1

http://www.youtube.com/watch?v=W4u0WK-epHM

Dundee United feature interview

Action features

http://www.youtube.com/watch?v=q1okFH2hi9Y

Dundee United v Borussia MG, 0–2

Last-minute goal

http://www.youtube.com/watch?v=93S0WAUMQq8

Rangers v Dundee United, 2–3, Aug 1986

Last-minute goal

http://www.youtube.com/watch?v=9MghmFUkBc8

St Johnstone v Rangers, 3–3

Last-minute goal

http://www.youtube.com/watch?v=5YGDYymqvHQ